NAVY SEABEE VETERANS OF AMERICA, INC.

"WE BUILD, WE FIGHT"

TURNER PUBLISHING COMPANY

TURNER PUBLISHING COMPANY

412 Broadway • P.O. Box 3101
Paducah, Kentucky 42002-3101
(270) 443-0121

Copyright © 2001
Publishing Rights: Turner Publishing Company
This book or any part thereof may not be
reproduced without the written consent of the
publisher.

Turner Publishing Company Staff:
Editor: Randy Baumgardner
Designer: Peter Zuniga

Library of Congress Catalog Card No.
00-112289
ISBN: 1-56311-696-0
ISBN: 1-68162-136-3

*MCB#6 Prepared for a Pass-in-Review on
deployment at Antigua British West Indies in 1955.
MCB#6 is formed for Inspection by Cdr. W.B. Short,
Cdr. CB Lant. Courtesy of Cdr. LaVern Pyles, Jr.*

Table of Contents

INTRODUCTION

The Navy Seabee Veterans of America, Inc. is a not for profit, Fraternal organization made up of Navy Seabees from WW II (both in the Pacific and European theatres), Korean Conflict, Vietnam, Gulf War, and peacetime Seabees.

They are a special breed of men and women. They know the Construction Trades and how to fight to protect what they build.

As you read this book you will learn about the SEABEE, where the name "Seabee" came from and some of the most crucial projects that were done in all the Wars that were fought, under the most treacherous conditions.

You will learn how and why the Seabees were formed and who was the first "King Bee". Also, how many Seabees were there during WW II and what the Marines, Army and Air Force thought of them.

Where are the Seabees today? Just pick up a newspaper or watch the television, and wherever you see a Natural Disaster, you will find the Seabees already at work. In peacetime they do humanitarian work.

The Navy SVA is a very PROUD organization; we are proud of our achievements, and of all Seabees from 100 years old to 17 years old.

The Navy SVA would not be where it is today were it not for some of our National Officers. The National Secretary Mel Ramige, for one, is one of the most respected, hardest working Seabees in our organization. His job description would undoubtedly take two pages to list. He also takes care of our 1-800-SEABEE 5 telephone. All the past National Commanders and the present Commander contributed their Leadership ability to the successful growth of the Navy SVA.

In this book you will read about some of our members, and see how they looked before and now. These stories will not be found in the history books at today's schools.

To those WW II Seabees who built those Airport runways, fuel stations, hospitals, water wells, roads, bridges, and the "pit" on Tinian where the "A" bombs were assembled and lifted into the bellies of the B-29s, we thank you and all WW II veterans.

For more information about the Navy SVA, check our web page, www.nsva.org.

Jack Brandt

John W. "Jack" Brandt
Past National Commander
Navy Seabee Veterans of America

PUBLISHER'S MESSAGE

It is indeed an honor to present this commemorative book to the veterans and families of the Navy Seabees Veterans of America. It can be said that WW II was won on the backs and shoulders of the Seabee Corp, because her men built the roads, runways, bridges, hospitals, and bases that kept the whole operation together. The Seabee mottos, "We Build, We Fight!" and "Can Do!" are well–deserved…fitting tributes to this rare breed of sailor.

It has been a pleasure working with the Navy Seabee Veterans of America, Inc. My father, John Turner, Sr., was a WW II Seabee, and it is his memory that compels me to preserve the history of all our Nation's heroes. May this book serve as a source of remembrance and inspiration for years to come, a shining example upon which future generations can build.

Special thanks go to Mr. Jack Brandt, Past National Commander, for his help in making this book a reality. Jack served as our point of contact throughout the publishing process, and this book could not have developed without his efforts.

I must also thank the hundreds of Seabees whose biographies, stories and photographs fill these pages, as well as the thousands of other Seabees who answered the call when our Nation needed them most.

On behalf of the entire Turner Publishing family, congratulations on a job well done!

Sincerely,

Dave Turner
President

WHAT IS A SEABEE?

Between the awkwardness of a soldier and the dignity of a Marine there is a questionable character called a Seabee.

SEABEE come in assorted sizes, shapes, and weights, but all have the same code: to enjoy every second of every hour of every day, whether at work or at play, and to protest by griping (their most beloved privilege) when issued an order.

SEABEES are found everywhere: on top of, inside of, climbing on, swinging from, running around, or more likely than not, turning to.

Mothers and sweethearts love them, Fathers are proud of them, Brothers look up to them, Sisters admire them, Airdales hate them, Company Commanders tolerate them, and Chief Petty Officers drive them.

A SEABEE is a composite; he has the appetite of a horse, the digestion of a sword swallower, the energy of a pocket-sized atomic bomb, the curiosity of a cat, the lungs of a dictator, the imagination of Paul Bunyon, the slyness of a violin, the enthusiasm of a firecracker, and the spirit of a fighting cock. He likes: liberty. Leave, holidays, weekends, girls, chow, beer, movies, gedonks, swimming, pin-ups, sleep, and comic books.

He isn't too hot for: duty nights, watches, taps, reveille, routine, discipline, officers, drills, or secured heads.

Nobody else is so early to rise without actually wanting to get up. No other person gets so much fun out of liberty of Shore Patrol. No one can have so much fun on so little money.

A SEABEE is a magical creature; you can chew him out, but you can't get the work done without him; he is dirty, unpolished, unkempt, often overbearing, and sometimes reluctant.

A SEABEE is a man of magical abilities; he can weld, build, drive, repair and fight, he can wreck or he can beautify, he can make something out of nothing, work never tires him nor does he seem to tire of it.

His motto is "CAN DO", to which has added "HAS DONE" and "DID": this frequently miraculous occurrence is recognized in the form of a "WELL DONE" by everyone from the Commanding Officer down.

The average SEABEE is a thickheaded individual of a variety of nationalities. He won't admit it to anyone or anywhere except in the defense of his Corps that his is the best job in the Navy. Without him, the Fleet would have nothing to gripe about. Marines would have nothing to talk about, and history would have nothing to write about.

U.S. Navy photo. Courtesy of M.J. Etters, Jr.

Acknowledgments

To all you SEABEES who sent your stories and pictures to the editor to make this book a reality, I thank you.

People have heard about the SEABEES during the wars, but not too many know about us after the battles were won. In this book you will see that we believe "Once a Seabee, Always a Seabee." We have built bridges, runways, hospitals and schools while on active duty, and today we keep our Seabee friendships alive in this GREAT organization called the Navy Seabee Veterans of America, Inc.

The Navy SVA conducts an annual Convention/Reunion somewhere in the U.S.A. Hundreds of Seabees and their spouses gather to renew old acquaintances and meet new friends.

The camaraderie is so great that no one wants to ever miss a Convention, no matter where it is held. The Navy SVA Auxiliary, made up of Seabee spouses, mothers, sisters and daughters, is very active also. It has been a tradition that they make a donation each year, at the National Convention to the SMSA (Seabee Memorial Scholarship Association). At the present time, the Navy SVA owns 18 of the 85 scholarships, and five are awarded to grandchildren of Seabees. We also support the CEC/Seabee Historical Foundation, which has museums in Port Hueneme, California and Gulfport, Mississippi. The east coast Seabee base, Davisville, Rhode Island, was closed and seven acres of land were donated to Island X1, Davisville, which is being

made into a Memorial Park by its members.

We owe this book to all that donated material to make it what it is.

A special thanks to our Founders and all who followed, who in any way held our organization in such high esteem and made it into what it is today.

You can reach us at 1-800-SEABEE 5 or our web site nsva.org.

Jack Brandt

John W. "Jack" Brandt
National Commander
1998 to 2000
Navy Seabee Veterans of America

Courtesy of Joe Rubin.

7

Following WWII, Seabees prepare to board for the long trip home. Courtesy of Bill Patrick.

SEABEES
HISTORY

United States Navy Construction Batallions (CBs)

Seabees—The Early Years

In October 1941, with an eye on developing storm clouds across both oceans, Rear Admiral Ben Moreell, Chief of the Navy's Bureau of Yards and Docks, began laying the foundation of the Naval Construction Force. With the Japanese attack on Pearl Harbor and our entrance into the war, he was authorized to organize the Construction Battalions that would be necessary to prepare for the long march to Tokyo and Berlin.

The earliest Seabees were recruited from the ranks of the civilian construction trades and were placed under the leadership of officers of the Navy's Civil Engineer Corps. With emphasis more on experience and skill than on youth and physical standards, the average age of Seabees during the early days of the war was 33, giving rise to a famous Marines Corps barb: "Don't strike a Seabee, he just might be a Marine's father!"

Over 325,000 men served with the Seabees in World War II, fighting and building in over 400 places before the war ended.

The Seabees list of accomplishments is impressive. In the Pacific, where most of the construction work was needed, the "Bees" built 110 major airstrips, 700 square city blocks of warehouses, hospitals for over 70,000 patients, storage tanks for 100,000, 000 gallons of gasoline and other fuels, and with housing that allowed over 1,500,000 men to call home while fighting the enemy.

The Seabees landed with the Marines at nearly every invasion in the Pacific and proved their value in both the Asiatic-Pacific and European theaters many times over.

With the general demobilization following the war, the "Bees" were all but disestablished, with only 3,300 men left on active duty in June 1950.

In Korea as in WWII, the Seabees performed admirably, landing with the invading forces at Inchon, providing pontoon causeways during and after the hours of the initial landing.

With the end of the Korean War, Seabees demobilization was not repeated as it was after World War II. The old Naval Construction Battalions (NCBs) gave way to distinct Seabee Units: The Amphibious Construction Battalions (ACB's) and the Naval Mobile Construction Battalions (NMCB's).

NMCB's are responsible for land construction of a wide variety, including military camps, roads, bridges, tank farms, airstrips, and docking facilities. ACB's are landing and docking units and have the mission of placing causeways and pontoons, performing other functions necessary for landing personnel and equipment in the shortest possible time. Both are highly mobile units whose mission includes maintaining a high state of readiness to perform any mission,

Ben Moreell
Vice-Admiral, C.E.C., U.S.N.

including disaster recovery, in a minimum of time.

The lessons learned in WWII and Korea were learned well. During the years of peace following Korea, Seabees deployed to nearly every major Naval Base outside of the Continental United States, including Alaska and Hawaii, building and training to be ready.

With the escalation of the Vietnam War, Seabees proved their readiness. They built from the Delta region to the DM2, providing airstrips, camps, hospitals, exchanges, roads, warehouses, storage tanks, towers, and anything to do with fighting a war or providing creature comforts for American forces.

While Civic Action programs are nothing new to the American fighting man, they played an important part in Seabee tasking in Vietnam. Civic Action Teams (CAT's), or Seabee Technical Assistance Teams (STAT's), now called Seabee Teams, were a result of President Kennedy's goal of providing organized civic assistance to the people of Vietnam. The 13-man teams, throughout the war, provided schools, health programs, dental care, and similar village improvement projects, lending a friendly hand to the people of a war-torn land.

Since the end of the Vietnam War, SEABEES have maintained a high degree of readiness, and have helped, meet construction needs in the cold of Antarctica and the heat of the Philippines and Diego Gatcia.

The Story of the Seabees

reprinted from Camp Endicott, Naval Construction Training Center, U.S. Navy Department

In July 1942, a detachment of U.S. Marines assaulted Segi, New Georgia. At dawn the Leathernecks splashed through the water and came tearing up the beach looking for Japanese. They did not find any Japanese, at once. Instead, a group of white men, looking very much like Americans,

stepped from behind trees and shouted to them. Cautiously, the Marines advanced, behind aimed carbines. One of the party came forward.

"Colonel," he said, "the Seabees are always happy to welcome the Marines!" The Seabee was Lieutenant Bob Ryan. The Marine leader was Lieutenant Colonel Michael Currin.

A Seabee boatswain's mate walked over whacked a Marine private between the shoulder blades.

"What kept yuh, bud?" he inquired.

The South Pacific air turned sulfuric as Marine Corps adjectives withered the fronds off the nearby palm trees. Since the beginning of time, Marines had always been everywhere first. It was legendary that when the soldiers and sailors got to Heaven, they would find Marines guarding the streets. Now, here was a group of surveyors intimating, and not too subtly, that when the Marines got to Heaven, they would find that the Seabees had already built the streets!

The Marines were taken back, but not for long.

"Seabees!" one of them cracked. "And what do you think you are doing in here?"

"What are we doing in here? Why, we were rushed out here to protect you Leathernecks!"

It looked as if the brawl might start any minute. Then a slow-spoken Marine sergeant relieved the situation:

"Take it easy, fellows," he said. "We ain't goin' to hit no Seabee. He might have a grandson in the Marines."

A grizzled ex-sand-hog bristled up. "Young whippersnappers!" he started. He seemed to have some trouble with his teeth. Everybody laughed.

"Lookout, grandpop, you're losing your upper plate!" a Marine chortled.

"Are we really THAT short of men back home?" another inquired. The loosened dental plate had fixed everything up. The Marines and Seabees were friends again.

What had happened was that a Seabee surveying party had managed to make a secret landing at Segi Point. Their assignment was to lay out a fighter strip to provide closer escort for bombers striking at Munda. Ten days and 22 hours later, fighter planes were taking off from that field. The Seabees had been surveying the site when the Marine Raiders came storming unknowingly ashore.

A somewhat similar occurrence was Bougainville. A Seabee road crew was cutting a road through heavy jungle when a Marine patrol slithered up. The flabbergasted Leathernecks ordered the Seabees to get back. The road they were building extended 700 yards BEYOND the front lines. The road gang paused momentarily. One of them aimed a contemptuous stream of "Copenhagen" (snuff, to you) at a distant tree, and suggested that the Marines hurry up and capture the road before the Seabees completed it.

Courtesy of Rudy Haukebo

The Fighting Fortieth

The conduct of the "Fighting Fortieth" Seabee battalion (so christened by Brig. Gen. William C. Chase) won it a Presidential Unit Citation. The construction men moved onto Los Negros Island in the Admiralties while the Army's dismounted cavalry was resisting a determined Japanese counterattack. The Army was hanging on desperately to a strip of land half a mile long and varying in width from 50 to 300 yards. Momote airstrip, which the Seabees had been sent in to repair, was no-man's land. Mortar shells were falling on it. Snipers were taking pot shots. The Seabees had long wanted action, and this was it.

Down the ramp of their LST roared two bulldozers, then a ditch-digger. This giant contraption, defying a cone of sniper fire, lumbered to the north end of the airstrip, started digging three-foot trenches. As rapidly as they could be scooped out, the fighting construction men jumped in with their machine guns and grenades to form a support line for the Army. They fought for two nights and helped break up three Japanese attacks.

The first night was a tough one. Through the darkness came word that the Japanese had broken the Army's line at one point. Seabees and soldiers let loose with everything they could throw. Chief Petty Officer G.O. McEwen of Spokane, WA, who earned the DSC in World War I, moved up with his Seabee crew into an abandoned position and started sending toward an enemy machine gun nest. Daylight showed seven dead Japanese at the base of the gun. The Army line had held.

Meanwhile, other members of the battalion got construction underway. They stopped their bulldozers and graders only long enough to return a few shots at the sniper-infested coconut grove adjoining the strip. They scraped the topsoil from the whole area to reach a suitable landing base. They filled bomb craters and erected a signal tower. They cleared firing lines in front of the Army positions, constructed gun emplacements, dug pits for Army doctors to tend the wounded, and they buried Japanese.

They had their own dead to bury, too. Shrapnel bursting in the trees above the bivouac area exacted its toll, but the work kept

Courtesy of Bill Patrick

on. Fighting by night and working by day, the Seabees soon produced visible results. By the end of the second day, a mobile machine shop was going full blast. It quickly restored to operation 18 badly needed guns, included 13 cannons.

Work on the airfield rushed along during all daylight hours. Six days after the Seabees first landed; a Mitchell medium bomber came in for a successful landing. Two more arrived the next day, and on the next a squadron of P-40s commenced regular operations from the field.

When the Japanese were finally wiped out and an American base had grown out of the shell-torn island, Major General Innis P. Swift of the Army wrote a recommendation that the Seabees, commanded by Commander Irwin S. Rasmusson, CEC, USNR, be given a Presidential Unit Citation. The General pointed out that casualties had cut the battalion's strength by almost 17 percent. He commented that "the battle services performed by the members of the CB, while possibly motivated to some ex-

tent by an overwhelming desire for souvenirs, were entirely voluntary."

He then concluded with an apt description of the Fighting Fortieth:

"The cheerful and uncomplaining attitude of these engineers, and their outstanding esprit, were noticeable to all associated with the unit and gave great encouragement to the troops in combat."

The citation awarded by President Roosevelt to these skilled American workingmen who had built roads, bridges and cities before they had transplanted their genius to combat areas, said in part:

"Notwithstanding the fact that the area was still under enemy fire, the battalion immediately on landing assumed its assigned work in clearing and preparing the airstrip...it became commonplace for the operators to return the fire when continuing their work.

"It soon became evident that cavalry patrols operating against the enemy required fire lanes into the jungle to permit concentration of automatic weapons fire against the enemy. The Fortieth Construction Battalion no sooner learned of this need than they turned their bulldozers into the jungle, and cut the required fire lanes in superb disregard of the enemy fire–in particular the operation of the bulldozers into the teeth of the enemy's position was most inspiring and heartening, and created an immediate resurgence of the offensive spirit in weary troops."

How They Were Born

The Seabees cherish that account of how they greeted the highly touted Marines at Segi. They repeat with relish how Aurelio Tassone, machinist's mate, drove his bulldozer down the ramp of an LST, lifted its blade for protection and leveled a Japanese pillbox, burying its 12 occupants alive.

They gleefully tell how Seabee Leslie E. Sammons of the 77th Battalion brought in a

Kwatalew, Oct. 1945, The 141st NCB built this parking area. Courtesy of Gino R. Sacchetti.

Co A-6, 79th USNCB on training maneuvers, Feb. 1943, Camp Bradford, Virginia. Courtesy of John H. Taggart.

Japanese whom he flushed out while uprooting coconut trees with a bulldozer. The Japanese soldier had been hiding in a treetop when the bulldozer shook him out. As he hit the ground, Sammons charged him with a monkey wrench. He meekly gave up.

These tall tales are all true. But, for the sake of historical truth, it must be made clear that these incidents are rare exceptions. Actually, the Seabees are not primarily combat men. The Marines and the Army win beachheads. The Seabees improve them. In the field the And, the Marines are equally quick to admit that there is no substitute for experience in the construction business. They freely confess that six Seabees can out-build five times their number of combat troops.

The Seabees, drawn from more than 60 different constructive trades, are top-flight builders who have been given enough military training to be able to defend themselves and what they build.

To understand just what they are, and how they came into being in the dark days immediately following Pearl Harbor, it is necessary to review some Naval history. From the first our Navy had to construct and maintain shore facilities. Prior to Pearl Harbor, the building of docks, warehouses, radio stations and the drydocking and repairing of ships was done by civilian labor under private contract. The Navy, in 1842, created its Civil Engineers Corps. Thereafter, a few officers from each graduating class at Annapolis were assigned to the CEC, and given an additional three-year course in civil engineering, at some top ranking engineering school, usually Rensselaer Polytechnic Institute. Upon graduation, they became officers of the CEC, staff officers who planned and contracted for shore installations authorized by Congress and ordered by the Secretary of the Navy.

Because under policies enunciated in the Monroe Doctrine, our Navy was considered a defensive weapon, not an offensive weapon, little was done by way of extending our naval establishment before World War II. As late as 1930, the entire planning and administrative program was carried on by 126 officers. For the 20-year period ending in 1938, there was extremely little development of our naval shore facilities.

In the wave of Pacifism that followed the end of the First World War, the CEC like all branches of the Navy felt the pinch of a financial straightjacket. On June 22, 1940, when France fell, the United States Navy, ashore and afloat, was a superannuated, defensive organization unable to wage modern war at any distance from the U.S. mainland.

Our most advanced base in the Atlantic was Puerto Rico. In the Pacific we had Pearl Harbor, and that was about all.

We had a weak line running through Midway, Wake Island and Guam to Cavite. Congress reneged at appropriating money with which to fortify Guam. Our airfields in the Philippines were little more than cow pastures.

Vice Admiral Ben Moreell, then chief of Civil Engineers and chief of the Bureau of Yards and Docks, had long feared the consequences of our unsympathetic policy of marking time. He became at times downright belligerent in his efforts to change it. He had joined the CEC during the First World War. When it was over he campaigned to improve our defenses in the Pacific Ocean. His motto was "Let's get in, or get out!" He pleaded fervently in early 1930s for greater emphasis on naval aviation.

When in 1940 war seemed probable, it became the problem of Admiral Moreell and the CEC to build five roads over which the United States could project her industrial might against her enemies—two roads to Germany, and three to Tokyo. These had to be long roads, through steaming, dense jungles, over ice-capped mountains, and over great stretches of water. They had to be wide enough to accommodate a great flow of weapons and supplies.

The Navy was still using the private contractor and civilian labor to build both continental facilities and advanced bases. Under the Navy set-up, it had to be that way. CEC officers, being staff officers, could not command Navy personnel.

While war clouds gathered, cost-plus-fixed fee contracts were quickly negotiated with private contractors, who started at once to recruit workmen for overseas assignments. High wages and the call of adventure soon had thousands of men sailing for Newfoundland, Iceland, Britain, the West Indies, Sitka, Kodiak, Dutch Harbor, Pearl Harbor, Midway, Wake, Cavite, Palmyra and Samoa. In 1941 we had 70,000 civilians at advanced bases.

Admiral Moreell had his doubts about civilians for advanced base work. They were not under military discipline. They were free to throw up their jobs at the first attack of homesickness, with no greater penalty than loss of pay. Admiral Moreell wondered what would happen to these civilian workers under a bombing attack. In December 1941, he got his answer. The Japanese swarmed onto Guam. Without means of defending themselves, the civilian construction workers were an easy conquest.

Not only did they lack weapons and knowledge of how to use them, but also, lacking uniforms, they were without the protection given a soldier under International Law. Had they elected to defend themselves by arms, they would have been classed as guerrillas and shot. They had no choice but to surrender at Guam, Wake and Cavite.

The Navy thereupon concluded that defenseless laborers would have to be replaced by construction men who could fight as well as build. On December 28, 1941, formation of the first regiment of Seabees, with 3,300 men and officers, was authorized. Three years later

Guard duty, Port Hueneme, California, 1944. Courtesy of Alan Burns.

this nucleus had grown to an Army of 230,000 enlisted men and nearly 9,000 officers of the Civil Engineer Corps. (In October 1944, there were about 235,000 men and 8,500 officers.)

Under direction of the Navy's Bureau of Yards and Docks, this hard-working, high-speed outfit of skilled artisans proceeded at once to outbuild the Japanese, just as the U.S. Fleet proceeded to outfight them. Their two mottoes from the first were "Can Do" and "We Build, We Fight." Rarely have mottoes been so completely lived up to.

Time was of the essence. It was imperative to build at once a fuel base along our lifeline to Australia, toward which the Japanese had started. The first detachment of Seabees did not have time to wait for training, nor for proper outfitting. They had little more than their courage, plus their skill as experienced construction men, when they left an East Coast port bound for the Panama Canal.

From Panama they headed toward Bora Bora Island in the Society group, armed with just 13 Springfield rifles. The island's defenses consisted of a dozen 3-inch antiaircraft guns with enough ammunition to last SIX MINUTES! The Seabees completed their assignment in Bora Bora. They built the fuel tanks. And those fuel tanks were soon to serve the American fighting forces well.

A state of extreme urgency still existed when the first regular battalion sailed from Norfolk, VA, for the South Pacific. It was on its way a bare two days after it was commissioned. Soon, however, training camps were put into full operation. Most of the Seabees received their training either at Camp Allen, near Norfolk; Camp Peary, just outside Williamsburg, VA; or at Camp Endicott at Davisville, RI. Other Seabee activities are located at Camp Parks, CA, a replacement center where battalions returning from overseas are reorganized and given a chance to recuperate; Quoddy Village, ME, where veterans suffering from malaria are rehabilitated; and the Advance Base Depots at Hueneme, CA; and at Davisville, where battalions are stationed pending embarkation.

In the training program, the military was stressed over construction. The bureau's procurement bureaus obtained men with adequate experience in building. Consequently, the brief training period of from eight to twelve weeks was devoted principally to teaching these construction men how to defend themselves, and to acquainting them with new types of equipment, and with war-time adaptations of equipment they had handled in civilian life.

These men were given regular Navy ratings corresponding to their skill as civilians. Chief carpenter's mate ratings (pay $126 to $138 per month) were given to small contractors or foremen of proven ability to handle men. Journeymen carpenters were given ratings of carpenter's mate first class or second class (with pay ranging from $96 to $114). Apprentice carpenters were given a third class petty officer's, or a seaman's rating (with pay from $54 to $64).

In "boot" camp, after being inoculated and given butch haircuts, they were taught close

Returning from Cat Island, Gulfport, Miss.; 4 Dec 1943. Courtesy of Alan Burns.

Construction Recruit (CR) Russell A Mazzeo facing inspecting officer at his first personnel inspection in 1954, at C.B. Div. 3-22, Waterbury CT (NRTC). Courtesy of Cdr. Russell A. Mazzeo.

18th Battallion Carpenter Shop Crew: On Tinian 1944-45. L-R Fielder, Chief Hilderbrand, Smokey Powers, Blith, Crowman, Flick, Angeworth, Angelberger, unknown. Courtesy of Harry E. Fielder.

order drill, the manual of arms, basic extended formations, use of the carbine, the bayonet, and hand grenade. They were ordered on practice marches and taught military courtesy.

About halfway in the training period, the men were organized into commissioned battalions under their own officers. They then began six weeks of advanced training. Half of this period was devoted to additional military training and the other half to technical training, including instruction in the use of machine guns, automatic rifles, mortars, and .20 and .40 millimeter anti-aircraft guns. Only picked men in each battalion were given this specialized training. Other men in each battalion who showed special aptitude were instructed in chemical warfare, judo, field fortifications, and

extended order operations.

Men showing special aptitude were given instruction in camouflage, communications, diving, drafting, mosquito control, water pro-

curement, and air raid protection. Others were taught refrigeration, seamanship, signaling, rigging, tank construction and heavy equipment repair. In all, about 40 special courses of instruction were given, so that enough skills were developed in a construction battalion to make it a self sufficient unit on any kind of advanced base assignment. If battalions had been organized solely for one specific type of construction, the valuable factor of maneuverability would have been lost.

The Seabees took their construction skill as a matter of course; the military stuff was new to them, however, and therefore quite glamorous. Their heroes became, not the men who devised quick ways of licking tough construction jobs, but such men as Aurelio Tassone, mentioned earlier in these pages, who drove that bulldozer into a Japanese pillbox and buried those 12 Japanese alive. Another of their top heroes was Carl Hull who went into the jungle at Bougainville with only an axe and came out with a badly unnerved Japanese prisoner. And Leslie Sammons who subdued a slant-eye with a monkey wrench. The Seabees proved so eager to get into the fighting that, many times, they would work hard all day at appointed tasks, then beg permission to spend their free time up on the front lines with combat troops.

One Headquarters Company and four construction companies comprise each Seabee battalion. In a headquarters company are 165 men—draftsmen, bakers, cooks, gunners, yeomen, storekeepers, mail clerks, etc. The construction maintenance company numbers 227 men; a general construction company, 189; 261 form a company whose specialty is roads, airfields and excavations; 240 in a water front construction company. The total complement of a battalion is 1,082 men and 34 officers. The officers comprise 27 from the CEC, two doctors, two dentists, two supply and disbursing officers and one chaplain.

In general, the first battalions to leave the country reinforced or replaced contractors' civilian forces at our established bases such as Pearl Harbor, Midway, Palmyra, Johnston, etc., in the Pacific; Dutch Harbor, Sitka and other bases in the Alaskan sector; Bermuda, Trinidad and similar bases leased from Great Britain; at Argentia, Newfoundland; in Iceland, and in the United Kingdom. The work they undertook was not the glamorous type. But it was essential to expand these bases so that more supplies and material could be stored for later shipment to battlefronts.

Facilities at Pearl Harbor, for example, not only had to be rebuilt, but also tremendously

Erection of a 100-ton floating crane in New Guinea, 1944. Courtesy of Hoyt Bryson.

Blasting coral to build an air landing strip. Courtesy of Albert Chomor.

The first B-29 to land at Tinian, adopted our 13th NCB black cat insignia. Courtesy of Robert T. Dunn.

increased, to accommodate the flow of men and materials and ships which use it as a staging base today. Defense of these bases also had to be constructed.

The story of the Seabees' construction in the South Pacific is probably the most significant, for there a pattern of advanced base building was developed. The story starts with the arrival of the first naval Construction Battalion in the New Hebrides. The Japanese were driving inexorably toward Australia, had already captured Guadalcanal and were busily constructing a bomber strip there. On May 4, 1942, the same day the Japanese landed at Guadalcanal, and the day on which the Battle of the Coral Sea began, Lieutenant Commander Samuel J. Mathis, CEC, USNR, landed with a detachment of the first Seabee Battalion at Efate in the New Hebrides Island. His job was to open up airstrips from which the U.S. bombers could start bombing the Japanese.

Let Commander Mathis tell his own story:

"The war down there was just a race between the Japanese and the Americans. If the Japanese could put Henderson Field into operation before we could start bombing them from the New Hebrides, then the Japanese would run us out. If we got our planes over Henderson Field before the Japanese could complete it, then maybe we could pave the way for a landing..."

"All through June our PBYs kept bombing Guadalcanal from Havannah Harbor, but it was a 1,400-mile round trip, and we knew we were going to have to have an airfield closer to Guadalcanal before we could bomb the Japanese effectively. So on June 28, the base skipper, myself, and a British intelligence officer named Josslyn set out to explore the islands north of Efate in an effort to find an airfield site as close as possible to Guadalcanal. We flew up to the Espiritu Santo, the northernmost tip of the New

Hebrides—it's about 500 miles north of Efate and about 500 miles from Henderson Field.

"We had wanted to get closer to Henderson Field, but it was impossible. Vice Admiral John S. McCain came up and told us the field at Espiritu Santo had to be ready on July 28. We arrived at Espiritu on the afternoon of July 8. There wasn't anything there but jungle. We began unloading and clearing; we set up floodlights and worked around the clock. I had 12 Seabees who operated nine big pieces of equipment 24 hours a day for a month. You can figure out how much sleep they got.

"We cleared and surfaced 6,000 feet of runway, but we didn't cover the runway with Marston mat. We didn't have any mat. We just graded and rolled the coral. On July 28 we made our deadline. The first squadron of fighters came in. Then on July 29 the big boys came in—one squadron of B-17s. We fueled them from drums, and on July 30 they gave the Japanese the first big pasting. We had to work around the clock right on, getting the fuel supply lines set up. During the next seven days we did little else than lug bombs and gasoline.

"By August 2nd or 3rd it seemed that the whole Air Force and Marine Corps were pouring into our camp. Our little 35-man galley went on a 24-hour schedule of its own, feeding those air squadrons. On August 7 the Marines began landing at Henderson Field, and our field at Espiritu Santo became the vital link between our fields at Houmea and Efate and Henderson Field."

The Seabees won that race. Bombers from Espiritu Santo took an effective part in the recapture of Guadalcanal, and prevented the Japanese from completing Henderson Field. Within three weeks after the Marines had established their beachhead on Guadalcanal, the Sixth Battalion of

Seabees were on their way to consolidate the position by completing the airfield the Japanese had started.

The Seabees were driven at a killing pace not only to finish the field, but keep it in operation. The Japanese, enraged, bombed it continuously. Even the Seabee yeomen and cooks were drawn into the repair crews to fill up bomb and shell craters so that our planes could continue to use the field. With loads of dirt, they would stand by at the edge of the field, while the bombs came down. Then they would rush out and fill the craters fast enough to enable our own planes to land. To provide proper fighter protection for the bombers, additional fighter fields had to be built nearby. Other battalions were rushed to the island. Japanese bombed and shelled the work, but they couldn't prevent its completion.

Meantime, the Seabees built roads up to the front lines; they unloaded supply ships; they constructed a gasoline tank farm. The erection of this tank farm was an outstanding example of Seabee ingenuity, of which more will be written later in this history. The Seabees were ready to begin work when a Japanese attack drove out to sea the ships, which carried the tank farm materials. Instead of delaying construction, the men went to work camouflaging the tank sites and preparing their foundations. Then when the ships finally returned to discharge their cargoes, the Seabees went to work under the camouflage. The Japanese never did find out where the tanks were located, and day after day they would lob shells far over the place where 800,000 gallons of gasoline were stored.

Bridges had to be built over the sluggish jungle rivers. Few materials were available. The Seabees used captured Japanese stuff and cut their own lumber from mahogany and teak and other precious woods native to the area. It has been estimated one bridge they built over the Lunga River would have cost a half million dollars in the States. It was built of solid mahogany.

The Seabees went on to construct piers, utilities and storage facilities. They built personnel structures and a hospital and a railroad. One battalion undertook to drain the swamps and bring malaria under control. Finally, Guadalcanal was developed into a base from which operations could be carried on to the north and west.

The construction men hopped next to the Russell Islands. A fighter strip was

74th CB bulldozer blasted by Japanese land mine. Operator survived but lost all hearing. Courtesy of Ken Beatty.

needed to send up fighter planes to escort bombers from Guadalcanal in their attacks on Japanese bases farther up the line. The Seabees landed in a Russell Island jungle one morning at daybreak in the rain. Thirteen days later, despite 16-1/2 inches of rain, the first plane landed on the new strip.

With Guadalcanal well consolidated, the United States forces proceeded to advance up the "slot" of the Solomons for the big Japanese air base at Munda on New Georgia Island. Our heavy guns would be able to reach Munda from Rendova. D-Day on Rendova was July 1, 1943. At dawn the rain was falling in torrents. Marines, soldiers and Seabees left their transports and plowed through heavy water toward East Beach. Behind rain-soaked bulldozers, the tense builders watched the beach come closer. Japanese in palm trees sent .25 caliber bullets spitting into the water all about them. As the Yanks landed, there was a brief but bitter fight. The Japanese who remained alive took to their heels. Seabees worked with a frenzy to unload trucks, tractors, heavy guns and supplies. They had to get the stuff off the beach and hidden quickly.

This was an unusually tough job because of the marshy condition of the beaches, which were too soft for the steel matting, which the battalion had brought. The Seabees, while Japanese planes bombed and strafed them, cut down palm trees and built a corduroy road over which guns could be unloaded and put in place to defend the beachhead.

Commander H. Roy Whittaker, CEC, describes the difficulties:

"All day long we sweated and swore and worked to bring the heavy stuff ashore and hide it from the Japanese bombers. Our mesh, designed to 'snowshoe' vehicles over soft mud, failed miserably. Even our biggest tractors bogged down in the muck. The men ceased to look like men; they looked like slimy frogs working in some prehistoric ooze. As they sank to their knees they discarded their clothes. They slung water out of their eyes, cursed their mud-slickened hands, and somehow kept the stuff rolling ashore. The Japanese were still sniping, but in spite of this the men began felling the coconut palms, cutting them into 12-foot lengths and corrugating the road. Our traction-treaded vehicles could go over these logs, but the spinning wheels of a truck would send the logs flying, and the truck would bury itself. To pull the trucks out we lashed a bulldozer to a tree, then dragged the trucks clear with the dozer's winch."

"When night came we had unloaded six ships, but the scene on the beach was dismal. More troops, Marines and Seabees had come in, but the mud was about to lick us. Foxholes filled with water as rapidly as they could be dug; the men rolled their exhausted mud-covered bodies in tents and slept in the mud. As the Japanese would infiltrate during the night, the Army boys holding our line in the grove would kill them with trench knives.

"Next day the Japanese planes came in with bomb bays open. All of us began firing with what guns had been set up, but most of the Seabees had to lie in the open on the beach and take it. We tried to dig trenches with our hands and noses while the Japanese poured it on us. The first bombs found

It took six months to build this airstrip on Truk Island. Courtesy of Albert Chomor.

Blasting coral for an air strip on Truk Island, 1945. Courtesy of Albert Chomor.

our two main fuel dumps, and we had to lie there in the mud and watch our supplies burn while the Japanese strafed us."

"One bomb landed almost under our largest bulldozer, and the big machine just reared up like a stallion and disintegrated. A five-ton cache of our dynamite went off, exploding the eardrums of the men nearest it."

Two Seabee officers, Lieutenant Irwin W. Lee and Lieutenant George W. Stephenson, and 21 Seabees were killed during this attack. Many more were wounded, several missing and some were out of their heads. All the galley equipment, most of the supplies, and all the men's seabags and personal belongings were destroyed. All that night the medics worked with the wounded.

"The biggest job," continued Commander Whittaker, "was to get them clean. That's one thing about being a Seabee. Aboard ship you bathe, wash down with antiseptic, and put on clean clothing before an action. In the Air Force you can take a bath before you take off. But when a Seabee gets hit, he's usually on a beach in the mud. Mud seems to be our element. When we die, we die in the mud.

"Next day, while we worked in relays, chaplains from the Army and Marines helped us bury our dead. Three more had died during the night. Not one of these boys would have ever thought of himself as a hero, but I felt proud to have been their commanding officer. They were construction men, mostly from the oil fields of Oklahoma and Texas, and, with never a complaint, they had died in the mud trying to get a job done."

On the fourth day after the landing the Seabees had opened a road, of sorts, to West Beach, had snaked big 155s through two

miles of mud, and the Marines set them up. Late that afternoon the big guns started pounding Munda. The Seabees halted work, cheered madly. "No group of men," declared Commander Whittaker, "had ever endured more in order for guns to begin firing."

"They kept on firing for days. Word came that 5,000 Americans had landed on New Georgia near Munda. The Japanese knew Munda was doomed, if we could hold out. They sent their planes over the Seabees and the Marines repeatedly. By the sixth day, American planes were able to take up the fight, and they tangled with the Japanese right over the Seabees' heads. The Seabees lay in muddy foxholes for an hour and watched the air battle. They cheered loudly each time a Zero would burst into flames. Afterward, the Japanese tried to raid repeatedly, but few planes got close enough to cause much damage. Seabees in the Munda operation lost an average of 21.8 pounds per man."

While all this was going on at Rendova, another battalion of Seabees, unobserved by the Japanese for the first eight days, were building an airstrip out of the jungle at Segi Point, so that our bombers coming up from Guadalcanal could have fighter protection over the target. An initial area of 250 by 3,500 feet was cleared; the area was graded and drained. Coral was laid over a minimum area of 100 by 2,500 feet, 12 to 18 inches deep. Marston mat was laid over most of this. On July 11 a Navy Corsair fighter pilot made an emergency landing on this strip and pronounced it ready for use. This was 10 days, 22 hours and 12 minutes after the first landing boat had slid into shore.

The Seabees, Marines and soldiers on

Rendova had so monopolized the attention of the Japanese by their incessant shelling, that the Seabees at Segi Point virtually had their field completed before the Japanese found it. When they finally did find it, they hit it hard, exploded a dynamite dump and a fuel dump and peppered bulldozers and trucks with shrapnel. But they were too late. The fighter planes from Segi had helped relieve the Japanese pressure on the men-in-the-mud at Rendova. Three weeks after the opening of the airstrip at Segi Point not a single Japanese remained alive on Munda.

Advanced platoons of the 73rd Seabee Battalion started rebuilding the airfield at Munda, which the Japanese had not been able to use for eight weeks because of the blasting we had given it. The Seabees were given exactly nine days in which to have the field in operation. Round-the-clock work started. The nine days were not needed. American planes began landing at Munda on the afternoon of August 13. The 24th Battalion, which had been on Rendova arrived on August 15 and the two battalions set to work to make Munda a major base. Many Japanese had died from our flamethrowers in an elaborate tunnel system in the coral. Seabees removed the roasted Nips and transformed the tunnels into fancy living quarters. There they slept, without once having to jump up and run for a foxhole.

Admiral William Halsey in November 1943, pronounced the Munda Air Base one of the finest in the South Pacific. "I had to run most of the time," the Admiral recalled in a radio interview, "to keep from being shoveled into the ocean."

The Admiral cited Commander Kenrick P. Doane, who led the 73rd Battalion, in part as follows:

"Prior to his commencing work at Munda, there were no roads, and the airfields and taxiways were unusable due to the bombardment and shelling of the area by our forces prior to its capture. In spite of shortage of personnel and equipment, and faced with a task of great magnitude, Commander Doane was able, nevertheless, by virtue of his planning, leadership, industry and working 'round the clock' to make serviceable the Munda Airfield on August 14, 1943, a good four days ahead of the original schedule. Though subjected to shelling and bombing, both in the camp area and on the airfield, Commander Doane and his men have expanded the size and facilities of the airfield at a phenomenal rate. In addition, the all-weather road net and the Air Housing Area have been completed far faster than had been hoped."

Commander Doane, who helped plan and superintend the building of La Guardia Airfield at New York City, replied to this citation as follows:

"It's easy to perform construction miracles with men like the Seabees. They are the world's finest construction men...when we took men like this and put them into one organization, we loaded the dice against the Japanese."

Bougainville

Bougainville was the next important jump ahead. With the first wave of Marines who landed on Torokina Point November 1, 1943 was a detachment of the 75th Seabee Battalion. Lieutenant (jg) Robert E. Johnson, who commanded the detachment, described the operation:

"The five officers and 95 men who composed our landing detachment were all volunteers. We came in with the Marines on the USS President Adams; *and for the landing we divided ourselves into four units—one to unload ammunition; another to unload fuel; another to unload rations and packs; and the Fourth Seabee unit manned the machine guns on all Higgins boats and tank lighters.*

"We were to follow ashore immediately behind Company C, First Battalion, Third Marine Division, which was the only assault force expected to meet any opposition. Our landing craft were ordered to pass through the narrow channel between Puruata and Torokina Islands. The Japanese had machine-gun nests on the inside of both islands, and they fired heavily on our first assault boats. Japanese planes also strafed us on the run-in. Our Seabee gunners made those Japanese machine guns ineffective and helped to drive off the Zeros. One landing craft was hit by artillery fire, and we had to unload the wounded from it under rather desperate conditions.

"At the beach, Seabee gunners provided cover while the Marines advanced to erase the Japanese with grenades and flame throwers. When a Marine was shot from a crippled tractor, which was pulling in the first load of ammunition, a Seabee leaped to his place, repaired the tractor, and delivered the ammunition.

"The Seabees dug foxholes not only for themselves but also for the Marines and for all casualties who were unable to dig their own. When a group of Marines was about to be wiped out because of lack of supplies, there were three Seabees that managed to get through with ammunition and to bring back the wounded.

"A part of the area selected for the Torokina fighter strip was beyond the front lines. One Seabee was captured by the Japanese while clearing the strips. This was the area where the Marine patrol ran into the Seabees, and upbraided them for being out of safe territory. As if danger from Japanese were not enough, the Seabees had to work under the active volcano, Mt. Bagana, which towered near the area. Seabees, who were cutting a road in advance of the front lines, and their Marine guard, were attacked by Japanese. Seven of our men were killed and 20 were wounded. All might have been annihilated if Chief Carpenter's Mate Joseph R. Bumgarner and a crew of Seabees, who were building a bridge had not heard the firing, and gone to the rescue. They helped chase the Japanese, and carried out the Marine and Seabee casualties."

Three Seabee battalions, the 25th, 53rd and 77th, came in to help the 71st and 75th convert the Empress Augusta Bay area into a major base. They built the Piva bomber strip, and provided two bomber strips and an additional fighter strip from which to assault Rabaul. Japanese artillery fire and bombs pounded the airstrip, but Seabees repaired the damage so rapidly that during all the counterattacks the field was never out of use for longer than half an hour.

Still other Seabee battalions moved in to accelerate the Solomons campaign with bases on New Britain, the Green Islands and the Admiralties. In each case the job was the same, to get supplies ashore, construct or repair airfields, build roads, camps, supply dumps.

Farther north, during the invasion of the Gilberts, Seabees set to work of Betio airfield before sniper fire had been quieted. Seventy-eight hours later the field was in condition to receive American planes. In the Marshalls at Kwajalein and at Roi and Namur, the Seabees first took an important part in the landing of supplies and equipment over pontoon causeways, to be described in detail later in this account. Here they undertook the quick repair of badly damaged airfields. Shell fragments played havoc with tires, and dud shells and bombs slowed the going, but Seabees soon had removed the debris of bombardment, and had a new naval base well under construction.

Recapture of Guam and construction of airfields there gave the Seabees a great feeling of personal revenge. The whole Seabee organization as related earlier had grown out of the tragedies of Guam, Wake and Cavite where construction men had been unable to defend themselves. On the day Guam was reclaimed, nearby Saipan was already being converted into a base. Repairing the damage of our own bombardment, Seabees

had Isley field in operation days before it was even certain that Saipan's capture was assured.

Just what the Seabees did to help rebuild air and naval facilities at Palau has not been revealed in detail as this is written. But Seabees were in on the operation from the start, and it is known that another repair job is well underway there.

Such has been the story of Seabees at work in the Pacific, where their relationship has always been close with the Marines. There has been a generous amount of ribbing, mostly good-humored, between the two services. Whatever may have been their first appraisal of one another, the relationship soon reached a plane of high mutual respect. The Seabees are, on the average, much older men. Personnel in the early battalions averaged about 35 years of age. The oldest Seabee is 63. Marines, of course, are in their teens or early 20s. Consequently, Marines usually refer to the Seabees as "Old Folks." The Seabees appoint themselves as the Marines' "protectors." That leaves the score on repartee about even. The fine relationship of the two branches is well expressed by two signposts on Bougainville. One, erected by the Marines, states:

"When we reach the Isle of Japan,
With our caps at a jaunty tilt,
We'll enter the city of Tokyo
On the roads the Seabees built."

The other signpost, erected by Seabees, is a plaque simply dedicated to "our protectors–the Marines."

In the Aleutians

Simultaneously with their labors in the South and Central Pacific combat theaters, Seabee battalions were shoulder deep in the rough battle of the Aleutians. In his book, Can Do, *a lively and comprehensive account of the Seabees, Lieutenant (jg) William Bradford Huie, CEC, USNR, describes the Aleutians as a "prehistoric connecting link between two land masses which modern man was willing to ignore as worthless" until the Japanese jumped on us.*

The battle here was not against the Japanese in person, but against impossible weather and horrible soil conditions.

This road from Seattle to the Aleutians was one of the five great highways which it was considered necessary to build toward the homeland of the enemy. It is often called "the northern highway to victory." Largely volcanic mountaintops, the entire area was barren and uninhabited until the Seabees piled in at the war's outbreak to replace civilian employees working on Navy contracts. They found endless stretches of tundra, but not a tree nor a shrub west of Dutch Harbor. They went to work immediately enlarging old facilities and building new ones, wharves, fuel storage facilities, warehouses, camps and airstrips.

It is said the Aleutians are the source of more high wind even than a professional Texan. The "williwaw" is an unpredictable gale that strikes that area with terri-

The 1040 detachment while being transferred from one town to another on the 40 and 8 railroad. Africa, 1943. Courtesy of Paul Crepeau.

Shore Patrol during a beer party, French Morocco, North Africa. Courtesy of Hugh Acton.

fying suddenness. Seabee William J. Fox, CM1/c, is an authority on them. He actually rode one like a "magic carpet" from a warehouse he was helping to build to the side of a mountain 150 feet away. The involuntary ride occurred when he and three mates were nailing asbestos roofing on the warehouse. The force of the gale tore loose the holds that Fox's companions had on the sheet, permitting it to go sailing 20 feet off the ground against the mountainside, with Fox aboard.

Fox was unhurt except for a bump on his head. "The only thing I regret," he said, "is that it didn't blow me right back home to Montana!"

Another Seabee, Archie A. Lamb, SF1/c, figures he is living on borrowed time. He was working on a dock in the Aleutians when a williwaw sprang up, forcing him to head for shore. He had scarcely left when a cargo ship, dragging anchor, crashed into the dock, and destroyed the section he had just vacated. Another time, during a dense fog, Lamb was on a sand spit working on floating docks. While the fog didn't bother the construction workers, it did confuse a group of fighter pilots trying to land on an island.

The airfield was close by and several of the fighters, mistaking the sand spit for the field, came in to land. Diving over an embankment, Lamb and his mates barely avoided the whirling propellers. The Seabee's last close call occurred during a williwaw at night. Suddenly Lamb discovered he was sharing the back of the truck with a loose, bouncing 2,000-pound bomb. At every jounce the bomb changed position, and so did the Seabee! The truck was moving too fast to risk a jump in the dark, and the noisy williwaw drowned out his shouts to the driver. Lamb continued the deadly game of leapfrog until camp was reached.

Today the Aleutians road is a finished highway, starting in Seattle, continuing to Sitka, to Kodiak and to Dutch Harbor (which is farther west actually than Pearl Harbor) and then to Umnak, Amchitka and as far as Attu. From Attu it is but 700 miles to the Kuriles where the Japanese have their advanced base at Paramushiro, and only 1,900 miles to Tokyo—ultimate end of the Seabee road.

It took time, of course, for Seabees on bulldozers to advance our bomber lines, but they helped make it possible for our P-38s to fly from a factory in California and be in action over Paramushiro 24 hours later; for our B-17s to fly out of Seattle in the morning and drop explosives on Paramushiro the same night.

The greatest landing difficulty in all the Aleutians was the watery conglomeration of grass and mud called tundra, which lies from six to thirty inches deep on top of sand and volcanic rock. Vehicles with rubber tires could not negotiate it. So the first job was to build roads over which trucks could move supplies inland from the beach.

Laboring almost a year with hand picks and hand shovels, the Japanese had built about 26 miles of temporary roads at Kiska. These were thin, one-way strips of rock laid over the tundra. These roads would not support the heavier American machines. The Seabees found a rocky hill nearby and started blasting it away during the first hour of landing. Under floodlights, they continued working all night. Dump trucks next day carried the broken rock away from the hill and re-enforced all the Japanese roads in the area. They became two-way thoroughfares. Within a week, jeep, half-track, bulldozer and truck traffic was so heavy the Shore Patrol had to get on the job as traffic cops.

The Japanese left their communication line in almost perfect condition at Kiska. Knowing they would find no trees in the Aleutians, they had brought creosote poles from Japan and had strung many miles of line. About all the Seabees had to do was to reset a few of the poles, attach portable generators and turn on the lights.

Mediterranean Area

Naval construction battalions were busy on the other side of the world, too. Forty Seabees, who billed themselves as the "Dirty Forty," were the first to serve across the Atlantic. They arrived at Kissy Flats, near Freetown, Africa in August 1942. Their assignment was to build some docks and develop port and fueling facilities, and build the bases from which Allied forces could attack the not-so-soft underbelly of Europe. From Agadir to beyond Cape Bon Peninsula, they developed port facilities, fuel stations, airfields, ship repair point, and other installations necessary to launch the attack.

Seabees loading pontoon on side of LST in Africa before invading the south of France, 15 August 1944. Courtesy of Paul Crepeau.

Hauling cement in Tilbury England. Courtesy of Raymond B. Dierkes.

Seabees south of France invasion, 15 August 1944. Pontoons causeway manned by Seabees. Courtesy of Paul Crepeau.

Seabees at play after the invasion of Europe, using German uniforms and guns on the French Riviera. Courtesy of Paul Crepeau.

The North African operations were a British and U.S. Army show, but Seabees built the installations for the U.S. Navy. The battalions which labored there were the 54th, which landed at Arzew, Algeria; the 70th; and the 120th which landed at Casablanca, French Morocco, with the invasion convoy on November 8, 1942.

The "Dirty Forty" didn't wait for their promised new equipment to reach them at Freetown. They understood how German submarines sometimes caused delay or disappearance of supplies in transit. So they set about repairing some old steam shovels. They soon had them coughing away, tearing up the face of Africa. The natives were fascinated by the Seabees, some of whom must have read how Mark Twain's hero got the fence white-washed. For soon the natives were working with the Seabees, hewing gumwood piles, 50 to 80 feet long. These piles were capped with iron so that they could be driven into the volcanic lava that composed the harbor bottom. Cigarettes acted like a supercharger on the natives. A Seabee handed out a Kool one day. The native who smoked it appeared to be in seventh heaven. News of the new cheroot got about that night. Next day half a hundred Africans showed up clamoring for work and Kools!

A discovery, which the 120th Battalion claims to have made at Oran, may bring a post-war boom there rivaling anything Miami ever knew. They claimed that bald-headed Seabees grew new hair once they tarried thereabouts. A certain combination of balmy sea breezes and medicated sun was given the credit for restoring life to dead cells and producing the luxuriant new topping. It also was declared to have eradicated freckles. The authenticity of these claims have not been approved by any better business bureau, but it is a fact that these reports, which circulated among Seabees everywhere, brought an avalanche of applications from hundreds of billiard-topped builders asking to be assigned to duty at Oran.

While the 54th, 70th and 120th battalions toiled in Africa, the 17th, 64th and 69th built the base at Argentia, Newfoundland. The 9th and 28th battalions built the vast Navy installations in Iceland.

The 31st and 49th battalions worked in Bermuda, repaired damaged ships, restowed cargo in vessels buffeted by heavy weather, built wharves and dry docks. The big base at Trinidad was constructed by the 30th, 80th and 83rd battalions. The lonely assignment to the Galapagos Islands, which guard the Pacific approaches to the Panama Canal, fell to the 1012th Detachment, which had previously worked in Honduras, Nicaragua and the Canal Zone.

The Seabees' Magic Box, The Pontoon

Much of the credit for our successful landings at Sicily, Salerno and Anzio undeniably must go to the Navy pontoon, and the manner in which the Seabees used it. This five-by-seven-by-five-foot cube of sheet steel has been compared with radar and the Sperry bombsight in its influence on our fortunes of war. The Germans figured the shallow water off the Southern Sicilian beaches would preclude any possibility of our landing there. LSTs can drive their ramps right into the beach where water deepens normally, but around Licata, Sicily, for instance, the landing ships would ground as far out as 300 feet from shore. The Germans reasoned that the Allies would not try to negotiate such a perilous ship-to-shore problem under their bombs. They looked for us to land farther north.

Once we landed in Africa, our experts set out to find a way to put the tanks, bulldozers and trucks within "wading distance" of the beach at Licata, Sicily. The Army had a system of laying their famous steel treadways across rubber doughnuts, so the Army engineers started experimenting with them. The Navy put the problem up to Captain John N. Laycock, who had designed the Navy pontoon in 1941, after the CEC had foreseen that new devices for beach operations would be imperative in case war broke out in the Pacific.

It was foreseen that floating piers, dry-docks, causeways and barges would be needed in great numbers. Captain Laycock set out to devise one section, which could be prefabricated and made the basic part of all this beach equipment. A barge, it was argued, would have to be a welded, riveted unit to be strong and rigid enough to sustain great weight. Captain Laycock was determined to find a way to impart the rigidity of a single box to a combination of boxes. He started collecting cigar boxes, experimented with them, found a way to bolt many together and have the resulting string of boxes almost as strong as if it were in one piece. He put his conception of the pontoon unit on paper. It was to be built of sheet steel and would weigh about 2,600 pounds. The pontoons were to be connected by self-tightening, interlocking bolts and straps. He designed a 50-ton barge, a 100-ton dry-dock and a seaplane ramp—all three structures to be built from the pontoon boxes.

A contract was let to the Pittsburgh-Des Moines Steel Company in February 1941. An outboard propulsion unit was built by Murray & Tregurtha, boat-builders of North Quincy, MA, at the same time. In late spring all the items were ready to be tested. They proved completely successful in tests. So impressed were the British, they ordered 3,000 pontoons at $700 each, on the spot.

Seventy-five firms are now engaged in the manufacture of the pontoons, and their connecting jewelry. The Navy in 1944 paid $100,000,000 for pontoon gear. The assembly of the pontoons and their structures is an overseas Seabee responsibility.

Captain Laycock discovered that to make a steel causeway wide enough for tanks and trucks, it would be necessary to fasten two pontoons together, to get a width of 14 feet. It was found that the maximum safe length to which these two-pontoon sections could be strung was 175 feet. They were flexible in that length, but could withstand considerable stress.

"Then we hit upon the slide-rule idea," said Captain Laycock. "If a 300-foot structure was too long and too flexible to withstand surf action, why not use two 175-foot assemblies, overlap them and make their combined length adjustable. We set the Seabees to practicing with such an arrangement and then we arranged a dual demonstration."

Our tactics in Sicily and, in fact, our LST landing tactics for this war were determined by that demonstration. Along Narragansett Bay two LSTs approached a beach at full speed. The Army Engineers with their treadways and rubber doughnuts were aboard one. Seabees were aboard the other LST, which towed two 175-foot pontoons assembled in slide-rule position. Seabees rode the pontoons.

Both ships grounded 500 feet from the shore. The Engineers dropped their front ramp, threw their doughnuts over the side, and shoved the treadways out. As soon as the Seabees' LST started to ground, the men on the pontoons cut them loose and allowed them to drive on toward the beach under their own momentum. They ran the front end of the leading causeway into two-foot water and grounded it. A line ran from the stern end of the trailing pontoon section to the LST. The Seabees quickly unlocked their two causeways, and pulled the rear one back toward the LST, thereby lengthening their pontoon "slide rule." They quickly clamped the two 175-foot sections together again, where they overlapped. A big anti-tank gun charged out of the LST, negotiated the steel causeway and reached the beach in just seven minutes after the LST had grounded.

"We all gasped at that demonstration," said Captain Laycock. "We knew we had a surprise for the Germans."

A total of 5,760 of these pontoons, made up into ninety-six 175-foot causeways, were assemble in North Africa. En route to the landing scene, it was found that a convoy could move faster if the pontoon causeway were slung on the sides of the LSTs, rather than towed. They were both towed by tugs and carried by LSTs in the new side-carry manner when the great armada sailed for Sicily in July 1943. Next morning the LSTs were disgorging vehicles of war by the hundreds. The Germans couldn't believe their eyes. When one LST was unloaded, the causeway would be unfastened and swung around to a waiting ship. A total of 11,500 vehicles were unloaded onto Sicily in this manner.

Two officers and 34 Seabees rode each causeway-carrying LST. A few miles off the invasion beaches, the Seabees cut the cables holding the causeway sections with axes, and allowed them to hit the water. Then they opened the bow doors, lowered the ramp, and "let the duck out." The duck is an amphibious tractor. Using it for towing purposes, the Seabees then maneuvered the two sections into the slide-rule position along one side of the LST, and the ship ran for the beach. One officer and 24 Seabees were lying belly down on each causeway as the LSTs sped in. At the exact moment, the Seabees cut the causeways, and rigged them up to the beach. The unarmed daredevils, who rode these surf-buffeted contraptions through bombs, shell and mines, were as exposed as lizards on a flat rock. Their casualties were relatively light in Sicily, but not so

at Salerno and Anzio where the Nazis waited for the causeways with countermeasures.

The first vehicle to land on the continent of Europe was a Seabee bulldozer driven by Raymond J. Calhoun, MM1/c, of Troy, NY, who went in at Salerno.

In the initial Italian operation, the 1006th Pontoon Detachment of 28 officers and 300 men suffered 23 percent casualties.

One officer and seven men were killed as the Germans bombed the causeways to tear them loose. Nine officers and 57 Seabees were awarded the Purple Heart in this action.

The Salerno operation was one of the bloodiest of the entire war. The Germans were well entrenched in the hills and poured a terrific fire down on the beach, where the Seabees were unloading supplies, clearing debris, setting up dumps, building dressing stations, and keeping traffic moving. It was after watching the Seabees on the beaches and manning the exposed pontoon causeways that a young paratrooper made the classic remark: "And," he said, "I thought we were the worst fools in the war!"

The 1006th Detachment, led by Lieutenant Willis H. Mitchell, Warrant Officer Richard A. Look and Lieutenant Commander W.A. Burke Jr., was the first to go into North Beach, Salerno.

"We were following the course of the YM mine sweepers," Commander Burke later reported, "when, about a mile off shore a large size Italian mine which had been swept to the surface but had not exploded, loomed in the path of the ship. The forward lookout made a frantic effort to veer the ship to port but the curved end of the inboard causeway hit and rode up over the mine which bounced along under the bottom for about 70 feet before going off against the side of the ship. Thinking 'we've been hit by an aerial bomb', I threw myself to the deck. There was a blinding glare and air, water and oil fell on us. The ship was still under way, but the causeways were gone and rapidly drifting astern. A pontoon or two were drifting free, but we did not at first realize that those shadows piled on the forward weather deck were pontoons blown from the sea. A couple of small craft in the vicinity went to the assistance of the Seabees aboard the wrecked causeways.

"We found out later that there was sufficient warning of the explosion for the men to run to the extreme aft end of the causeway where, though they were violently stunned by the terrific detonation, only two were killed. Dick Look's eardrums were punctured and several others were seriously wounded.

"We did not know whether the ship would stay afloat long enough to reach the beach as she was listing badly. We grounded, without our causeways, some 250 feet off the shoreline with about 11

feet of water at the bow ramp. It was immediately apparent that the beach had not yet been taken. Batteries of 88s and mortars had the range of the beach and kept up the shelling all through D-Day; it was decided to retract and attempt to put our combat cargo ashore over one of the other sets of causeways or via LCTs.

"When we were about half a mile off the beach, a British destroyer laid down a smoke screen which protected us from further fire from the shore and enabled us to anchor in the transport area between the Flag Ship Biscayne and the Monitor Abercrombie, transferring our cargo to LCTs."

A second LST running to North Beach had better luck. Lieutenant Harry Stevens Jr. was officer-in-charge of the causeways. The other Seabee officer was Ensign M.T. Jacobs who told the story:

"At H-Hour-0330 our LST had moved into within three miles of the Red section of North Beach. We were carrying men of a Hampshire regiment. On the tank deck we had six Shermans, with a lot of half-tracks, Bren gun carriers and ducks.

"The 16th Panzers were ready for us with big guns, 88s and machine guns—our warships returned the fire. The Savannah had pulled into within a few hundred feet of our LST, and she was blasting with everything she had.

"German bombers started coming over, so even the guns on the LSTs started firing. It was hot! And right at that moment we got the order to prepare to launch causeways; we opened the bow doors and let our duck out. I had to direct the rigging and ride the causeways; shells were popping all around us, but while you are rigging you are so busy you don't mind it so much. It's when you start into the beach and have nothing to do but hold and pray—that's when you really get scared.

"All 25 of us who were lying on the causeways were dressed in two-piece coveralls, helmets and life jackets. We had canteens and 45s on our belts; no other arms. You don't need anybody to tell you to lie flat on that causeway, because you feel like the most exposed man in the whole harbor. You look at a Stillson wrench lying in front of you, and it looks big enough for you to crawl under it. Honestly, you get the idea that wrench gives you some protection.

"About 0620, just before sunup, we hit the beach full speed. We cut the causeways loose, but our luck was holding; our LST slid right on up to the water's edge, and we didn't need the causeways for her. All we had to do was throw a few sandbags under her ramp and spread the mat. We grabbed shovels and dug slit trenches while shells were bursting all around us.

"Seven or eight Hampshires decided that they'd brew up a spot of tea on the beach. They built a fire and had the water boiling when one of them called to me, 'Say, chappie, come and have a spot o' tea.'

"I started walking toward them and was within 50 feet of them when a land mind went off right under that fire. The explosion knocked me flat and when I got up every one of those Hampshires was dead and mangled. Late that afternoon our men established a bivouac about 300 yards from where we had landed.

"We stayed there on the beach for 10 days during which the bombing, shelling and fighting continued almost constantly. The crisis was on the fifth and sixth days, when it appeared that perhaps we were going to have to pull a Dunkirk, but those British's finally turned the tide. We Seabees had no further casualties on the beach, but we had some close calls."

Following the Mediterranean landings, several of the veteran pontoon units embarked for England where they commenced assembling pontoon gear for the invasion of France. They also taught English sailors how to assemble and operate the pontoons.

Several new uses were developed, and the most spectacular of these was the Rhino ferry. Instead of a narrow bridge of pontoons, like the causeway, the steel boxes were built into great barges—six pontoons wide and 30 long. They could be propelled either by inboard units or by large outboard motors.

In addition, the maneuverability was increased by a small pontoon tug. The Seabees rode these fully loaded, across the English Channel. After unloading them, they used them as ferries operating back and forth to the ships lying off shore.

It has been estimated that during the first critical week at one of the Normandy beaches, 85 percent of the vehicles unloaded were brought ashore through means of pontoon gear.

They contributed tremendously to the success of the initial landing operations. And the Seabees, who manned them, in some instances as many as 80 hours at a stretch, were given unstinting credit for their work.

With landing operations at Normandy running smoothly, other Seabee units went to work helping restore the port of Cherbourg. Many were skilled construction men possessed of skills at welding, carpentry, demolition and diving.

The Stevedore Battalions

Preceding pages have dealt exclusively with the fighter-builders on construction assignments. Another group of Seabees, the "Special Battalions," have undertaken one of the most important, if least glamorous, jobs of the war - loading and unloading ships in the combat zones. At one time our inability to handle cargo at its destination threatened the success of all our operations. Ships which had run the submarine and mine gantlet with supplies representing sacrifice and hard work on the home front, lay fully loaded, at anchor, veritable clay pigeons for enemy aircraft.

It was clear by late 1942 that the Navy would have to organize special battalions to handle the huge piles of freight. Civilian ship crews were not able to do the job, even though they had the courage to work under the bombs and were willing to work long hours. The work was hazardous. There had been no time to build piers on the Pacific islands, and when a freighter arrived at, say, Guadalcanal, she was obliged to anchor offshore and dump her cargo onto heaving barges. The barges then had to be gotten somehow to the beach, where the cargo then had to be transferred to trucks, all of which doubled the normal amount of stevedoring.

At the worst of the unloading crisis, when 83 ships were lying at anchor in the South Pacific waiting to be unloaded, a construction battalion was ordered to lend a hand. The Seabees, although few of them had ever handled cargoes, were able to do the job in HALF the time the civilian crews had been requiring. Seabee enthusiasm compensated for their lack of experience. They pitched in with a great deal of profanity, "Copenhagened" the clock, and defied the weather. That was the tip-off. The Civil Engineer Corps thereupon singled out 95 men with experience as stevedores who had enlisted in the construction battalions.

It hand-picked 900 others who had some knowledge of rigging and handling barges and small boats, and dispatched them to the Pacific. They were later joined by the Second, Third and Fourth "Specials." These men, who had volunteered to build and to fight, were not too happy at first over their new and less exciting assignment. But, seeing the need, they quickly went to work, and are credited with playing a brave and vital role in turning our fortunes of war in that area. They quickly cleared the bottlenecks that were strangling our entire war effort in the Pacific.

One liberty ship captain reported: "The manner in which the men of the First Special accepted duty during an attack on us by 12 enemy aircraft was unsurpassed. Gangs were organized as ammunition carrier, magazine loaders, and at fire stations. Some men took positions on the 20-mm guns, some on the 3-inch guns, and some as corpsmen at the First Aid station."

Said another master: " During the course of a raid, while enemy planes were forming for another dive on the ship, the First Specials calmly removed broken booms and rigging from the hatches and lashed them to the deck for safety. During the night they stood guard watch, relieving the gun crews in order that they might be in best form when needed."

Lieutenant Commander James E. King, of the Coast Guard, was captain of a cargo ship that put in at Bougainville when Japanese mortars were making it unhealthy for the stevedores. This is what he reported:

"I would like to take this opportunity to state that they (the men of the Special) are without doubt the finest unit that has ever handled the loading or discharging while I have been in command of this vessel. Their teamwork is really a pleasure to watch, and the amount of cargo discharged per gang hour is far in excess of any stevedoring done in this area.

"The stevedores that worked this ship in the States would be put to shame if they could see these boys in action. When I look at your outfit, I feel proud to be an American."

A training program was started for the Specials once the first extreme emergency had been relieved. The Bureau of Yards and Docks appealed to the steamship and stevedoring companies to give up some of their top men to become officers of the special battalions. The companies came through like the real Americans they are. A few experienced officers and men were assigned to each battalion (1,010 men and 34 officers). Volunteers who comprised the remainder of the battalion were trained on shipboard. The inexperienced men were conditioned on two "dry-land Liberty Ships" put together at Camp Peary, VA.

Seabee Specials handled 112,407 tons of cargo from 33 ships during the first three months in the Pacific. When the First Seabee Special arrived at Noumea, 66 ships clogged the harbor. Thirty days later, there were 30 fewer ships there. In another month, they were being discharged as fast as they came in. Since then, backing up our fighting men in every war theater, 30,000 Specials have truly "kept the hook moving."

Seabee Ingenuity

Wherever you find a Seabee, you will find a bulldozer. That is his flagship. He has the same feeling about it that a flier has for his plane. The things he can do with it are numberless. And it is said that the Seabee has one thing even more valuable—his own ingenuity. He has an incredible capacity for finding a way to do the thing that just can't be done. Herewith are just a few examples of almost endless Seabee resourcefulness:

An LST was lying helpless off the shore of a South Pacific Island over which Japanese bombers had had a field day. The LST's propeller had been put out of commission, and there were no tools with which to remove it for repair. Having no alternative, the horrified captain watched Seabee divers go down and pack dynamite around the propeller. They put in just the right amount in the right places. The blasts blew the propeller off. The ship was not further damaged. The Seabees carried the damaged part away, repaired it, and restored it to the LST.

The Seabees claim that they can solve any construction problem in the world, given two things: enough junk piles and half enough time. What they do with old oil drums staggers a layman's imagination. With them, they have improved drainage ditches for airfields and roads; they have used them as roofing, chimneys, sewer pipes, stoves, shower baths, furniture, and at least 1,001 other purposes.

At Vella Lavella a landing ship grounded too far from shore to unload its cargo. Japanese bombs were falling around it and on the beaches. Herbert F. Minster, chief yeoman, figured that the palm trees at the water's edge, if properly felled, would reach to the ship's ramp. They bridged the gap. The cargo was quickly rolled ashore over the felled palm trunks.

When an LST beached 60 feet off a central Pacific Island, Seabees ran two strings of pontoons between and made a road out to the ship. Over this they unloaded 2,800 drums of gasoline, 100 tons of wire and all the rest of the cargo in less than 10 hours, including the time it took to build the road.

During the fighting for a beachhead, a bulldozer's transmission was damaged. With Japanese bullets whistling by, two Seabees used an ordinary screwdriver to shift gears and the job proceeded.

Seabees were temporarily out of drainage pipe while building a hospital at Munda. Two officers noticed a huge pile of empty Japanese shell casings. They cut and welded the casings to make a deluxe brass pipe 2,000 feet long. The cut-off ends were fashioned into ashtrays by individual Seabees who sent them home as souvenirs.

The Japanese had left behind a damaged concrete mixer when they scampered off one Pacific outpost. Taking a 20-foot length of 4-inch pipe, the Seabees patched the holes. When the mixer's mangled gasoline motors would not start, the Seabees powered the machine with a belt attached to the rear wheel of one of the their own trucks. Pouring some salvaged Japanese cement and some coral into the revitalized mixer, the Seabees commenced pouring a concrete galley floor within 48 hours after landing.

Once the Seabees had to build a bridge before their own equipment arrived. They hooked up a captured Japanese motor to a portable sawmill and started cutting planking out of solid mahogany. A destroyed Japanese hangar provided beams for trusses, a Japanese winch was used for power, and material for the grading work was hauled in captured Japanese trucks.

They have built many other bridges, warehouses, and comfort stations out of precious woods. A statistical report sent to Washington by one Seabee officer proudly called attention to the luxury of solid mahogany "heads."

The Seabees made themselves a sightseeing boat by raising a sunken barge.

There is a rumor that enterprising, if conscienceless, Seabees have copied Japanese shipping directions from old packing cases onto phony Japanese flags, which the Seabees made, and have traded them profitably to the unsuspecting.

When a palm tree is found that is too tough to be knocked over by the power of a single bulldozer, they attack with three machines. With blades raised, they hit the tree simultaneously. If that does not topple it, earth is bulldozed into a ramp leading to a higher point on the tree where better leverage may be had. Seldom do they have to resort to saws, axes and dynamite.

Lacking drills to make holes for dynamite, Seabees fired shells from an M-4 tank to puncture a hillside.

"They're the cat's whiskers" was almost an accurate phrase when used to describe Christmas toys made by the 120th Battalion Seabees for French and Arab tots in Algiers. Short of paintbrushes, Seabee Frank Weideman ran down three cats, plucked hairs from their backs, and fashioned the delicate brushes with which the toys were painted. Everybody had a good time-except the cats. Weideman also supplied his buddies with fishing flies made from bird feathers.

The 64th Battalion's machine shop got a man-sized job when handed a pile driver piston, which had split in half. It was made of tool steel, 18 inches in diameter, three feet high, and weighed 800 pounds. Welders worked continuously for 106 hours, used 300 pounds of welding rod.

How to do their washing with the least effort challenged the inventiveness of Don Litrell, J.F. Glass and T.H. Sontag of the 56th Battalion on "Island X." From a junk pile the embryo Edisons salvaged a G.I. can, a refrigerator belt, a truck tie-rod, a worn-out concrete vibrator motor and an old washer agitator. Mixing well before using, the Seabees came up with something, which didn't closely resemble

a washing machine, but it did the job ship-shape.

When a pal's watch broke down for want of a jewel, Charlie L. Zacek of the 56th Battalion, a former watch-repairman from Texas, simply snipped the head off an ordinary straight pin, dressed it down and set it in place. The watch has not lost a second nor missed a tick since.

James M. Hallowes Jr. has small feet. He had never been able to get GI shoes that fit. In French Morocco, he had to bargain for a pair of native-made sandals to continue working. In Oran, he talked the Army out of a coupon to buy a pair he described as "only a little too wide." Then, while on liberty, he saw a WAC walking down the street. An idea was born, a proposition was stated. For the rest of his tour of duty, Hallowes got around very nicely - in the shoes of a sympathetic WAC.

The problem of how a section of heavy steel could be cut 20 feet under water out on a Southwest Pacific Island without any tools for the job was dumped in the lap of L.E. Damm of San Francisco. He decided an underwater cutting torch was the best answer. He took the problem to H.O.T. Ridlon who scratched his head, went to work. Taking and ordinary blowtorch, he enclosed the cutting tip in a compressed air bell, which he was obliged to make on the spot. The torch worked.

The "Sea Hag" is not listed in "Jane's Fighting Ships," but it is a familiar sight in the forward fighting zones of Pacific. The 200 Seabee stevedores who landed on a British-mandated island in the Central Pacific found a lack of housing facilities. Grabbing a 1,500-ton lighter lying at anchor, and appropriating the necessary land-based construction battalion gear, the unit started building itself a houseboat.

Bulldozer stockpile, Davisville, RI. Courtesy of Ernest B. Hauer.

Upon arrival to Camp Endicott, a Seabees first task was to find his duffel bag. 27 OCT. 1944. Courtesy of Raymond Dierkes.

Seabees 1040 DET front of Quanset Hut in Davisville, RI. 1943. Courtesy of Paul Crepeau.

A double-effect salt-water evaporator, with gadgets to prevent water spilling into the distillate line due to the roll of the lighter, was installed as the fresh water supply system. Salt water was pumped aboard by a converted submersible bilge pump. Seven field ranges, welded to the deck, became the nucleus of the galley. Addition of a rack to the forward side of the ranges made direct serving, cafeteria style, possible without use of a steam table. Air pressure was supplied by a shallow diving pump.

Piping was used for drains; hatches were cut in the deck; companionways led to the deck below, which was turned into crew quarters. Steel bunks were fitted in. Portholes and passageways were built.

Cargo dunnage was procured to construct the house. Laid out in sections, it included engine room, galley, mess hall, supply and disbursing office, post office, sick bay, ship's service store and other compartments. If has officer's and chief's quarters, and a signal bridge. Pontoons were used as storage tanks. Oil drums, tops and bottoms knocked out, were welded together and installed as ventilation funnels from hold to topside. Not a pretentious craft, but she is extremely livable. It has been towed to three forward areas, covering more than 1,800 sea miles. Skipper of the odd vessel is Lieutenant Edward Norton, of Belmont, CA.

One group of Seabees, bothered by rats, built an earth ramp leading to the brim of an oil drum half filled with water. A collapsible plank was suspended from the edge to a choice tid-bit. When one victim ventured out and fell into the water, the plank bounced back into position to receive the next.

A dishwashing machine was made out of discarded oil drums, piping, wire baskets and metal frames.

One battalion retrieved a Japanese truck from the junk heap, remodeled it into a traveling library van to make books available to isolated work parties.

In the Green Islands a trombonist couldn't find a suitable mute for his instrument. Using a pork-sausage-can, studded with automobile head gaskets, he now gets the desired pianissimo.

At a North African base, a Seabee made a bull fiddle out of an discarded oil drum. Coxswain T.W. Montgomery carved a violin out of native mahogany on Guadalcanal, using teakwood for inlay work and bridge, and balsa for the chin rest. The instrument's ribs were boiled and lashed around beer bottles. The rest of the violin was finished with a couple of files, a knife and a coping saw. Strings are still lacking, no cats being available on the island.

On Bougainville, where the Japanese bombed the Seabees 60 times, Lieutenant Sidney Mauk remembered a certain delicacy he used to eat in a drug store in New Rochelle, NY. He and his machine shop crew sawed native teakwood and fashioned a 50-gallon tub. They welded a lattice work paddle into a 30-gallon stainless steel cooking kettle. They rigged a bearing and shaft to rotate the kettle inside the wooden tub. A worn-out bulldozer supplied a fan belt; a portable generator supplied a one-lunged air-cooled engine. The transmission and differential from a bomb-wrecked jeep were added. A belt connected the transmission and engine. The transmission was connected to the differential by shaft and the differential to the inner kettle by a universal joint. The outer tub was filled with ice. Into the cooking kettle went 30 gallons of a certain white powder mixed with water. The one-lunger was cranked, the jeep was put into high, and guess what happened? The Fighting Builders, half an hour later, dug into 30 gallons of the world's smoothest ice cream.

Some of these examples of ingenuity seem trivial when stacked alongside more substantial Seabee achievements, but they reveal the spirit of the men. How are you going to discount men who can go through 60 bombings and come out making ice cream?

The Early Years of Camp Endicott

reprinted from Camp Endicott, Naval Construction Training Center, U.S. Navy Department

On June 9, 1942, the Secretary of the Navy authorized the establishment of the Naval Construction Training Center at Davisville, RI. This new center, Camp Endicott, named after Rear Admiral Mordecai T. Endicott, first Chief of the Bureau of Yards and Docks, was a 500-acre camp site consisting of farmland, low, rocky hills, woods and swamps.

Sixty-four days later, the first battalion came aboard for training.

The intervening two months had been hectic. Construction began June 22. Quonset huts and long, green buildings began to appear overnight. Roads were roughed out, swamp areas were ditched and drained, the ground was criss-crossed by the deep furrows of water and sewage systems. Bulldozers and draglines began to level drill fields.

On August 3, the first contingent of enlisted men arrived. They were prepared for the commissioning of the station August 11 and the arrival, 24 hours later, of the 18th Construction Battalion for advance training.

Battalions coming in during the fall of 1942 were ushered into a confusion of muddy roads, gaping waterline ditches, half-finished buildings and hastily erected facilities. But battlefronts were crying for Seabees and there was no time to waste.

The first two or three battalions came to Camp Endicott already formed and ready for advanced training. Thereafter, men began pouring in directly from the recruiting stations.

Shedding civilian clothes, they went into their "boot" period—their first four weeks of Navy life—that time of getting accustomed to barracks, uniforms and orders, to the sting of hypodermic needles, to the endless, orderly routine of the service. Then they were organized into battalions for another four weeks of training—advanced.

During these eight weeks, raw recruits were converted, under pressure of time, into fighting builders. They were indoctrinated in the principles of modern warfare. They were led through the intricacies of close and extended order drills. They were taught to shoot, to throw hand grenades, to fight with bayonets, to defend themselves with judo in hand-to-hand combat. They sweated and panted through the torture of combat obstacle courses. And they came through prepared to function as military units.

At the same time, they were becoming familiar with the specialized machinery and equipment they were to use later on beachheads, battlefronts and foreign bases. This part of the training was not strange to most of them, because the majority were skilled construction men as civilians.

Battalions training in the fall and early winter of 1942 had an opportunity to get a glimpse of—and to participate in—one of the minor miracles of construction for which the Seabees were to become famous all over the world. The camp was literally being built around them.

One group of buildings, the first group to be completed, included the administration building, station force barracks, mess hall, recreation building and station dispensary.

Stretching away in orderly rows from the central group came other building groups, serving as unit areas for battalions. Each unit area was complete to its own barracks, mess hall, and administration building. Each had its recreation building, with ship's store, library, theater, bowling alleys, billiard room and class rooms.

In the meantime, here and there about the camp, groups of Quonset huts had been erected to serve as school facilities and warehouses. Extensive drill fields, great drill halls, and a baseball field were coming into being. Later were to be added such refinements as a bathing beach on Narragansett Bay, the world's largest indoor swimming pool and a golf course.

While Camp Endicott was started only in June 1942, in less than six months it was operating at capacity, training its full complement of battalions by early December of that year. By early spring of 1943, construction of the training center was virtually complete, although improvement of the grounds and minor alterations of facilities continued. There were paved streets, lights, neatly painted buildings, trim lawns, profuse plantings of flowers, and other evidences that the camp was approaching maturity.

By April 4, 1943, the camp presented an almost finished appearance and was ready for its formal dedication by the late Secretary of the Navy Frank Knox. Present for the ceremony, besides Mr. Knox, were Rear Admiral (now Vice-Admiral) Ben Moreell, CEC, USN, Chief of the Bureau of Yards and Docks, under whose cognizance the Seabees came. Other high Naval officers present included Rear Admiral (now Vice-Admiral) Randall Jacobs, Chief of the Bureau of Naval Personnel. Miss Grace Endicott, daughter of the late Rear Admiral Endicott, was a guest of honor.

In the spring of 1943 the days of Camp Endicott as a "boot" training station came to a close. Thereafter, the base was to concentrate on advanced training of battalions about to be shipped overseas.

This meant greater attention was to be paid to the camp's rifle range, located four miles northwest of Davisville, RI, and commonly known as the Sun Valley Rifle Range. Seabees first began firing on the range about February 22, 1943, and housing facilities were installed there in May.

Preoccupation with advanced training also meant the later addition, in the summer of 1944, of special facilities for use of stevedore battalions. Across the tracks from Camp Endicott proper, two "training ship" units were built on dry land, and budding stevedore units spent long days loading and unloading the "material of war", which one day they would unload half way across the globe.

Well into its program of giving advanced training to outgoing battalions, Camp Endicott also became center for "refresher" courses for Naval officers, for training of groups of midshipmen and of groups of newly commissioned officers. It became likewise a reception center for battalions returning to the United States from duty overseas.

During its brief span of existence, Camp Endicott was an important part of the program of training, equipping and receiving back into this country more than four score of Seabee Battalions and numerous specialized units.

Its outstanding success was largely due to the direction of the man who was at its helm since its very beginning—Captain Fred F. Rogers, USN (Ret), Commanding Officer.

Sergeant of the guard, Davisville, RI; Courtesy of Hugh Acton.

Seabees pose in Davisville, RI; Courtesy of Ernest B. Hauer.

Seabees duck used during invasion of France, 15 August 1944. Courtesy of Paul Crepeau.

SPECIAL STORIES

The Sawmill Gang, location unknown, 1943. Front row: Mr. Blackridge, Smitty, Corp. Engelhardt, Burns, Mitsing, Fortner, Smitty, Auclaire, Morton. Rear row: Chief Eckhardt, Mr. Darnell, Chief Crockett, Barton, Panonski, Rothman, Chief Bahhen, Sandy, Trouche, Morten, Gallagher, Kennedy, Murphy. Courtesy of Alan E. Burns.

The Seabees

by James C. DiPietro

The Navy needed fighters
And they needed working men,
So they organized the Seabees,
Who could work and fight to win.

They took riggers, welders, carpenters,
And cooks and bakers, too.
They put them in the Navy,
And showed them what to do.

With machine gun and rifle,
The Seabees learned to shoot.
They learned just how to guard themselves,
And other things to boot.

They learned to drill and march all day.
They learned just how to dress.
They even learned the Navy's trick
Of "seconds at the mess."

They learned the Navy lingo,
Called it "head" and "deck" and "swab,"
They learned just how to "knock it off"
Like any other gob.

They learned these many different things
In thirteen weeks or less;
And what they learned they practiced
By putting to the test.

With training done, they left the States,
And went to Island X
They took their own equipment
It filled the holds and decks.

The Japanese were on the island,
When at last it have in sight.
The Seabees had a job on hand,
So they prepared to fight.

They landed under heavy fire,
Among the shot and shell;
They charged across the rock beach,
And gave the Nippers hell.

At last the Nippies were wiped out,
Then came the time to work.
Every Seabee did his duty,
Not a one was seen to shirk.

They built a landing field and decks,
Mess halls and barracks, too.
They piped in water, wired up lights,
They had a lot to do.

At last the place was "squared away."
Twas pretty to be seen,
And then a ship came sailing in,
And brought the first Marine.

They followed up the Seabees
(Though they said they came before),
And they found a base awaiting,
Room for them and many more.

From the Halls of Montezuma
To the shores of Tripoli
It used to be the Leathernecks,
But now it's all Seabees.

And when at last we're called above,
And stand at heavens scene.
There'll be a Seabee waiting there,
To greet the first Marine.

The Birth Of The Bee

Reprinted in part from the March/April issue of the Navy Civil Engineer

There have been many stories, some almost legendary, of how the famed Seabee emblem was created. Here, in his own words, is the factual account of the "birth of the Bee" from the creator of the design and term itself—Frank J. Iafrate.

"During the early part of 1942, I was employed as a clerk at the Naval Air Station in Quonset Point, RI. I was in charge of an office that held a large file of confidential drawings of naval dock installations, both throughout this country and overseas. It was basically a reference file, and both naval CEC officers and ci-

vilian draftsmen could refer to them for a possible solution to a particular problem(s) they had encountered.

"It was not long before (at least to the men who had access to my office) I became known as an artist-of sorts.

"One day I heard some scuttlebutt about a special group of Navy men who were not only being trained in construction work by civilians, but also were receiving military training from Marine units. This special group was referred to as Construction Battalion men.

"Soon after learning of this new outfit, a Lieutenant Schilstone came to my office and asked if I would make up an insignia for a group of 250 men he was in charge of. Lieutenant Schilstone explained his unit was one of four being separately trained to be later formed into the first Construction Battalion. These new units were to replace civilian workers the Navy had then recently lost on such islands as Wake and Guam. Lieutenant Schilstone further explained that these men would be used to build forward bases and would go ashore in the second wave after Marines. The task of the Navy men was primarily to build airstrips, docks, roads, etc., but they would also be trained and ready to fight defending what they had built.

"The type of insignia he was looking for was a "Disney type" insignia and mentioned if a name could be coined instead of the cumbersome one of Construction Battalion. I said I would very much like to give it a try and would report to him as soon as I had a rough.

"After discarding the beaver as the main theme for the insignia," Mr. Iafrate goes on to say, "The next day, while still searching my brain, I happened to think of a busy bee who works industriously and yet is capable of stinging you when you try to claim his property. It seemed to fit with the Construction Battalion concept. I thought a white Navy hat on an animated bee to make him strictly Navy; a hammer and wrench on a couple of "hand" legs to show his construction abilities; and a submachine gun in his front "hand" legs to show his military powers. This bee, I thought, should have a determined look on his face to show he meant to do what he set out to do, in the shortest time possible.

"I had no idea at the time it would be used by other groups. I remember being so enthused with this mental image that I went home that night and started to do some rough sketches. While doing this I remembered I also needed a name. As I looked at the rough pencil sketch insignia, it occurred to me that Navy brings to mind the sea and that my main character was a bee. Thus, a phonetic rendering of the initials "C" and "B" became Seabees. It seemed

Seabee field practice.

Co. D-5, 133 NCB in Gulfport, Miss. Nov. 1944. Courtesy of Wilfred MacGiffert.

John Taggart and Leon Bittinger during road construction. Okinawa, May 1945. Courtesy of John Taggart.

to fit—short, easy to say and remember. Now, I felt I had it, the complete insignia.

"Instead of doing a rough sketch for the lieutenant, I went right into a finished watercolor drawing and brought it to work the next day. I contacted Lieutenant Schilstone and he came to my office, where I explained my thinking in the make-up of my "Seebee." The lieutenant seemed very pleased and suggested we show it to the officer in charge of construction.

"As I remember, it was a Captain Miller, who after seeing it suggested it be sent to Rear Admiral Ben Moreell, CEC, USN, who was Chief of Yards and Dock in Washington, D.C. This was done, and after a few days I received a thank you letter from the admiral for the Seebee insignia.

"Mr. Iafrate's insignia was later used in a large recruiting drive to obtain men for the Con-

struction Battalion Forces. The only part of the design that Mr. Iafrate was not responsible for was the hauser rope encircling the Seabee and the lettering of Seabee."

He himself served in the Seabees and was discharged a chief petty officer late in 1946. Soon after he was discharged he was awarded the Secretary of the Navy's Distinguished Public Service Award Medal for his design of the now famous Seabee insignia.

A Jungle Christmas Celebration

Chaplain Joseph Degi, Colonel (Ret) US Army

In addition to the fascinating experience I learned from Seabee "Can Do" there was great camaraderie, but one lifelong incident is etched in my memory. This unexpected inspiration happened on Christmas Eve. The 119th Seabee Battalion arrived in March 1944, in Milne Bay, New Guinea, where it seemed to rain constantly. In May, the battalion received orders to move north to Hollandia, Dutch New Guinea to build the Advance Naval Headquarters, the nerve center of the South Pacific operation where the invasion of the Philippines was planned. Upon arrival at Hollandia, the Battalion was divided: the main body at Hollandia to build the Seventh Fleet Headquarters, A Company with elements of Headquarters Company were deployed to Tanah Merah Bay some 25 miles north to build a tank farm for storage of high grade fuel for fighter planes. A torturous road had to be cut through the foothills of the Owen Stanley mountains that would connect Hollandia Bay to Tenah Merah Bay.

At Tenah Merah Bay camp, we established in the midst of the jungle, on top of the mountain where a winding road would lead down to the Bay. We were completely cut off from any form of civi-

lization. A permanent camp of tents for 250 of us was quickly built and all possible comforts were provided. Every day, seven days a week with long hours of labor was our routine. One relaxation after the evening meal was to watch rerun movies. During the day we would on occasion see natives, "Fuzzy-Wuzzys" scantily dressed, walking in groups along the jungle path but neither ever tried to communicate with one another nor to trade for "cat eyes." We were instructed that these natives were at one time head hunters, and it may be dangerous to confront any of them.

On Christmas Eve, 1944, the heat, mosquitoes, jungle rot on our bodies, exhaustion and plain homesickness occupied our thoughts. No mention of doing something special for Christmas Eve, for it was just another routine day. We did have a battalion chaplain, but he was at the Main Camp in Hollandia and he rarely ventured down the 25 mile jungle road to our small, isolated camp, This was to be like all other nights, and we gathered in the clearing for the rerun movie to relax and ponder what about our world. Suddenly, out of the edge of the jungle came what seemed like an attacking army of natives, but without any weapons or visible signs of hostility. There were about 50 men who, without any attempt to inform us of their intentions, gathered together as a group, and to our astonishment, began to sing. They were singing a most beautiful, harmonious rendition of all our familiar Christmas Carols (O Come All Ye Faithful, It Came Upon A Midnight Clear, Silent Night, etc.) with the same tunes but in their native language.

This continued for 45 minutes as we with tearful eyes, stunned and perplexed, tried to understand what was happening here 11,000 miles from our homes, in a God forsaken, uncivilized jungle. Our memories went back to the many Christmas Eves we had with our parents, our families and how we wished that we could be back there with them for this Christmas Eve.

We heard from various sources that there were missionaries back in the jungle somewhere. It became obvious that these missionaries preceded us into this hostile dark and fearful part of God's creation, and they accomplished what we would think impossible. We were the most civilized, educated, advanced people on planet earth and yet, we of the western civilization were be-

Main Street, New Guinea, 1944-45.

Philippines. Summer 1945. Courtesy W.C. Snefkev.

Officers and men P.A.D. 3, New Guinea, 1944-45. Courtesy of Hoyt Bryson.

ing reminded by natives what made us great. The uneducated, half-civilized bushmen of New Guinea reminded us who we were. Of all the exciting adventures I had with the Seabees, Christmas Eve 1944, stands out in my heart and mind as the best Christmas, ever.

Uninvited Guests

by Richard Zander

I was a 19-year-old Seabee crane and shovel operator, but driving supply trucks at the time. I was stationed on Guam with the 41st Naval Construction Battalion. Our primary job was building Quonset huts for storage, road building and site demolition. Our camp was close to overgrowth.

The evening chow line started at 1700 and ended at 1800. There was usually a long line at first since everyone was very hungry. Then they would spend the rest of the evening relaxing. That meant writing letters,

playing cards, baseball, or going to whatever movie was showing that night.

One evening I went late to eat. The late comers were called stragglers. As it approached 1800, more stragglers seemed to get in line. Something strange began to happen. The three men at the end of the line huddled together and seemed to shy away from the others. They also were very dirty and had welder's goggles on their foreheads. They did not talk at all among themselves. Most of our battalion knew each other by name or face, but not these three mates. The Shore Patrol was alerted and surrounded them for a closer look. They were asked for their dog tags. They could not speak English and immediately held up their hands. They were Japanese soldiers who came out of the jungle and tried to sneak into the chow line to get a meal. They were taken to the POW camp on the island.

We were surprised that there were Japanese still in the jungle on the island. Especially since Guam had been secured

on August 10, 1944, about eight months earlier. They hid well. Actually a Japanese soldier, Shochi Yokoi, was captured 29 years after the war ended. He had hidden in the jungle and existed that long without realizing the war was over.

A Navy Seabee Can-Do

David A. Morrison USN Seabee

The slogan, "A Navy Seabee Can-Do," is typical of many of the Seabees that served in WWII in the USS, Europe, Africa, South America and the Aleutian Islands.

In 1991, I learned from the Navy Bureau of Records, that the Pontoon Assembly Detachments had received a Navy Commendation, a special Navy Commendation, and a Navy Citation from the Commander of the South Pacific.

In 1996, I also learned from the Navy Seabee (Command) Historian that there was

H. Hoyt Bryson at work, 100 ton floating crane, New Guinea and Samar, 1944-45. Courtesy of Hoyt Bryson.

Courtesy of Gino R. Sacchetti.

Bob Dunn, 13th NCB. Courtesy Robert T. Dunn.

50x100 Quanset Factory PAD # 2, Bienka, Russells 1943. Courtesy of D.A. Morrison.

Bobcats at their reunion in Branson MO, 1999. Courtesy of Albert Travgott.

Philippines Summer 45. Courtesy of W.C. Snefkey.

a PAD #6 in the South Pacific. When you consider the total production of all six PAD units, the total could have been 20,000 tons of steel used.

In the early part of 1942, the slogan of the Seabees was, "The Difficult We Do Immediately, The Impossible Takes Us A Little Longer." Today, 1997, the Seabees are still active and their slogan is, "Can-Do."

I am very proud to say that I am a "Seabee," and I cherish all the friends that I made during my years in the U.S. Navy. We can hold our heads high as we all served our United States of America well.

What is a Navy Bobcat?

submitted by Harold E. Williams and Albert W. Traugott

A Navy Bobcat was a member of the first naval construction unit organized and sent overseas in World War II. The unit was called the First Naval Construction Battalion. It was not a battalion, as it had only 250 enlisted men and six officers. The term "Seabees" was not coined and approved by the Bureau of Navigation, until March 5, 1942, so the men called themselves "Bobcats" after the designated code name for their first destination, Bora Bora.

The unit was commissioned in Charleston, South Carolina, on January 21, 1942 and shipped out for Bora Bora, Society Islands on January 27, arriving there on February 18. They proceeded to unload ships, construct Quonset huts and a fresh water system, build roads, construct a seaplane base, and a refueling station of 22 fuel tanks. When that was done, they built an airstrip.

On March 26, 1942, the unit's name was changed from the First Construction Battalion to First Construction Detachment, and the name First Construction Battalion was given to a battalion in training at Camp Allen, Norfolk, Virginia.

After 19 months on Bora Bora, the Bobcats were sent to American Samoa to join the 22nd Marine Regiment Reinforced. During the next seven months, the Bobcats performed general construction work and also saw action with the Marines during the campaign in the Marshall Islands, on Eniwetok, Parry and Engebi Islands. After 26 months of tropical campaigning the Bobcats were

detached from the Marines, returned to the States and inactivated at the Construction Battalion Replacement Depot at Camp Parks, CA.

The Bobcats now go by the name Bobcat Battalion, because even though they were a small unit, they think they earned the name.

Now you have the answer to the question, "What is a Navy Bobcat?"

Note: This article was brought to our attention by Catherine McCabe, Director, Rochester Council Navy League and submitted by Harold E. William

Spare The Seabee

Annonynous. Submitted by Will Barker

Whatever the publicity about the Navy, there is one branch that without it we could not have won the war in the Pacific during World War II. Today it is solidly institutionalized and yet scarcely noticed. We refer, of course, to the Construction Battalion Units, better known as Seabees, whose motto is "We build and we fight!"

Okinawa, mines and traps. Courtesy of Ken Beatty (far left rear).

27th N.C.B. Gally Tulagi, Oct. 1943. Courtesy Paul Kaplan.

Results of a Pacific typhoon bent these steel girders in Okinawa, 1945. Courtesy of Raymond Dierkes.

Engineering Department 41st Naval Construction Battalion-Guam 1945. Back row: L-R: Ch. Carl Bench, Ch. Lynch, Ens. Rehkoff, Lt. Orville Christensen, Ch. William Cover. Front row: L-R: Ch. Criss Runge, William Malone 1/c, Carl Hendrickson, 1/c, Ch. Harry Johnson, Ray Cronin 1/c. Courtesy of William Malone.

At work they sort of dress like Army combat engineers but talk like sailors, wear Navy rating badges and marks, yet as often as not hang out, off duty, with their traditional friends, the grunt Marines.

Today, Seabees are received and trained as such. But when formed in 1942, the entire notion of Navy builders was brand new and their famed founder was Vice Admiral Ben Moreell.

CSC, USN had to start from scratch to get the massive number of already experienced men needed to support the long train of island-hopping amphibious attacks being planned. His answer was to bypass the age limits and recruit straight out of construction sites and union halls.

They signed up with alacrity—from dam sites, oil fields, high iron jobs, mines, etc.—and what he got were thousands of the toughest, meanest and best heavy construction men on earth, most of whom were old enough to be the fathers (in some cases the grandfathers) of young new men elsewhere. None, before or after Navy indoctrination, gave a tinker's damn about details, much less regulations. They ignored saluting, ceremony, mud, bugs, and bombs about equally, while becoming noted for practical jokes, horrible eating habits; the ability to steal or create anything that would make their lives more comfortable. They were also known, for having short fuses if fired upon: they were known to use bulldozers as tanks. Being peculiar sorts, Seabee units often kept goats as mascots and their collective reputations soon preceded them.

The story goes: On one contested Pacific Island shortly after the Marines got done, gangs of natives were mopping up Japanese stragglers when they came across one of the Seabee goats. After observing it

curiously, they returned to their chief for instructions as to whether or not they should kill this strange and irritable creature.

"What manner of beast is it?" asked the chief.

"Oh, he's very strange, majesty" the native replied. "He has fierce eyes, long horns, a shaggy beard, will eat anything and stinks like hell."

"Spare him," pronounced the chief, "Don't kill him whatever you do. He's what the Americans call a "Seabee.""

The Ironworkers

by James C. Di Pietro

Four o'clock comes and we trudge back to our tents or some of us to the beer hall, where we just sit and shrug off the weariness of a good day's work. Home is a canvas covered (usually leaky) place, where we have the entire contents of our private lives locked in a footlocker.

Some of us fall asleep and miss chow, much to the delight of the mess cooks, but some guys make up for the lost food by their tremendous appetites, and store tons of food in their bottomless pits.

The men in the showers are a little frustrated because they can't get the water just right, it's either boiling or freezing.

The storekeeper at the beer hall has lost his mind because no less than a thousand cans of beer have gone over the counter in 10 minutes flat. The corpsmen close sickbay after nursing half the battalion and wonder if they are going to sleep all night.

One by one, the dirty mess of grease becomes a human body of men, tired, but refreshed, and some sick from eating too much for fear of starving before breakfast.

Clockwise from left: Anthony Sommese, George Spafford, Frank Solitario, and Joe Stefano. Okinawa, April 1945. Courtesy of George Spafford.

You might be a little lucky today, because you got a letter or two or maybe you don't have duty section till the day after tomorrow. The movies start, and everybody wants to see what's playing. Between the moans and the groans because the picture is flicking on and off and cursing the rain we have to sit in, we watch it anyway because there's nothing else to do. But, we stop griping the second we think of the poor guy on the rock crusher watch. Some of us play cards, write letters, look at pictures or just think of going home.

If Jimmy D. decides to get his drums out, everybody gets headaches.

Come back to the tent and before you can do anything else, some pest comes barging in and yells "lights out." Sleep is a precious thing and you try to grab all you can, but it's even more precious because you can be anything or anywhere in the world, except here. London, Paris, Rome or New York, or maybe some small town with a population of a hundred.

You can be a millionaire or sometimes be walking into a night spot with a beautiful girl on your arm, and then just as you are going to kiss her good-night, you're being pulled out of bed.

You see some of the most beautiful sunrises in the world, but hate them because it only means another day working in the field, earning the taxpayers money. You stick your tongue out at yourself through a cracked mirror, wash up, and head down to the chow hall with a growling stomach. Everything else is routine. Quarters, absentees, lectures, sick-bay, boss's, ditches, trucks but at 0800 there seems to be a beautiful break in the day, which almost explains all this crazy run-a-round. The stars and stripes are going up, and like the pig you are, you stand there saluting with a greasy hand or an unshaven face. You are the headaches and praise of the officers, the filth and grime from the grease pit, the ugly slob that fleet sailors hate, and the cream of American mechanical talent.

MCB#7 is a city in itself, with courts and laws, celebrities and lowbrows, places of worship and heretics, and just about everything that can be thrown in a melting pot, in which the only thing that seems to survive, is the tough miserable chief who is always on our backs. I don't know about the rest of you, but when I go home, I'm gonna brag about it, cuz I'm a Seabee.

The NCTC Diving School

by Thomas M. Ansbro, BM1/c DT, USNR (1942-45)

History: NCTC Davisville was not created in one fell swoop. Seabee trainees frequently arrived in camp before housing and training facilities were entirely ready for them. Barracks and school buildings construction ran into mid-1943. The technical training schools came together as the instructor-qualified personnel, related equipment, and training materials were acquired-some by unconventional means of supply.

Early diving gear. Note the oil on this Seabees' body after diving on a sunken vessel. Courtesy of Ken Beatty.

Potential instructors were occasionally transferred to tech training faculty directly out of boot camp. Until classrooms were built, classes were held out of doors or under any available shelter and with whatever equipment could be assembled to do the job.

No exception to this new rule, the NCTC Diving School was operated from early 1942 almost to the end of its first year without any standard Navy diving equipment, any official Navy training text or related official literature, and without a single Navy-trained or Navy-qualified instructor. Fortunately, the instructor staff was composed of experienced divers, but they were all recruited from civilian construction or salvage activities. The Navy itself was short

of divers, and there were less then 500 civilian divers in the U.S. when the war began. Consequently, the available practitioner talent pool was a small one. The school did not have a permanent home until September '42, when the staff was assigned to one end of a new hangar shared with the Heavy Equipment Maintenance School occupying the rest of the building. At that point, classes moved indoors. Construction of an indoor, heated, 30-by-33-foot diver training tank partially sunk below the concrete floor, plus classrooms outfitted with compressed-air-and-oxygen piping facilities was complete by early December. For diver safety and to combat caisson sickness (bends), the school needed a recompression chamber.

One, a large 20-footer was located in reasonably salvable condition in storage in nearby Massachusetts. We trucked it in, assembled, piped and refitted it in the new school building. While the hangar was constructed by contractors "according to Hoyle" (as per the government's agreement with the unions), the tank, classrooms, equipment, etc. were all constructed by Diving School and other Tech School personnel on base. Our friends in the adjoining school in our building found us a huge air compressor and rigged it outside the building. In addition to our main building, we had a seagoing adjunct classroom built–a diving barge built of Seabee pontoons and powered by the biggest outboard motor in the world. The heavy equipment guys next door found us another monster compressor and rigged it on the barge. We could now train divers in the tank and outside in Narragansett Bay.

Meanwhile, diving training went on, as well as possible. The school's director (principal instructor) was BMC Elmer Brunette (Wisconsin), his assistants were BM1/c Bill Davidson (Texas), BM1/c Jack Gulledge (Texas), BM1/c Harry Homer (New York), GM1/c Frank Landers (Pennsylvania), BM2/c Ed Newman (Texas), CM21c Joel Montgomery (Iowa), BM2/c Walt Waterman (Washington), CM2/c Ted Cetner (New York), SF3/c Ed Lucier (Massachusetts), and S1/c Tom Ansbro (New York). All of the above were divers from coastal and riverine shipyards, salvage and marine construction activities, bridge caisson work, submarine tunnels, and even oil field activities. Nearly all had experience with explosives, some had worked with newly-developed and primitive underwater welding and cutting equipment (both oxy-hydrogen and high-amperage oxy-electric), and all had worked with heavy hoisting equipment, cranes, derricks and rigging equipment. Not one had ever worked with or in standard Navy deep-sea diving equipment. Some of us had never even seen it. This didn't matter very much in 1942 because we didn't have any. We had the Miller-Dunn helmet (used in the Miami Seaquarium in clear water), good for not much more than sitting on the bottom of the sea and watching fish swim by. We had a new "shallow-water diving mask," an early demand–breather mask connected to the surface air system by welding hose, which could also be used in shallow water with welding or aviator's breathing oxygen. It was good for limited activity in warm water, with reasonably clear visibility, of dubious value in cold, deep, or murky, polluted water. Wet suits did not exist.

To dive in cold water without the conventional fully enclosed dry gear, we coated our bodies with vaseline and donned the Navy's blue "long Johns," woolen underwear. It actually worked for short-duration shallow water dives. Not great, but OK. Limited to the sparse gear so far furnished by the Navy, we got a break. We learned that the Navy Mark V gas mask had been converted to shallow water diving use in Pearl Harbor salvage activity. No details, just a rumor. We jumped on it, made our own conversion with a minimum of tamper-

A souvenir from Tarawa.

War booty from Tarawa.

ing with the structure of the mask itself. It worked better than what we had been officially given, and it found its way into our instruction. I had an old 1920 model civilian diving helmet-and-breastplate at home, rescued from my former employer's desire to junk some of the company's older equipment. I got it sent up to the school. Among the faculty, we scrounged the rest of the "deep sea" gear (all civilian type), enough to dress out one diver and put him safely over the side. We did what we could with what we had. What we had, among other things, were green woolen uniforms and coats from the Civilian Conservation Corps (CCC, known as FDR's Tree Army). There weren't enough Navy Pea coats to go around until late 1942, so some of us wore the "greenies." Not in town, of course. The greenies were our secret. They were serviceable and warm. However, Navy Supply soon caught up with us, and we got our Navy uniforms.

Eventually, in early 1943, the standard Navy deep sea gear arrived, complete with modern telephones installed in the helmets, and even with the 1864 model hand–operated diving air pump

(four-man pumping–primitive, but workable). Modern–day portable air compressors had not been invented yet. Other things not yet then invented: SCUBA gear. But other brand-new stuff came in: swim fins, snorkels and masks, as well as plastic explosives and shape charges, just in time for the UDT (underwater demolition teams, also a new idea).

The Navy apparently having discovered that we existed, decided that we could use some Fleet Navy divers in the school, so we received four recent graduates of the new Salvage Diving School conducted on the sunken wreck of the French liner Normandie, at that time resting on her port side on the bottom of New York Harbor. We absorbed the new arrivals (Fleet divers Ed Nolan, Dave Brunton, Ed Beshara and Jim Boliver) into the staff, and the entire staff became recognized and appointed as Diver, Salvage (DS) and eligible for hazardous duty pay. The Navy soon found other assignments for the Fleet divers, and they were duly transferred elsewhere. BUPERS sent representatives of the advancement in rate

examination staff to coach us in writing examinations for the Seabee ratings. We wrote the exams, they were accepted by BUPERS, and some of us took our own exams to attain promotion (I went from third to first class on my own exams. The war ended before I could take the chief's exam). In general, things settled down, and from mid-1943 until Camp Endicott eventually phased out training, the Diving School practically functioned on automatic. In addition to our regular student training duties, we trained some personnel who went on to the new UDT training in Fort Pierce, got to use the Seabees' unique floating 75-ton crane in an interesting salvage job, hunted for drownees to aid the local police, blasted away old waterfront structures, salvaged a few sunken Navy aircraft and harbor craft, went out on a couple of classified underwater projects, raised storm-sized floating construction equipment, built a seawall and marine railway, rode out a hurricane in Narragansett Bay in our diving barge and a tugboat, and on occasion, braved the Atlantic on our barge. We also were invited to the Navy Submarine School during a hiatus between classes. We enjoyed making dives in the famous submarine escape tower, where we tried a few new wrinkles like "blowing and going," going both up to the surface and down to the submerged escape hatches without diving gear. Tricky stuff for those times. We all learned a lot.

Invasion

by Kenneth Beatty

The convoy with the LST's lay over at Funa Futi in the Ellice Islands for several days. On the night of November 13, 1943, "Sewing Machine Charlie" came over (presumably from Tarawa) and dropped a number of bombs near the airstrip. It was our first taste of danger in an act of war.

As the entire world remembers, the Marines went in on Betio, November 20, 1943. Two of the 74th CB LSTs entered the lagoon that afternoon to discharge their deck load. It was not until three days later that the island was declared secured; Tuesday afternoon, the 23rd, the 74th began unloading the LSTs at the edge of the reef, at the same time some stood guard duty ashore that night.

By the 24th the defense battalion moved in to share their duties. The ensuing months the Marines held that defense with the 74th CB, and at the same time sharing their food, clothes and friendship, plus sharing the duties operating the anti-aircraft batteries. The Marines set up detection units and communications and provided a military defense while the 74th attended to their work.

At this point it is appropriate to relate of the difficulties faced by the battalion personnel. The island of Betio was only 285 acres, also in massive ruins; not a single tree remained undamaged, and huge piles of burned and decaying food in Japanese supply dumps. Flies, mosquitoes and rats infested the entire

Clearing anti-tank and invasion mines on Tarawa. Courtesy of Ken Beatty.

island. Japanese soldiers remained in hiding for some days and came out at night—a menace to security. We were in an exposed position in the Pacific. Tarawa was the curtain–raiser of the Central Pacific Campaign, and was in flying distance of enemy held islands as Nauru, Kusai, Marshalls, Mille and Maloelap. It was a possibility that an assault by the Japanese fleet might take place.

Most of the Americans and enemy dead were properly buried by the end of the second week and speedy construction of an air base was underway and the threat of Japanese snipers soon had been dealt with.

On December 3, enemy bombers flew over Betio and dropped their bombs squarely on the runway area. From that day through January 17, raids occurred every two or three nights, and sometimes on successive nights. On December 23-24, four separate raids occurred and no one slept more than an hour or two. There were also many false alarms that had to be treated as raids.

During this time all Seabees worked 12 hours a day, seven days a week, including Christmas and New Years. Night crews were more fortunate than the day crew, for the raids and alerts came when they were at work. The day men lost their sleep, however.

Through all of this, the morale was high. Food began with K-rations, and very slowly progressed toward the levels of good Navy diet. In time we went from foxholes to shacks to tarpaulins, while others covered with galvanized corrugated iron. Sudden violent showers inundated these dwellings and in time were replaced with tents on platforms screened from insects. Showers came in the twilight or after dark, and the men would take off their clothes and stand in the rain with a bar of soap.

In three months, the 74th Seabees constructed airstrips to be used by fighters and bombers alike, laid out camp stands, repair shops, administrative buildings, defense fortifications, a hospital, and revetments for ground planes against night bombing. Now we were ready for the Marshall Islands.

My Little Seabee

Taken from a South Pacific news letter WWII and submitted by Ben Bauer

You can have your Army Kaki
But I'll take my Navy blue;
For there's still another fighter
That I'll introduce to you.

His uniform is different
The best you'll ever see;
The Japanese called him a Seadog
But his real name is Seabee.

He was trained in Virginia
The land that God forgot;
The mud is 14 inches deep
The rain will never stop.

He has set many a table
And many's the dish he's dried;
He also learned to make a bed
A broom he sure can guide.

He's peeled many an onion
And twice as many spuds;
He also spends his leisure time
Washing out his 'duds.

Now darling take a little tip
That I'm handing out to you;
Just get yourself a good Seabee
For there's nothing he can't do

And when he gets to heaven
To St. Peter he will tell;
Another Seabee reporting, Sir
I've served my time in Hell.

13th Battalion The Story of the Four Helmets

by Fred Tanner

Located on the Island of Tinian at the original site of the camp of the 13th Battalion Navy Seabees, which later became the 509th Composite Group.

We honored four of our comrades by retiring their helmets in the latter part of 1944. It was my privilege to have had a part in honoring these men. One day some individuals from Headquarters Company came to our welding shop and asked us to weld the four helmets on stakes so that they could be erected near the walkway in the Headquarters area. Though somewhat deteriorated and rusted, the helmets still stand today. They are located at the original site of the camp of the 13th Battalion Navy Seabees that later became the 509th Composite Group Camp.

Of the four helmets that we retired, only one belonged to a comrade who lost his life. His name was Lewis Ray Freye. Lewis was assigned to driving a dump truck hauling coral from Pit 16

Fred Tanner in photo of four helmets retired to honor four men who were sent home. Courtesy of Fred Tanner.

to various areas of the airfield construction. These trucks ran 24 hours a day, and Lewis was on the day shift. On this particular day Lewis' truck was the last one loaded before the 12:00 lunch hour. When he failed to come in for lunch, some of his crew became concerned. As soon as possible they went out to check on him. They knew that he was to unload the coral at a certain hardstand that was under construction. His truck was there, and they found him pinned underneath the bed of the truck. It was common for coral to get stuck in the hinge of the dump bed, keeping it from coming back down after dumping the load. Evidently this was the case, and Lewis was trying to dislodge the coral when the bed came down on him, taking his life.

The following day we held a Memorial Service for Lewis, led by our Chaplain, Lieutenant Bond. Lewis Freye was buried in the American Cemetery that was located near the 13th Camp just west of the traffic circle on 8th Avenue. (The Americans buried in this cemetery during the war were later exhumed for reburial according to families' wishes.)

Another one of the helmets represented a young man whose last name was Money. Though he was not on duty, he was riding along with his buddy, who drove a water (sprinkler) truck on the night shift during the construction of North Field. We had outfitted this 10-wheel International truck with two six-foot cubicle pontoons. These pontoons carried a tremendous amount of water, thereby making the truck extremely top heavy. Money and his buddy had just refilled at the water tower and were heading back to their construction site, driving along one of the cross section taxiways, when they detected a "bump-

ing noise." Concerned that it might be a problem with a tire, they stopped immediately. (During this time, there was a great shortage of rubber, and tires were at a premium, so we had to take every precaution in protecting our tires. We discovered that by putting an endless chain around the tandem wheels of the trucks it would eliminate coral getting stuck between the tires. All of our trucks were equipped this way.) Money and the driver thought that maybe the chain had broken and a piece of coral had lodged between the tires. The driver asked Money to check it out. In checking to see if the chain had broken, he stooped down between the tandem wheels. As he did, a small drainage ditch next to the truck caved in, causing the truck to overturn. Money could see that the truck was coming over on him, and he dove between the duel wheels. This quick-thinking saved his life, but his legs were crushed under the pontoon tanks. He was also caught by the endless chain trapping him between the wheels. A bulldozer nearby was able to lift the truck off of his legs, but they couldn't free him from the chain. The warrant officer on duty, who drove a jeep raced up to the welding shop, and told us what had happened. As fast as we could, we grabbed a cutting torch, a set of tanks and gauges, and necessary tools, threw it all on the jeep and hauled back as fast we could go. By the time we got there, I had the torch all set up and geared with goggles, gloves, and lighter, I was able to cut the chain and release Money from under the truck. Fortunately, we had a well-equipped hospital by this time, and Money was taken there. As soon as he was stabilized, he had to be sent back to the States for further care. We never heard how he got along after he left Tinian.

The other two helmets represent two of our chiefs who developed bleeding ulcers and had to be sent home. One of these men was our welding chief from Potstown, PA. We called him "Dutch," his last name was Slueter. The other man was the chief of the light equipment mechanics shop. I do not recall his name.

The 13th Battalion also lost one man on Okinawa, where we were sent after we left Tinian. His name was Maurice Booth Grindstaff. He was operating a shovel during the night shift at the Schuri Coral Pit, when he was shot by a sniper.

While these deaths were tragic, we are very proud of the fact that out of our 13th Seabee Battalion of 1,200 men working day and night under hazardous conditions, we lost only these two men. This phenomenal statistic also includes our first cruise in 1942-43 to Dutch Harbor, AK where there was no loss of life.

Military cemetery at Los Negros.

In Memoriam

U.S. Veteran Seabees killed on Truk.

Seabees Killed In Action

Avila, George Joaquin, S1/c, June 16, 1944, on Saipan.

Bowen, Thomas Houston, EM2/c, February 12, 1944, on Roi Island.

Egner, Joseph Douglass, S1/c, June 16, 1944, on Saipan.

Fields, Edward, WT1/c, June 17, 1944, on Saipan.

Gammon, Robert Douglas, S1/c, June 17, 1944, on Saipan.

Gebhardt, Henry Anthony, Sl/c, June 15, 1944, on Saipan.

Hacker, Donald, S2/c, July 11, 1944, on Saipan.

Hebert, Ellis John, S1/c, June 16, 1944, on Saipan.

Hunter, Sam Eugons Jr., Sl/c, June 15, 1944, on Saipan.

Hutchman, John Donald, Ptr1/c, June 26, 1944, on Saipan.

Luchs, Tilden LeRoy, MM3/c, June 15, 1944, on Saipan.

Montesi, Marcello Gino, F1/c, June 16, 1944, at sea off Saipan.

Pettypiece, William John, CM3/c, February 12, 1944, on Roi island.

Willcutt, Boyd Bates, MM3/c, June 15, 1944, on Saipan.

Seabees Who Died While In Service Overseas

Cline, Roy Clark, BMl/c, October 16, 1944, on Tinian.

Hemphill, Tipton, S1/c, March 21, 1945, on Tinian.

Lupton, Harold Lawson, CEM(AA), March 25, 1944, on Maui, T.H.

Myers, Hollace Holland, GMl/c, August 2, 1944, on Tinian.

Stephens, James Little, SF3/c, April 19, 1945, on Tinian.

5th Marine Cemetary; also some Seabees and regular Navy, late February 1945.

Awards and Medals

Navy-Marine Corps Medal

Woodward, Muriel S.
Atkins, Eugene E.

Bronze Star

Flinn, Thomas H., Lt. Cmdr.
Faust, Floyd H.
Pfaff, Henry W.
Partridge, John W., Lt.
Fitzgerald, Thomas V.
Phillipson, Paul L.
Rist, Lawrence M., Lt.
Frasier, Joseph H.
Pillsbury, Stephen F.
Woodrich, Warren B., LTJG
Gans, Donald F.
Taylor, Kenneth F.
Fiske, Charles C. LTJG
Hager, George R.
Thornburg, Claud A.
Jackson, Norman M., LTJG
King Clarence G.
Vaughn, Vernon C.
Hammerman, Willard S., Carptenter
Korn, Joseph A.
Wardzala, Theodore J.
Nilsen, Harold C.
Wadsworth, William F.
Block, John L.
Nolan, Thomas W.
Watson, Frank P.
Brunk, Allen W.

Purple Heart

Devore, Cecil C.
Geoghegan, A.R.E.
Hines, W.E.
Jackson, N.M.
Rist, L.M.
Adams, James S.
Bell, Sidney
Bocholtz, E.P.
Brown, H.G.
Buskey, Thomas F.
Campbell, G.E.
Capkovic, Robert J.
Carlo, Louis G.
Carmody, Thomas J.
Carr, James L.
Cassidy, Vincent F.
Chmielewicz, Frank J.
Colflesh, Paul W.
Dalcin, J.
Dorato, L. J.
Ernst, Richard E.
Gahagan, Joseph
Glazik, J.S.
Goodell, H.A.
Graham, Cecil B.
Gray, W.E.
Guthrie, William P.
Hamp, Boyd M., Jr.
Hargrove, C.P.
Hartmann, Ervin D.
Holloway, Joseph B.
Hopkins, William W.
Horak, William
Hord, Stewart W.
Keough, Paul J.

Purple Heart

Korczynski, David J.
Kratcoski, Leonard J.
Lawson, Monroe A.
Lemoine, Jdmas E.
Lenart, Albin S.
Litwin, John Jr.
Lowery, Raymond F.
Madinger, Charles E. Jr.
Mellino, Anthony J.
Miller, J.D.
Naum, George J.
Neiderer, Thomas B.
Nitzberg, Howard A.
Nordstrom, Reynold L.
Ott, Charles R.
Partridge, Jack
Pickett, Louis L.
Pillsbury, Stephen F.
Price, Charles A. Jr.
Radcliff, D.D.
Ridling. J.B.
Ronaldo, James W.
Russell, S.W.
Salinkas, A.A.
Schildknecht, Eugene O.
Sedgwick, K.W.
Smith, Charles A.
Scott, William J.
Sutton, W.L.
Taylor, M.G.
Thomas, E.N.
Truss, O.T.
Van Damm, Lovell H.
Yoracek, W.R.
Wilson, F.W.

Courtesy of M. Ramige.

FIRST NATIONAL CONVENTION
SEABEE VETERANS OF AMERICA
LASALLE HOTEL - CHICAGO, ILLINOIS - OCTOBER 9, 1948

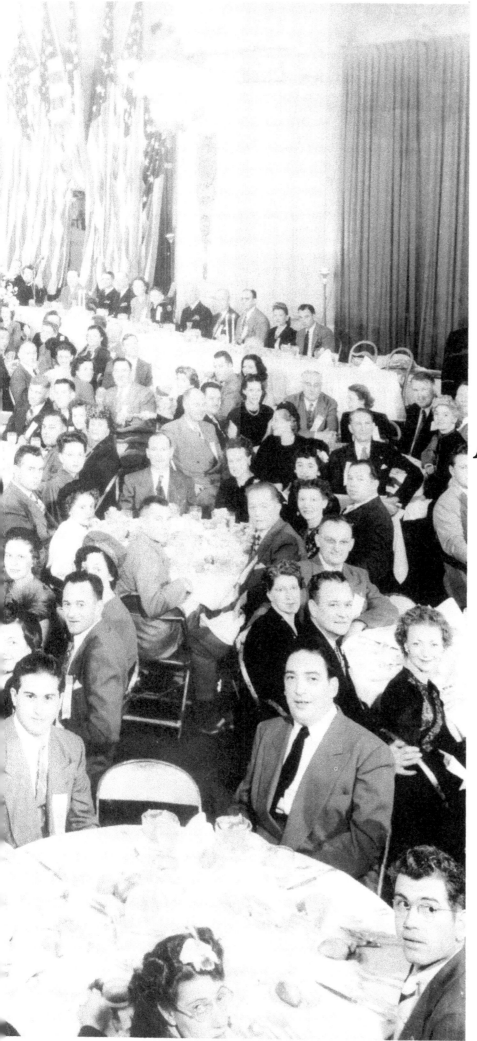

SEABEES ASSOCIATION HISTORY

Formation of National Seabee Veteran's Association

A Gathering in Chicago

When writing of the early days of the original few whom worked and laid the groundwork for the present Navy Seabee Veterans of America Organization, there is one name that will always be in our hearts and minds. That name belongs to a leader, the late Captain Howard P. Potter, CEC, USN.

Captain Potter was instrumental in not only bringing the Seabee Veterans together in units called Chapters to further their fellowship, he envisioned the need for a national Organization that would be exclusively for the World War II Seabee Veteran. In 1948 he called and gathered together the Men of the Chapters within the Chicago area for the purpose of developing a National Organization. They realized that the problems and difficulties involved in implementing an organization of national scope would demand considerable time and effort; however, they felt that the groundwork for a national organization would best be started by organizing state and local chapters where Seabees and CEC's could be found within the USA. Then, and only then, could these state and local chapters be welded into a national association.

The development of a National Association was to follow the generally accepted democratic process employed in the United States, that of implementation by Constitutional Convention. This method insured that the resulting organization would represent the will of the majority.

From these considerations, a National (Constitutional) Convention was called. This convention was held at the LaSalle Hotel in Chicago, May 8-10, 1948. Over one hundred members and delegates from thirteen states were in attendance, and a constitution was drawn up, revised, and accepted by the Convention.

From this Constitutional Convention, the date and place were voted upon to hold the Association's first Annual National Convention. The attendees at the Constitutional Convention chose October 8-10, 1948, at the LaSalle Hotel in Chicago, as the first site to begin the 50–plus year history of the Navy Seabee Veterans of America.

Hundreds of Seabees and their guests enjoyed the planned programs, along with many other special attendees. Our old boss during the war, Vice Admiral Ben Moreell, was among the guest speakers. An address by Rear Admiral John J. Manning, CEC, USN, Chief of the Bureau of Yards and Docks, was also one of the many highlights of the evening.

Those who attended did a terrific job in laying the foundation for our permanent National Organization. A vast amount of practical planning and business was accomplished in a short period of time. The outstanding features mentioned were again the same shown at the Constitutional Convention held the previous May: enthusiasm, loyalty, fellowship, and common determination to build a permanent, enduring fraternity.

The early make-up of our Organization set the pattern from which our present day National Organization evolved. Although tithes may change, the position description and duties remain fairly standard. In 1948, our Officers were: a national president as the executive head of the Seabee Veterans Association, vice presidents, a secretary, treasurer, counselor, chaplain, and mascot. Our Committees consisted of convention rules and procedures, finance, membership, legislation, insignia and emblem, nomination, publicity and publications, conventions, and finally, resolutions.

A notable item on the light side of the 1948 National Convention is that the finance committee estimated the cost for the Convention would be approximately $2,500. When all the expenditures were added up and deducted from the income, the Convention realized a tidy sum of $104.97 profit. How they raised these funds is also interesting. They went to every Chapter and asked that each active member send a $1.00 donation to the National. The per capita payment totaled at $1,149. Registration fees produced an additional $961, making their income total $2,610. Would you believe the Finance Committee missed their estimation by only $5.03?

The 1948 Constitution and Bylaws recommended that units be known as Island X's, because most Seabees were shipped to islands of the Pacific. Therefore, the drafters thought the term Island X-? would be more appropriate. It was also decided that if there were two or more Islands in a given state, Washington, D.C., zone, or territory, they could form into a Department. In 1948, the following states organized their Islands into Departments: Illinois, Indiana, Michigan, Ohio, and Iowa.

At the National Executive Committee Meeting held in Chicago on 4 February 1949, the members of the Committee stud-

Courtesy of Roland A. Swanson.

23rd NMCB-F1 Belvoir, VA. CM1 Ernie "Pap" Basser. Retiring from NMCB 23 April 2000, 20 years.

Dedication of the Seabee Monument, North Tonawande, NY; Admiral Nash just stepping down. Courtesy of R.E. Chrisey.

Dedication of the Seabee Monument, North Tonawanda, NY Courtesy R.E. Chrisey.

Wreath that was tossed into the water for those that died at sea. Courtesy of R.E. Chrisey.

Marching in Memorial Day Parade. Courtesy of R.E. Chrisey.

Forming for memorial services for those veterans that died at sea.

Island X-9 Kingston, NY. Working on our first project, rebuilding the Clifton Ave. ... Globe is an old Navy Anchor bouy. Courtesy of R.E. Chrisey.

Island X-9 Completed monument for the fourth ward, Kingston, NY, dedication day. Courtesy of R.E. Chrisey.

Members of Island X-9 Kingston, NY, end of parade. Note: We still have our M-1 carbines for Color Guard. Courtesy of R.E. Chrisey.

Remaining 20th Seabees. Courtesy of Earl R. DuPriest.

Island X-11. Courtesy of Roland A. Swanson.

C.B.M.U. 505 Taken Feb. 1986 at Shellhorn's, an impromptu get together. L-R: Hope Cambron-Tucson AZ, Charles Shellhorn-Gila NM, Hil Christiansen-Portland OR, E.E. Brown-Barnard VT.

Commanding oficer NMCB-23, Ft Belvoir VA, presenting plaque of job well done from U.S.N. to CMI E. Pap Basser.

ied the National Constitution and Bylaws "from stem to stem," and clarified, revised, and rephrased them as they felt necessary.

They discussed the per-capita tax or dues from the Islands to the National. They wanted dues cleared through the respective Departments before being sent on to the National no later than July of each year. It was decided that dues would be $1.00 for each new SVA member and $.50 for each yearly renewal. Additionally, they discussed a proposal to organize a disaster and mobilization unit within each Island, which could work with local Red Cross or rescue units in the event of a local disaster.

Who says that a National Convention is all business, no pleasure, and costly? "Your all-inclusive entertainment, a ticket costing $5.00 per person, included a ride in one of Atlantic City's famous rolling on the Boardwalk, admission to the world-famous Steel Pier, admission to two first-run movies, and an unforgettable ocean sightseeing trip on one of Captain Starn's big boats. Last, but not least, was a seat in the World's largest auditorium to witness the famed Miss America Pageant.

The climax of the Convention was an all-military services simulated combat landing on the sandy beaches of Atlantic City to set up a beachhead. Although residents of the city were alerted days in advance of this planned spectacular, the noise of the simulated bombing, aircraft flying overhead, ships landing troops and equipment over pontoon causeways, and demolition teams blowing up planted objects (during which explosions blew out windows along the Boardwalk and even a couple of blocks inland), some of the residents thought they were being invaded by enemy forces. Thank goodness, the Convention Committee had taken out an insurance policy to cover any damage sustained during the simulated "landing."

Other highlights of the three-day convention were a Boardwalk parade and an address by Rear Admiral John J. Manning, CEC, and USN. It might be mentioned that the Admiral, while addressing the Convention, spoke of plans for a Seabee Reserve to be authorized, trained, and ready in case of any future attack. Once formed, he said, "they (the Reserve) would not be used on any construction work that could be performed by union labor, and they would never be used as strikebreakers."

Recent Highlights

Jumping ahead 40 years, by the year 1987, the National Seabees Veteran's of America had more than 3,000 members. In 1989, it was announced that in 1992 the designated amount for funding a NSVA scholarship would be $25,000, and efforts to obtain a Seabees 50th Anniversary stamp were being made in 1990.

In the year 1991, a 40-year narrative, "We've Got You Covered" was completed with 3,000 copies printed. Association dues were increased to $5.

1992 marked the 50th Anniversary for the establishment of the Navy Seabees. The Navy S.V.A. membership passed 4,000, with a new

count of 4,245. By 1995 this number was increased to 4,993.

On November 11, 1997, the Navy Seabee Veteran's of America participated in the 15th Anniversary of the Vietnam Wall. The NSVA was only the 5th organization to lay a wreath out of 46 organizations.

May 8-October 10, 1998 marked the 50th Anniversary Celebration of the Navy Seabee Veteran's of America. In the years since, the Navy S.V.A. has continued to grow in size, activity and stature. At 2001 convention total N.S.V.A. membership is 5,520 members.

ISLAND HISTORIES

All Islands were invited to submit information on their organization, and the following represent those who chose to participate.

The 126th Naval Construction Battalion

by Lenno C. Johnston

The 126th Navy Construction Battalion had its beginning at Camp Perry in 1945. The battalion was stationed at Camp Endicott, Camp Parks and Port Hueneme, from where it was shipped to Island X, which was Engibi Island in the Eniwetok Atoll. Detachments served on Japtan, Parry and Hawthorne of the Atoll. Returned to Hawaii for a period of time before it headed for Okinawa, arriving there about the time of the Japanese surrender. As points were garnered, members left the battalion and headed home for a discharge.

The next activities for members of the battalion was in 1982, when Lenno Johnston organized its first reunion in Baton Rouge, Louisiana. For nine consecutive years the 126th won the attendance at the National Convention. In 1996, it received its charter as the 126th Battalion-at-Large. In 1999, it again received the attendance award. Since 1987 national offices held by members of the 126th are: National Commander, Joe Matthews and Lenno Johnston; Counselor, Harry Newman; Trustee, Bill Edwards; National Secretary for Islands - at-Large, Louis Ursillo; and Chaplain, Lenno Johnston.

The unit gives a U.S. flag to the youngest and oldest Seabee attending the National Banquet.

Island X-1 White River Jct., Vermont

by Dwight D. Harrington, Commander

Vermont is a small state with large distances between points. Island X-1 was formed in 1991 with the first meeting held in May of that year. The idea was conceived by Chief Warrant Officer James Hasson. Norm Hill's Island in Portsmouth, NH was used as a blue-

print. Our charter was granted in August 1991 and there are 18 names listed. The original objective was to have an organization in place in time to celebrate the 50th anniversary of the Seabees in 1992.

Island membership is drawn from the four corners of the state. With narrow roads and unpredictable weather, some members travel more than two hours to attend functions. We also draw our membership from across the Connecticut River and have several from our neighbors in New Hampshire. We have adopted National Commander Jack Brandt into our ranks, as he has a home here in Vermont. The high point of our membership was 61, but there has been in decline in the past few years. However, new members are being added as well and we are holding right around 40. The Ladies Auxiliary joins us in our functions and at our monthly meetings.

Dr. William Berg nominated Jim Hasson as the first commander of the Island. Jim is the Seabee's Seabee around Vermont, and he has provided strong leadership over the years. I am the second and current commander. Island secretary duties have been carried out by John Fielden, then by Dave Thurber, and currently by Norm Gassett. We have had but one chaplain, Mike Watson, who unfortunately passed away in 1999.

For the 1992 anniversary celebration, Governor Howard Dean of Vermont was made an honorary Seabee at a ceremony held in the capital city of Montpelier. During the ceremony, Governor Dean declared the month of March 1992 as Seabee Month throughout the state. The Island archives include the framed original proclamation from that event.

Normally, we hold our cold weather months' meetings at the Naval Reserve Center in White River Jct., VT. By meeting there, we can keep our close ties to the Navy itself, and there are fleet members as well as a detachment from RNMCB 27 on duty at the center. Jim Hasson and Island X-1 as a whole were instrumental in dedicating the drill hall within the reserve center to Roger Burnham, a Seabee from NMCB 12 killed in Vietnam. There is a granite plaque on display at the drill hall. The Island also participates in memorial ceremonies held at the local VA hospital, and has provided color guards for various ceremonies at the Vermont Veterans Cemetery. When Desert Storm came to a conclusion, the Island joined those in New Hampshire for a Welcome Home Parade for the returning troops.

The annual Seabee Birthday Party is the highlight of our year. Each one is a little different from the others. We have a social hour, a sit down meal, and a presentation from a guest speaker. Captain John Warner was a guest one year, Commander Larry Smith gave a presentation on his activities in Bosnia, and former Lieutenant Commander Gene Sevi spoke on his efforts while leading the Vermont Air National Guard in a recent ice storm emergency call up. Ed Lynch came by and presented much information on veteran's benefits to the group.

Our summer meetings take us to places around Vermont to experience our history. There are many historical sites and museums to visit. We have been to Ethan Allen's house (a founding father of Vermont), to the Maritime Museum to view an anchor from a British ship sunk in Lake Champlain during the War of 1812, and visited a French and Indian War era fort reconstruction. More contemporary sites are included in our trips, such as the U.S. Army Cold Regions Laboratory, the Vermont Yankee Nuclear Power Plant, the Catamount Brewery, (even though Seabees already know all about beer) and we have even been cruising on Lake Memphremagog on the Canadian border.

We meet each month throughout the year in various situations. When it is cold outside, we stay inside. During warm weather, we are out to enjoy the all too short Vermont summer. We provide support for each other in times of need and enjoy the company of all. Non-Seabee Naval personnel are always welcome at our events and the fellowship of old Navy comrades is everywhere when we get together. Our more distant members are kept informed with a monthly newsletter. Those large distances between points in Vermont have really been lessened because of our Island and its activities.

Island X-76 PA

by Ralph J. Storti

Island X-76 PA was founded on November 11, 1995 by John McGowan and Walt Wassel, our first commander and secretary-treasurer respectively. A meeting was held at the Willow Grove VFW Post 3612, with seven members in attendance. The Island then moved to the Willow Grove Naval Air Station Joint Reserve Base on May 11, 1996, and still continues to meet there today. Although they only had 11 members that first year, the roots were planted and the Island began to grow. On October 12, 1996, Sr. Vice Commander Larry Newell was elected commander of the Island. Under Larry's guidance membership and community involvement gradually increased. We closed out the year 1996-97 with 43 members.

Our biggest highlight came on April 12, 1997 when Chief Warrant Officer John Hunter (standing in for Past National Commander F.E. Jones) presented us with our charter. Membership for the period of 1997-98 was holding steady at 39. On June 13, 1998, then Sr. Vice Commander Raymond Fragassi was duly elected and assumed the role of Island X-76PA Commander. With Ray at the helm, things have really shifted into high gear. We now have a Ladies Auxiliary, Monthly Island Newsletter, Annual Picnic, Banquet, numerous committees and membership was at an all time high of 72 for the period ending June 30, 1999. If there's a job to be done, the Seabees of Island X-76PA are always there to do it.

Island X-8 NY
The Niagara Frontier Island
Tonawanda, NY

by Kenneth Wendt

Island X-8 was formed by six former members of Island X-5, West Seneca, NY. The reason was strictly a matter of geography. Western New York winters are not conducive to driving 35-40 miles for a meeting. When Island X-5 refused to move to a more central location, it was decided to form a new Island to serve northern Erie County and Niagara County.

The six formulators applied for a charter, and by the time they received it on November 13, 1993, they were 50 strong. They have since grown to over a 100.

The first major Island project was the building of a Monument, a tribute to all Seabees, past, present and future. The monument was built by Seabees for Seabees.

The second project was the remodeling of an empty piece of city property into a meeting hall. The hall is used for meetings and social functions and can seat 100 people. It has show cases and wall mounted memorabilia.

The next project was to relocate a Memorial to local boys killed in Vietnam. The original site was as obscure as the place where the boys were killed. It is now at a beautiful spot in the Tonawanda Riverfront Park.

The next project was the construction of a safe fishing dock for kids and handicapped persons, located in still water slip on the mighty Niagara River. The dock measures 150' by 10'.

Our next project is restoring a flatbed truck, on which we are going to mount a large Fighting Bee. This will be used in local parades.

What our next project will be? Only time will tell.

Of our over 100 members, over half are life members.

Island X-3 PA

by Jerry Montecupo, Secretary

The western Pennsylvania area was not represented by the NSVA until 1994. The Seabees from the western area of Pennsylvania who did belong to the organization (NSVA) were scattered throughout the U.S., because no one was able to get enough interest together to get an Island formed.

John Ware of Island X-1, Harrisburg, PA, contacted me when he saw my name on the roster of the Cumberland, MD, Island. He asked me if I was interested in forming an Island in the Pittsburgh area.

At the time I told him I was too busy, but if my workload slowed down I might be interested, John contacted me months later and asked me again. It just so happened that I was laid off from my construction job temporarily, so I told him I'd try. I also told him I had never had any organizational skills. He told me that he'd be more than happy to help. John gave me a list of 12 members of the NSVA who listed their addresses in the western Pennsylvania area.

I contacted the 12 Seabees and five agreed to meet on November 12, 1994 at the Brentwood, PA, VFW near Pittsburgh. The five founding members who met that day were Walter Bugielski, Dick Dively, Elmer Levendusky, Adam Belajac, Ted Vukelich and myself, Jerry Montecupo. John Whare chaired the opening of the meeting. The first item was to elect officers. We voted Walter Bugielski as commander, Jerry Montecupo as secretary and Dick Dively as Treasurer. We agreed to meet again on November 12, 1994 for our first regularly scheduled meeting at the Brentwood VFW.

At our second meeting, Dick Lindner NE vice-commander was in attendance. He welcomed our Island to the NSVA. We transferred and recruited 25 more members, bringing us a total of 30 members in the first month.

Since 1994 Island X-3, PA has moved it's membership up to over 120 Seabees from all over the U.S. We have an Honor Guard that marches in parades throughout the Pittsburgh area. We also have Island projects that we work on. We volunteer our construction skills at the YMCA Camp Kon-o-kwee north of Pittsburgh. It's a camp for children with and without physical handicaps. We have social events for the members.

The future of the Island looks good. Our members vary from WWII, Korean, Vietnam, and Desert Storm Veterans, to Reserve Seabees. We also have an active duty Seabee. We have a father and three sons and a father and son members. We are proud of our Island, its members and our country.

Island X-11, Chautauqua Region 1998 Review

by Roland A. Swanson, Commander

Navy Seabee Veterans of America Island X-11, Chautauqua Region, Jamestown, NY, began 1998 gathering Saturday January 3rd at the Holiday Inn for the WJTN Radio Breakfast party. Coordinator Clifford Hotchkiss assembled 22 individuals, including members and spouses.

January 26th Island X-11 conducted a shortened business meeting as a "potluck" dinner followed with 30 individuals attending. Guest speaker, Rolland Kidder spoke about upcoming Chautauqua County Veteran's Memorial to be erected on Tracy Plaza, Jamestown. A time of fellowship followed.

Seven members agreed to serve as funeral visitation representatives for Island X-11.

Island X-11 was represented at Chautauqua County Legislative meeting March 11 as the legislature contributed $25,000 to the Veteran's Endowment Fund, administered by Chautauqua Region Foundation.

Island X-11 was recognized in the CEC/Seabee Foundation newsletter for 1997 year end contribution. Following an April 27 meeting, Clifford Hotchkiss and Kenneth Douglas provided beef-n-wick sandwiches for refreshments.

Island X-11 members participated in town of Poland May 25 Memorial Day parade and cemetery observance. Retired CEC Captain H. Ford Stryker was keynote speaker.

Election of 1998-99 officers was conducted during May 18 meeting. Also distribution of scholarship award fundraiser tickets was begun by Chairman Ronald Marvin. Veterans Administration Health Enrollment has been stressed often by Service Officer James Snyder and others at meetings.

Island X-11 was represented at Department of New York Conference convention by six individuals during June 18-20 at Niagara Falls Air Force Base. Chautauqua County Veterans Service Agency Director Michael Suter installed elected officers during a June 22 meeting. Commander Swanson announced appointments prior to adjournment and time of fellowship.

Island X-11 had its second annual Family Picnic on Sunday, July 19, with 51 attendees. An abbreviated business meeting followed, at which time Ray Hulquist was recognized for his generous contribution of delicious steaks and hamburgers for attendees. Numerous prizes donated by members were awarded.

Island X-11 was represented at the NSVA National Convention at Biloxi, MS, in August. At this time Roland A. and Doris M. Swanson were named National Chaplains for NSVA and NSVAA respectively. They were the first husband and wife so named in the 50 year history of NSVA organization.

Island X-11 accepted its first female Seabee member, Laura Savko, at the August 24th meeting. R.A. Swanson, J.B. Logan and J.W. Hamilton were named as the Scholarship Award Criteria Committee in association with Dr. J.P. Hamels of Boces, Ashville. Island X-11 jackets were also presented for ordering.

North East District Commander Richard Lindner attended, and spoke during our September 28th meeting. Assisted by Ronald Marvin, Commander Lindner drew the winner's name for the "50/50" fundraiser to benefit upcoming scholarship award. The name drawn was Larry Logan of Claredon, PA.

Thomas Osborne, Roland and Doris Swanson visited the Eldred (PA) World War II Museum October 15 for purpose of presenting a copy of Rolland Kidder's A Hometown Went to War. *Director Kurt Pfaff accepted on behalf of museum library and conducted tour of facilities.*

The Department of New York authorized campaign service pins made available for ordering during fall season.

Island X-11 members participated at Jamestown's November 11 Veteran's Day services at Veteran's Park and downtown. This represented the first use of island's jackets at a public function. Student scholarship award criteria approved by committee, to develop application also. Island members assisted with Salvation Army Red Kettle bell ringing at two locations. The island was also represented at the Veteran's Memorial dedication November 21 at Jamestown City Hall.

Island X-11 representatives participated in Pearl Harbor Remembrance service at American Legion Post 735 in West Seneca, NY on December 7. Communicator Hulquist and Secretary Stafford created updated member roster listings indication 48 members of which 36 are life members. Treasurer Douglas established a certificate of deposit for scholarship award use to mature May 1999. Also approved during December was construction of four picnic tables for town of Gerry if further information received.

Throughout the year greetings and remembrances were sent to individuals, as well as numerous monetary contributions to several organizations.

Seacoast Island X-1

by Norman W. Hill

The Island was formed during the summer of 1989. During a visit to the National Convention of Navy Seabee Veterans of America at Tampa, FL, in August 1987, Norman Hill of Exeter, NH learned that only two other former Seabees from New England were present at the convention. On his return to Exeter, he decided to see if he could locate other former Seabees in his State. In September he wrote an article about the NSVA and sent it to be published in New Hampshire's largest newspaper, as he was aware the circulation covered the State. For reasons unknown, the article wasn't printed until sometime the following Spring. When the paper hit the streets, phone calls to Hill, inquiring about NSVA came in every day. With the assistance of Harmond Littlefield and others, Seacoast Island X-1 was formed. There was enough interest and membership to form two other Island X's at that time. These, unfortunately have phased out.

During the 50th anniversary of the Navy Seabees, celebrations were being held at Davisville, RI, Gulfport, MS, Port Hueneme, CA, and Washington, DC. The

NSVA received a great deal of exposure, and membership picked up. Hill was contacted by members from Maine, Massachusetts and Vermont to see if Islands could be formed in their State. Some membership was carried on the Seacoast Island roster until Islands were chartered. During that period, former members from other States also contacted Seacoast Island and were carried on the roster as members at large. At this writing, Seabees from North Carolina, Virginia, New York, Maine, Massachusetts and Tennessee have preferred to stay on Seacoast roster as member-at-large as no Islands are located in their home area.

Seacoast Island X-1 holds a membership of 90 plus members with about half holding a life membership. The Island publishes a bi-yearly newsletter, The Granite State Beeline, *that is sent to all its members and other supporting Islands and some of the National Officers.*

The Island holds its meetings at a local VFW Post in Exeter, NH. Each year on the last Sunday in July, a family picnic is held. Publicity is sent to local newspapers announcing the event and inviting Seabee families to attend. Invitations are also sent to the Islands in neighboring states to attend. Many years, the Islands has had as guests, Seabees from New York, Florida and Michigan. The 1999 Picnic was honored to have National Commander Jack and National Auxiliary President Cathy Brandt join us for the day.

The Island performs service projects for the VFW Post. In the near future, some members will turn to a construction project to build an addition on the Post Home. Members take part in community parades. Each year, books, magazines, clothing, and toilet accessories are donated to the New Hampshire Veterans Home.

Past commanders of Seacoast Island have been Harmond Littlefield, Raymond, NH 35th NCB; Herbert Tanner; E. Hampstead, NH MCB's 1, 6, 7, 58; Albert DiFazio, Seabrook, NH 49th NCB; Eugene Hill Jr., Portsmouth, NH MCB's 1, 6, 7, 11, ASA; Harold Ashey, Dover, NH MCB 11; Norm Hill, Exeter, NH 132nd NCB, ABCD serves the office of secretary each year. During the years 1990-92, Hill was elected to hold the office of National Commander of NSVA.

As members, the Island has a father and son: Leo Thomas of Rindge, NH served with 9th NCB in Okinawa. His son John of Fitchburgh, MA was with MCB 9 Vietnam. The two Young brothers of Belfast, ME served during WWII. Everett was with 88th NCB and Harold with the 92nd NCB. A writer and author of a number of books, two being about Seabee life is also a member. Hugh Aaron of Belfast, ME served with the 113th NCB WW II.

The goal of Seacoast Island X-1 is to keep locating recruiting and securing those former Seabees who are not aware that the Navy Seabee Veterans of America organization is an organization they can be a member of.

Island X-19
Syracuse, NY

by Jack Brandt

Island X-19 was the 2nd Island to be formed in New York. We chose the number 19 in memory of NMCB-19, of which we all belonged.

We were formed in 1984 and received our Charter officially in 1986. We started with 11 men, grew a little and always tried to keep it simple. We also formed an Auxiliary in 1991 while forming the Department of New York. Island X-19 held picnics, Seabee Birthday Balls, and get togethers at various times and places. We have a yearly project that we do. We get as many Seabees involved as possible. Every year we plant flowers at the Onondaga County Veterans Cemetery, the Monday before Memorial Day. We plant anywhere from 600 to 800 plants in about four hours.

In true Seabee fashion, we go in, do the job and go. We started doing this about 1989. We participate with Onondaga Council of Veterans and spearheaded the first Veteran's Day at the newly built Baseball Park.

This Island is also the home of the First Department of New York Commander and First National Commander from New York State John W "Jack" Brandt. Jack's wife Catherine is presently the National President of the Auxiliary; it is the second time in 50 years that there is a commander and president, husband and wife team. Jack is also the secretary-treasurer of Island X-19.

There are now 54 members in Island X-19, Syracuse, NY and growing.

Island X-9
Kington, New York

by Ronald E. Chrisey, Historian

Island X-9 Kington, New York received their Charter on October 15, 1994. It started with 33 original charter members. To date they have lost two, William Kaznowski and Anthony Luicci, both World War II Bee's, that served in the Pacific.

Our first project was to rebuild the World War II Monument at the corner of Highland and Clifton Ave. in Kingston, New York. Work began April 1, 1995, and was completed for dedication May 21, 1995.

That same year Island X-9 joined all the local veterans groups for the first time to hold memorial services at various points throughout the city of Kingston.

A color guard was formed and marched in the Island's first parade on Memorial Day 1995. The first social event was on June 10, 1995. Island X-9 joined the DAV and held a dinner dance at the Kingston V.F.W. Post.

In December 1997, Bruce Storey, one of our charter members was presented the New York State Conspicuous Cross because of all the other medals he had won. A frame was made for the award and presented to him, along with the certification from the Governor's Office.

Seabee Memorial Scholarship Association

In 1970 the Seabee Memorial Scholarship Association (SMSA) contacted the Navy Seabee Veteran Association (NSVA) asking the NSVA to appoint one member to the SMSA Board of Directors. A motion was then approved to nominate Willis Mitchell, and he was appointed by National President Dan Brumbaugh.

Two years later in 1972, the NSVA decided to authorize a donation of $100 to the SMSA if the funds were available. Later that year a resolution was passed that stated – if the NSVA ever ended in a dissolution, all funds left after paying bills would be donated to the scholarship fund. There also was discussion of a $20,000 scholarship. They knew at that particular time $20,000 would never happen. In fact, the scholarship fund remained dormant at $7,000 for quite a while. With hopes of raising the amount – the NSVA decided to open a SMSA Fund Account for receiving all donations and making sure that credit would be forthcoming from the SMSA.

1973 brought the first large donation in some time, and it was from Chairman Mitchell, a donation of $300 from the first monies of the NSVA. One year later there was a conflict with the NSVA and the SMSA. The Scholarship Association was not recognizing all of the donations made by the Veterans Association. At this time Delegate Frank Ware asked to be replace on the SMSA Board of Directors. It was two full years later when another donation from the NSVA was made in the amount of $217. In 1977 the donations came more frequently. $25 donation was made in honor of Irene Trarner, of NSVA National Commander Jim Trarner and a donation made from a calendar sale in the amount of $525.

In 1978 the Navy SVA Scholarship was ready to award its first scholarship. The amount needed for the scholarship was $7,000. By the time the deadline was up, only $4,000 was in the fund. The other $3,000 needed was voted to use monies from the NSVA General Funds. With in the next year the first NSVA Scholarship was completed with $7,000 and a second scholarship started with $2,700. The SMSA presented a special citation to the Navy SVA Auxiliary Treasurer, Mrs. Richard Grove, for the Auxiliary's outstanding record in raising scholarship funds. The first Nave Seabees Veteran's Association's scholarship was awarded to Ms. Janet P. Cardgon, daughter of CMCC Cardgon, WWII.

NSVA Commander Bill Baker noted that in 1980, a credit of $4,249 was set aside for the second ever NSVA Scholarship. The NSVA approved using the General Funds again to make up the difference in the second NSVA scholarship.

Two years later a procedure was established for the NSVA Treasurer to submit all donations on a 90-day basis of those funds donated towards additional scholarships. The financed were handled this way so that a certificate of appreciation could be made before forwarding the funds to the SMSA.

In 1984 the following were motioned, seconded and accepted. The number one NSVA scholarship would be named "Navy SVA Memorial Scholarship"; The number two NSVA scholarship would be named "Navy SVA Marvin Shields Memorial"; The number three NSVA scholarship would be named "Navy SVA Sunshine State Memorial". One year later it was decided that the fourth NSVA scholarship would be named "Navy SVA Ralph Richards Scholarship". That same year the number five scholarship would be named the "Navy SVA Robert Stetham Scholarship" and would be worth $10,000.

1985 was the first time that the NSVA asked the SMSA Board to consider having a scholarship for Grandchildren of Seabees & CEC's, and the SMSA Board accepted. As of 1987 the NSVA had not been represented on the SMSA Board of Directors since 1975,

Since 1987 it was decided that the NSVA would donate $100 to the SMSA when any past president commander passes away. This since has been expanded to include any national officer and spouses of present or past national commanders.

The Seabee Memorial Scholarship has continued to flourish through the past years and has helped many young people get a college education.

First loaded duck leaving LCT. Courtesy of Raymond B. Dierkes.

NSVA Past Presidents

Following are the names of the men who served as National Presidents of the
Seabee Veterans of America.

Howard Potter	Illinois	1948-1949
Leo Crowley	Michigan	1949-1950
Edward O'Rourke	Massachusetts	1950-1951
John Guminski	Illinois	1951-1952
J. Bert Knille	Ohio	1952-1953
Charles Hillhouse	Indiana	1953-1954
Don Engel	Illinois	1954-1955
Martin Richards	Ohio	1955-1956
Norman P. Sercombe	Michigan	1956-1957
Clayton Fralic	Wisconsin	1957-1958
Max Sherman	Illinois	1958-1959
Don Laubenz	Ohio	1959-1960
William McKnight	Missouri	1960-1961
Tom Reside	California	1961-1962
Edward Kipple	Illinois	1962-1963
Don Laubenz	Ohio	1963-1964
Willis Mitchell	California	1964-1965
Ray Gartski	Illinois	1965-1966
Willis Mitchell	California	1966-1967
Frank Ware	Texas	1967-1969
Dan Brombaugh	Oregon	1969-1971
Elmer Pegorsch	Ohio	1971-1973
Cecil Gould	Louisiana	1973-1974
James Sullivan	Florida	1974-1975
Jack Wright	Oregon	1975-1976
Dick Grove	Texas	1976-1977
Jim Johnstone	Michigan	1977-1978
William Baker	Louisiana	1978
Jim Johnstone	Michigan	1980-1981
Paul Simcoe	Louisiana	1981-1983
James Lindenmeyer	Florida	1983-1985
Joe L. Matthews	Texas	1985-1987
David Youngs	Ohio	1987-1988
John Fletcher	Ohio	1988-1989
Donald Clay	Florida	1989-1990
Norman Hill	New Hampshire	1990-1992
Lenno Johnston	Missouri	1992-1994
Paul W. Sutphin	Illinois	1994-1996
Ed Jones	Florida	1996-1998
Jack Brandt	New York	1998-2000
Richard J Schindler	Ohio	2000

NSVA National Conventions

1948 May 8-10	Chicago, Illinois	LaSalle Hotel
1949 September 9-11	Atlantic City, New Jersey	Clariridge Hotel
1950 September 22-24	Colorado Springs, Colorado	City Auditorium
1951 August 23-26	Boston, Massachusetts	Kenmore Hotel
1952 August 22-24	Milwaukee, Wisconsin	Schroeder Hotel
1953 August 21-23	LaFayette, Indiana	Fowler Hotel
1954 August 20-22	St. Louis, Missouri	Jefferson Hotel
1955 August 11-13	Jackson, Michigan	Hayes Hotel
1956 August 10-12	Cincinnati, Ohio	Sinton Hotel
1957 August 9-11	Detroit. Michigan	Fort Shelby Hotel
1958 August 14-17	Chicago, Illinois	Congress Hotel
1959 August 13-16	Toledo, Ohio	Commodore Perry Hotel
1960 August 18-21	San Diego, California	El Cortez Hotel
1961 August 18-19	St. Louis, Missouri	Statler-Hilton Hotel
1962 August 17-19	Phoenix, Arizona	Wetsward Hotel
1963 August 9-11	Miami Beach, Florida	Deauville Hotel
1964 August 13-16	Las Vegas, Nevada	Sahara Hotel
1965 August 19-22	Chicago, Illinois	La Salle Hotel
1966 August 19-21	Honolulu, Hawaii	Ilikai Hotel
1967 August 17-20	Dallas, Texas	Adolphus Hotel
1968 August 15-18	Philadelphia, Pennsylvania	Bellview Strafford Hotel
1969 August 7-10	Portland, Oregon	Sheraton Motor Inn
1970 August 13-16	Toledo, Ohio	Commadore Perry Motor Inn
1971 August 12-15	Kansas City, Missourri	Hotel President
1972 August 10-13	New Orleans, Louisiana	Jung Hotel
1973 August 9-12	St. Petersburg, Florida	St. Petersburg Hilton Hotel
1974 August 15-18	Portland, Oregon	Sheraton Motor Inn
1975 August 21-24	Dallas, Texas	Hilton Inn
1976 August 28-31	Kansas City, Missouri	Radisson Muehlebach Hotel
1977 July 27-30	Toledo, Ohio	Commadore Perry Motor Inn
1978 July 26-30	Louisville, Kentucky	Stouffer's Louisville Inn
1979 July 26-29	Chicago, Illinois	Pick-Congress Hotel
1980 July 30– Aug 3	Portland, Oregon	Sheraton Motor Inn
1981 July 30- Aug 2	Orlando, Florida	Orlando Marriott Inn
1982 July 29-31	Baton Rouge, Louisiana	Bellemont Motor Motel
1983 August 4-7	Oxnard, California	Casa Sirena Hotel
1984 August 2-4	Tucson, Arizona	Tucson Hilton Inn
1985 August 1-4	Fort Lauderdale, Florida	Marriott Hotel
1986 August 6-10	Tacoma, Washington	The Best Western Executive
1987 August 6-8	Tampa, Florida	The Holiday International Airport
1988 August 4-6	LaCrosse, Wisconsin	Mid-Way Motor Lodge
1989 August 2-6	Toledo, Ohio	Sheraton Westgate
1990 August 1-4	Sarasota, Florida	Holiday Inn
1991 August 7-10	Independence, Ohio	Holiday Inn
1992 August 5-9	Schaumburg, Illinois	Hyatt Regency Woodfield
1993 August 11-14	Buffalo, New York	Hyatt Regency Buffalo
1994 August 3-6	Tucson, Arizona	Holiday Inn Palo Verde
1995 September 18-22	Las Vegas, Nevada	Riviera Hotel & Convention Center
1996 August 7-11	ClearWater Beach, Florida	DoubleTree Resort Surfside
1997 August 6-10	Moline, Illinois	Holiday Inn & Convention Center
1998 August 8-14	Biloxi, Mississippi	Imperial Palace
1999 August 4-8	Albany, New York	Omni Hotel
2000 July 26-30	Buffalo, New York	Adams Mark Hotel
2001 August 15-19	St. Cloud, Minnesota	Kelly Inn

NSVA Auxiliary Past Presidents

YEAR	NAME	STATE
1948	Christine Dobbins	Ohio
1949-50	Marie Heimbrook	Ohio
1951	Arith Clark	Michigan
1952	Jane Hoffman	Kentucky
1953	Ellen Schultz	Wisconsin
1954	Jean Handel	Illinois
1955	Lorriane Supitilov	Wisconsin
1956	Magdalena Ade	Indiana
1957	Leona Taylor	Ohio
1958	Rose Sercombe	Michigan
1959	Bess Clayton	Wisconsin
1960-61	Edith McKnight	Missouri
1962	Marie Fish	California
1963	VirginiaKipple	Illinois
1964-65	Ivy Zanier	Illinois
1965-69	Edith McKnight	Missouri
1970-71	Emily Storeng	Texas
1972-73	Lydia Lake	Missouri
1974	Danny Gould	Louisiana
1975-76	Marie Simmons	Missouri
1977-78	Marie Gastfield	Illinois
1979	Maragaret Ocmann	Missouri
1980	Eileen Wright	Oregon
1981-82	Danny Gould	Louisiana
1983-84	Barbara Simcoe	Louisiana
1985-86	Marie Gastfield	Illinois
1987-89	Vyvian Davidson	Washington
1990-91	Ruby Turnley	Louisiana
1992-93	Barbara Simcoe	Louisiana
1994	Pinkey Matthews	Texas
1995	Joyce Linder	New York
1996	Lil Confrancesco	Florida
1997-98	Catherine Brandt	New York
1999-2000	Gloria Jones	Florida

Editors Note: All NSVA members were invited to submit biographies for inclusion in this publication. The following are those who chose to participate. These biographies were printed as received, with only minor editing. The publisher regrets it cannot assume responsibility for omissions or inaccuracies with the following biographies.

The first Seabee Rates to be promoted to one star (Master) Chiefs and two star (Super) Chiefs were instructors at U.S. Naval Schools, Constructions, Port Huenemen in 1961. Courtesy of Cdr. LaVern Pyles, Jr.

SEABEES
BIOGRAPHIES

HUGH "HUCK" ACTON, UT2/c, enlisted in the USN at Prescott, AZ, in March 1949. Boot camp at San Diego, CA. Naval Schools of Construction, Port Hueneme, CA. U.S. Naval Mobile Construction Bn. #1 at Little Creek, VA, later Davisville, RI.

Spent all of his enlistment in MCB #1 with operations in Vieques, Puerto Rico, three times Guantanamo, Cuba, Bermuda, Argentina, Newfoundland, Port Lyautey, French Morocco and was on nine different ships.

Discharged from the USN at NAS Jacksonville, FL, in 1953. Acton is a plankowner in MCB #1 and U.S. Naval Memorial.

Life member Navy Seabee Veterans of America, American Legion, NRA and charter life American Motorcycle Assoc.

At present he lives in Blanding, UT, and operates "Huck's" Museum and Trading Post.

BILL AKINS, born in Warren, OH, in 1948. Graduated from Mineral Ridge High School in 1966 and enlisted in the USN in June 1966. Attended boot camp at Great Lakes, IL, with Co. #396. Reported to Mobile Construction Bn. 71 at Davisville, RI, in September 1966. Served two tours in the Republic of South Vietnam with MCB 71.

Wounded in Phu Loc during second tour in August 1968. After second tour became member of CBU 201 in Davisville, RI. Honorably discharged in September 1969.

Married to the former Nedra Mitchell for 22 years. Raised three children: Shelley (31), married; Dawn Marie (27), married; and Mitch (15), a student. Currently living in Pataskala, OH. Employed with General Electric 20 years as industrial maintenance millwright.

Life member of VFW, DAV, Navy Seabee Veterans of America and Harley Owners Group. Member of American Motorcycle Assoc.

WILLIAM ANDREASSI, of Philadelphia, PA; present age 77. Served in 40th U.S. Naval Construction Bn. from Nov. 6, 1942-Jan. 6, 1946, as a boatswain's mate second class.

Commended for action as a member of first detachment of the battalion, which landed under fire at Los Negros, Admiralty Islands,

March 2, 1944, and immediately commenced work on air strip construction.

On Aug. 27, 1944, authorized by War Dept. General Order No. 54, dated July 5, 1944, to wear the Unit Citation insignia for unit action March 2, 1944, at Los Negros, Admiralty Islands. - O.F. Fried, by direction of the commanding officer.

Voyage One: Nov. 6, 1942, commissioned, Davisville, RI; Dec. 24, 1942, departed Davisville for Norfolk, VA; Dec. 27, 1942, sailed from Norfolk to Panama Canal; Jan. 3, 1943, sailed from Panama Canal to Espiritu in the New Hebrides; Feb. 3, 1943, set up camp and started construction on bomber three at Espiritu Santo; Nov. 13, 1943, completed assignment and then assigned to MacArthur's Sixth Army.

Arrived at Finschafen, New Guinea, Dec. 15, 1943. Work consisted of roads, bridges and staging area for their next major assault; March 2, 1944, landed at Los Negros in the Admiralty Islands. Lengthened Japanese airstrip for use of B-24s. Battalion lost 29 men and 45 received Purple Heart; April 20, 1944, B-24 Bomber crashed into the 40th NCB camp on takeoff with nine 500 pound bombs and 2,743 gallons of fuel which exploded; July 20, 1944, left Los Negros for New Caledonia; Sept. 5, 1944, sailed from New Caledonia to San Francisco; Sept. 18, 1944, arrived at Camp Parks, CA; Sept. 19, 1944, 40th NCB presented with the Army Presidential Unit Citation - "as public evidence of deserved honor and distinction for having operated effectively as combat troops on Los Negros in the Admiralty Islands." On "Voyage One" the 40th NCB traveled some 22,000 miles.

Voyage Two: Jan. 17, 1945, returning from 30 day leave, 40th NCB assigned to go to Saipan - pending transfer to final destination; Feb. 10, 1945, arrived at Pearl Harbor for 14 days; March 18, 1945, arrived at Saipan - assigned to Okinawa and the 10th Army; April 20, 1945, First Echelon arrived on Okinawa on LSTs 899, 850 and 763; May 14, 1945, Second Echelon arrived at Okinawa on the ship *Jasiah Snelling*; May 28, 1945, *Jasiah Snelling* hit by Japanese suicide plane at 0800 while being unloaded; July 1, 1945, completed main construction project, the Chimo Air Strip, which was now in operation as the nearest constructed airfield to Japan; Oct. 17, 1945, CNOB Okinawa requested authority to inactivate the 40th NCB; Jan. 6, 1946, returned home to Philadelphia, PA.

In response to the article, *We Build, We Fight*, the Seabees, which ran in the September 1996 issue of *Constructor*, another Associated General Contractors of America member has come forward with tales of his Seabee days. William Andreassi, chairman of the board of directors of Anvil Construction Co., Inc., Philadelphia, PA, served in the 40th U.S. NCB from Nov. 6, 1942-Dec. 25, 1946. His unit was awarded the Army Presidential Unit

Citation Sept. 19, 1944, and members of his unit claim four Battle Stars on their Pacific Theater Ribbon.

Andreassi's firm, which was founded by Andreassi after his discharge in 1946 and specializes in industrial and commercial construction, has represented Butler Manufacturing (a producer of pre-engineered metal building systems) for 33 years.

TOM ANSBRO, enlisted at New York City in September 1942. Active duty with 42nd Bn. in October, Camp Endicott, Davisville, RI. Transferred out of boot camp in October 1942 to serve as instructor NCTC Diving School. Eventually assistant principal instructor. Trained divers, designed/constructed training aids and devices, wrote curricula/tests/textbooks, conducted underwater salvage and construction activities. Received supplemental training in explosives and ordnance disposal.

Transferred to 64th NCB in August 1944. Further training in Chemical Warfare School and Field Sanitation and Malaria Control Schools. Served in Hawaii and Philippines, working in malaria control and on construction of waterfront facilities, pipelines, and a Navy base of operations for upcoming invasion of mainland China and the Japanese Home Islands.

War ended, sent home for discharge in November 1945. Some diving and ship repair work until re-entering college on GI Bill in 1947. Graduated from State University of New York (Champlain College) and University of Virginia in 1951.

Served 35 years as technical publications editor/writer and education specialist in U.S. Dept. of Defense (Depts. Army/Navy). Retired from federal civil service (Staff, Office of the Chief of Naval Education and Training) in 1986. Adjunct college teacher for 20 years.

KENNETH WALTER AUSTIN, born Sept. 17, 1927, in Mulberry, KS. Entered the USN Nov. 14, 1955, in Seattle and from there to San Diego for boot camp. After boot camp he went through so many kinds of schools that he began to wonder just where he was going to be assigned.

Finally, he was sent to CB School in Port Hueneme for Builders School; home for leave and then to Brooklyn Navy Base, NY, where he missed the rating exam (for second time) so assigned to scullery duty (second time).

Transferred to Newfoundland, landing at the port of St. Johns; from there to Argentina NAS (Navy 103). It was cold as all get out, so when assigned to the scullery again, he didn't mind as it was nice and warm (he missed the rating exams again). When he finished his tour in the scullery, he was assigned to the special services.

He relieved a third class damage control man and was told to either make the hobby shop pay for itself or they were going to close it down. He served there for two years and made grade from seaman second to second class petty officer.

He had one of the few blue liberty cards on the base which did not limit his travel as long as he was back for duty the following day. This was the best duty that he ever had in the service of the country.

He was sent to Davis, RI, for military refresher training where he spent some time marching in parades in the local events. From there he was sent to the Bahamas via Miami, FL, where he spent the last months of his enlistment helping build two bases, one for the Navy and the other a Loran Station for the Coast Guard.

He was sent to Jacksonville, FL, for discharge as builder second class. His time in the service was an experience that can never be forgotten as he holds fond memories of many places and people.

GEORGE WALLACE BALDWIN,

EO2/c, born Oct. 8, 1946, in Evanston, IL. Enlisted in the USN Oct. 21, 1965, at Norwich, New London, CT. He did two tours in Vietnam (Red Beach with the great MCB-58) seven miles north of Da Nang. His first tour involved well drilling which they did for Marine bases around Da Nang. He also drove transit miter hauling to Da Nang Air Base.

After his return home and schooling he returned to Vietnam arriving Dec. 16, 1967. Flight was delayed at Quonset Point due to a heavy snowfall for a day but they got there.

His second tour was spent building ammo bunkers at Da Nang Air Base and Marine support bases.

Baldwin was awarded the National Defense Service Medal, Vietnam Service Medal w/Fleet Marine Force Combat Operations Insignia and one Bronze Star, and RVN Campaign Medal w/Device. Released from active duty and transferred to Naval Reserve and was honorably discharged Oct. 20, 1971.

He now owns a general store in Preston, CT, works 16 hours a day and enjoys every minute of it. Thanks to Seabee 'can do' training he can handle it.

ELMER C. BARNARD, BUC, inducted

into the USN Jan. 15, 1942, at Quonset Point, RI. Served with 1st Bn. at Quonset Point; Auburn, NY; Camp Peary, VA; Tonga Tabu; Fiji; Efate, New Hebrides; and Camp Parks, CA. Also stationed in Hawaii, Saipan and Okinawa with 14th Bn.

Awarded the Good Conduct Medal, Asia Pacific Medal, American Defense Medal, Adm. Halsey Commendation and Army Unit

Commendation Special. Barnard was discharged in November 1945 at Boston, MA.

Memorable experiences: Operated pontoon barge at Fiji, unloading grounded liberty ship, *Thomas Edison*, between Japanese subs, coral reefs and hurricanes with 1st Bn.

He is national secretary of Seabee Veterans of America (life member #43) and state department president of Seabee Veterans of America, Michigan.

Civilian employment as salesman for Friden Co. and the last 24 years as sales representative for Pitney Bowes.

Barnard is married to Geraldine and has four children: Walter, Calvin, Allen and Laura; and four grandchildren: Marissa, Megan, Colette and Michelle.

ERNEST W. BASSER, CM1/c, born April

27, 1940, in McKeesport, PA. Inducted into the service in September 1979 at McKeesport, PA.

Military locations and stations were 1st Armd. Div., V Army Corp., 165th MI Bn., MCB 23, Ft. Belvoir, VA, FSU-I Manor, PA, Hoenfell, Germany and "Lukavac" Bosnia/Heneqouna.

First and only Seabee reservist called and volunteered for active duty, participating in Operation Joint Endeavor and Task Force Eagle, Bosnia (age 56 years). Assistant to U.S. Army Mayor of Camp Pauxtawny, largest U.S. Army camp in Bosnia (2,000 troops) serving as a Seabee engineer consultant and SerBiau/Bosnian interpreter and foot soldier. First Armd. Div., 165th MI.

Collision at Sea, "Merchant Marine Disaster," 1962, exiting Cape Cod Canal, MA. Serving as quartermaster and bos'n mate aboard M/V *Dynafuel*, U.S. Merchant Marine tanker ship, cut in half by Norwegian freighter, *Fernview;* M/V *Dynafuel* sank.

Awarded the Expert Rifle M-16-A2, Armed Forces Reserve Medal, USNR-MSM (5th), Sharpshooter M-16-A2, Bronze "M" for mobilization, Overseas Service Ribbon (1st), NATO Medal, Army Achievement Medal (1st), Armed Forces Expeditionary Medal (1st), Navy "E," Joint Meritorious Unit Award, Army Superior Unit Award, Armed Forces Service

Medal, Naval Reserve Merchant Marine Badge, Naval and USMC Overseas Ribbon, U.S. Merchant Marine Vietnam Service Medal, Sailor of the Quarter (2nd Quarter), Sailor of the Year, Military Outstanding Voluntary Service Medal, Army Battalion Coin for Excellence, Sea Cadet Navy League for CWO2, 165th MI Battalion Excellence Coin, Navy Achievement Medal w/Gold Star (2), Armed Forces Volunteer Medal, U.S. Merchant Mariners Badge, letter stating most decorated sailor in Navy Marine Corps Reserve Center (North Versailles, PA), and awarded second NATO award Operation Joint Endeavor, First Armd. Div., Ground Force.

Retiring in the year 2000 from USNR (10 years Merchant Marine, 21 years USN).

Married to Ann Rita with six children and 11 grandchildren. Civilian employment as a mechanic. Member of Armed Guard for 30 years, Armored Truck Co.

Basser is a member of VFW Post 914, service officer; Isle 3X, Pittsburgh, PA, service officer; instructor, NJROTC, North Versailles, PA; and PO1C NAVFAC Team, Naval Reserve and Marine Corps Center, North Versailles, PA.

CHARLES E. BATES JR., enlisted at

Mena, AR, Nov. 1, 1942. Served in the 7th Spc. NCB. Trained at Camp Peary, VA, then shipped out to Port Hueneme, CA. Served at Dutch Harbor, AK, for eight months, Adak for eight months and on to Okinawa.

Received Victory Medal, Asiatic-Pacific Campaign Medal, Good Conduct Medal and American Theater Campaign Ribbon. Discharged in January 1946 with rate of machinist's mate second class.

Married Gilda in 1947, the couple has two daughters and four granddaughters. Owned and operated two cattle farms for 45 years. Selected as Farm Family of the Year in 1985. Retired in 1993. Still active in church and community activities.

GLENN E. BATTSON, MM2/c, born June

4, 1916, in Great Falls, MT. Inducted into the service in October 1942 at Seattle, WA. Military locations and stations were Camp Peary, Camp Bradford, Port Hueneme, CA, and

Guadalcanal. Served as barber, seven months, ship's company; X-1W chaplain, two years; commander X-1, four years; secretary X-1, five years; and historian X-1, one year.

At Camp Parks for reassignment, he elected to serve at Port Hueneme as a barber. Thus he was denied the pleasure of his buddies from Guadalcanal. Ellen was 26 years old and he was 28 years young. They wanted to start their family, so they rented a house in Oxnard.

His First Special buddies are Victor Pritchett, Tom Denice, Ron Eldred (deceased), Harry Bennett, Bob Danley and Vaughan Stolsenberg (deceased).

He is the Seabee sailor who built a 10 place bomb shelter, and who gave free haircuts on the *Day Star*; who built sideboards on his bunk to ward off mosquitoes; who studied engineering books every night; who rigged an operating refueling barge; who drove the fuel truck around "Bloody Ridge" for barge gas; who knocked the hat off Walter Kayser in a "cocoa-nut" war.

Now he is again a member of 1st Spc. NCB Inc. Five of them have joined: Tom Denice, Glenn Battson, Ernst Lang, John Case and Victor Pritchett. They need more 1st Specialists to join! You won't be sorry!

Discharged in August 1945 at Bremerton, WA. Memorable experience was R&R to New Zealand, Barracks M. Arms Port Heuenme.

He married Ellen May 29, 1941, and has three sons and one daughter. Attended the University of Washington, Seattle. Employed as construction engineer from 1948-79. Retired to home and property development, builder, property maintenance. Member of the Methodist Church, VFW, 1st Special NCB, Lions Club and American Legion.

BENJAMIN F. BAUER, MM3/c, inducted into the service June 16, 1943, at Camden, NJ. Military locations and stations were Camp Peary, Super 7th Bn. training base, Williamsburg, VA, CBMU 519, CBMU 580, Solomon Islands, Munda, Segi Point, Okinawa, Port Hueneme, CA, and San Diego Naval Base, CA.

Bauer was awarded the Asiatic-Pacific Medal, Victory Medal and Good Conduct Medal. Discharged March 4, 1946, at Lido Beach, NY.

Memorable experiences: Locating a buddy through the Seabee Veterans Assoc., Howard Davis, who has since passed away. Joining with CBMU 520 reunions which was part of the 7th Bn. in Camp Peary before being broken up into CBMUs 518 through 521 and 580.

Civilian activity in the poultry business for 10 years and with Shell Chemical Co. for 21 years. Also was a plumber's helper and sold sewing machines. He loves fishing and bowling.

Bauer is married to Grace and has two sons, Robert and Bruce, seven grandchildren and two great-grandchildren.

KENNETH SEATON BEATTY, BM1/c, inducted into the service March 17, 1943, at Camp Peary, VA. Military locations and stations were Tarawa, Kwajalein and Okinawa.

Awards and medals include the American Theater, Asiatic-Pacific w/3 stars, Victory Bar, Occupational Force of Asia and three Unit Commendations. Discharged Nov. 11, 1945, at the Navy Center, Chicago, IL.

Memorable experiences: He belonged to one of the smallest units of the 74th Bn. USNCB units in diving and demolition duties. Time spent deactivating mines, salvaging equipment off the ocean floor, moving and sinking ships interfering with operations, installing underwater cable and pipe lines, retrieving lost articles, examining hulls of Navy ships with hits and near misses, retrieve bodies of downed bomber crews.

When his two year enlistment was up he volunteered to stay until the war was won. He served two years, seven months and 24 days which included four months of training and no leaves.

Retired from General Electric as field engineer in thermo-dynamics. He and Laura, his wife of 59 years, have one daughter, LeiLonie; one son, Jerry; two grandsons; and two great-grandsons.

RICHARD D. BENSON, BUL-CN (MCB 8), enlisted in the Seabees in 1965 and trained at Davisville, RI. He then was transferred to the West Coast at Port Hueneme, CA. From there he was shipped to Da Nang, Vietnam.

He then served a second tour of duty at Chu Lai, Vietnam and was honorably discharged in April 1967. He was awarded the National Defense Service Medal, Vietnam Service Medal and Ribbon (second award) and the Vietnam Campaign Medal.

Upon being discharged he joined the Carpenters Local 12 in Syracuse, NY. He then went on to start his own construction company building grocery stores in central New York. After almost 20 years, he is still operating this business and building grocery stores in New York, Pennsylvania and Ohio.

Married to Betty, the couple has two children, a son, Roy E.; a daughter, Susan M.; and one granddaughter, Emily S. Benson. He is a member of the Navy Seabee Veterans of America.

DON BENTLY, born in Cleveland, OH, Oct. 18, 1924, and was raised in Muscatine, IA. Inducted into the U.S. Navy in October 1943, Seaman 3rd Class. Trained in Camp Endicott, Signaling School, First Aid School, with advanced training at Port Hueneme, CA.

Assigned to Detachment 1038, later redesignated as the 302d Bat. During the war, was stationed in Hawaii, Saipan, Tinian, Leyte, and Luzon.

Of his many memorable experiences was Gen. MacArthur's arrival at Leyte and speech of liberation to the Filipinos, "By the grace of Almighty God our forces stand again on Philippine soil—soil consecrated in the blood of our two peoples...."

Don was discharged following the war as Seaman 1st Class. He went on found Bently Nevada Corporation, the world's leading provider of high-tech instrumentation, services and software for monitoring the mechanical conditions of machinery. He lives in Carson Valley, NV.

JOHN ALBERT BERGER JR., enlisted in CB Reserve at Ft. McHenry, Baltimore, MD, July 6, 1972; re-enlisted at Little Creek Amphibious Base, March 14, 1975.

Military locations and stations were boot camp, San Diego, CA; "A" School, Port Hueneme, CA; ACB-2, Little Creek, VA; "B" School, Gulfport, MS; Public Works Dept., USNAS, New Orleans, LA; Public Works Dept., Guantanamo Bay, Cuba; NMCB-133, Gulfport, MS. While attached to NMBC-133 served on *Diego Garcia* during the time of the attempted rescue of American citizens held by Iran; ended enlistment at U.S. Naval Station, Guam.

Awarded the National Defense Service Medal, Good Conduct Medal, Navy Expeditionary Medal, Sea Service Medal, Navy "E" Award and M-16 Rifle Sharpshooter. Discharged at Construction Battalion Center, Gulfport, MS, March 13, 1981.

Member Navy Seabee Veterans of America Island X-3, Cumberland, MD; past commander, VFW Post 11261; and member, American Legion Post 277, Pasadena, MD.

Berger has two daughters, Hattie Mercer (Mrs.) and Sara Ann.

JOHN ALBERT BERGER SR., SV3/c (SV rating now is EA), enlisted in CB Reserve at Ft. McHenry, Baltimore, MD, Aug. 8, 1950; called to active duty Jan. 2, 1952.

Military locations and stations were boot camp at Bainbridge Naval Training Center, MD; NAVSCON Port Hueneme, CA; MCB-4 Davisville, RI. With MCB-4 served at NAS Argentina Newfoundland, U.S. Naval Base Guantanamo Bay, Cuba.

Awarded the National Defense Service Medal. Released from active duty Oct. 12,

1953, Quonset Point, RI. Discharged Aug. 7, 1954.

Life member No. 273 Island X-3, Cumberland, MD; American Legion, Anne Arundel County Legionnaire of the Year 1998-99 and past service officer 1994-96. He is now service officer again for 1999-2000.

Married 47 years to Nancy (nee) Stickler. Has one son, John A. Jr. and two granddaughters, Hattie Mercer (Mrs.) and Sara.

CARL EVERETT BERGSTROM,

MM1/c, a plankowner in the 133rd Naval Constr. Bn. He went through boot training at Camp Peary, VA; advanced military training at Camp Endicott, RI; ABD, Camp Holliday, MS; and debarked from Port Hueneme, CA.

Arrived at NAS Honolulu, then to Fourth Marine Div. Base on Maui, T.H. The battalion shipped out for Iwo Jima, landing in the second wave. The 133rd suffered the highest number of casualties of any Seabee unit in WWII. Following the invasion of the island he returned to Guam and was discharged at Boston, MA, Jan. 31, 1946. He enlisted in the Naval Reserve and served until the pressure of civilian work made it impossible to keep up the requirements of the Reserve program.

Bergstrom earned the Asiatic-Pacific Theater Medal w/Battle Star, American Theater Medal and WWII Victory Medal. As part of the Fourth Marine Div. he would be entitled to any unit commendations awarded to the division.

Carl Bergstrom graduated from the University of Massachusetts, Amherst and was elected to the Stockbridge School of Agriculture Honor Society. He and Mimi Papacolas were married July 4, 1947, in Clinton, MA. In October 1949 he moved with his wife and baby daughter to Woodstock, VT, to manage the Billings Estate, and retired in 1991 as superintendent of the Rockefeller Estate, remaining as consultant. Carl's landscape designs may be seen today at the former Rockefeller Estate, now part of the National Park Service.

He joined the Navy Seabee Veterans of America, Island X-1 Vermont in 1994 and was a member at the time of his death, July 26, 1998, at age 82.

Bergstrom leaves his wife, Mimi Papacolas Bergstrom, Woodstock, VT; his daughter, Karen Bergstrom McKnight; her husband, Dr. John Michael McKnight Jr.; and grandsons, Dr. John Michael McKnight III and Carl Jason McKnight.

EUGENE-JEAN MARIE BERTRAND,

BM1/c, born Feb. 2, 1924, in Acushnet, MA. Inducted into the service Aug. 6, 1943, at Boston, MA.

Military locations and stations were Camp Peary, VA; 18th Spec. Bn. and Naval Constr. Det. 1034 Spec.; Port Hueneme, CA; Marshall Islands; Majuro; and Eniwetok Islands from February 1944-November 1945.

Awarded the American Area Medal and WWII Victory Medal. Bertrand was discharged Dec. 15, 1945, at Boston, MA.

Married Lina on July 24, 1948, and has five children and four grandchildren. They have celebrated their 50th wedding anniversary.

He is a retired stitching room machinist from E.T. Wright and Co., Rockland, MA, a men's shoe company. He now enjoys traveling, the family, gardening, fishing, walking, staying healthy and looks forward to receiving *Can Do* newsletter.

JOSEPH ALLEN BLAKE, BU2/c, in-

ducted into the service July 19, 1966, at Davisville, RI. Military locations and stations were USNAB, Coronado, CA; USNS, Adak, AK; and NAF Cam Ranh Bay, Republic of Vietnam.

Awarded the Man of the Month (November 1968) Award, National Defense Service Medal, Vietnam Service Medal and Republic of Vietnam Campaign Medal. Discharged Jan. 3, 1969, at Seattle, WA.

Memorable experiences: While stationed in Adak, AK, he met a classmate from home who was working for Civil Service. Reuniting with old buddies from home that also served in Vietnam. Having the opportunity to travel to the Philippines, Japan, Taiwan while on R&R.

Member of Lions, Masons, American Legion and VFW. Civilian employment as boatyard owner and other business investments. He has been married to his childhood sweetheart, Brenda, for 30 years. They have two children, Aaron and Charlinda.

JOHN WILLIAM "JACK" BRANDT,

CMCS (Ret.), USNR, born Aug. 25, 1933, in Syracuse, NY, to Anthony and Margaret Brandt. He enlisted in the Navy Reserves Sept. 14, 1950. He was activated for Korea and assigned to DER-391, a picket ship.

After his two years of active duty he joined the Fleet Div. in Syracuse. He and a former engineering officer talked about the Seabee program in Syracuse. The next month he was in their training and support company, cross-rating from engineman first class to CM first class. He served with NMCB-19, 13 and a short time with the 27th.

He was presented a charcoal drawing of the Seabee Memorial after being selected as Reserve Seabee of the Year 1973.

He made chief while with the 13th. He was the assistant officer in charge of "E" Co. and assistant officer in charge of the Bn. "Air Det." with 89 men, one officer. They won first place on the East Coast and also received recognition for being the first air detachment, active duty or reserve, to ever go out and return with a zero (0) dollar shortage. That year he made E8. He managed to be with the Navy for a total of 40 years. His last 21 years were with the Seabees.

He was a former Island X-19 commander, Dept. of New York commander, N.E. Dist. vice commander and national vice commander at large. He is presently the national commander of the Navy Seabee Veterans of America, Inc.

He and Catherine were married Aug. 11, 1956. They have three children: Ann Marie, Stephen and Mary K.; and five grandchildren. He retired from NYNEX after 35 years service.

HOWARD SHERIDAN BREWER, in-

ducted into the service Jan. 23, 1943, LB-1, Wescasset, ME. Military locations and stations were NCTC Norfolk, VA; NCTC Williamsburg, VA; 69th NCB; CEMU-636; Davisville, RI; England; France; and Germany.

Awarded the WWII Victory Medal, American Area Medal, EAME Medal, Good Conduct Medal, Point System. Discharged at USN Personnel Separation Center, Boston, MA, Jan. 25, 1946 as carpenter's mate second class.

Memorable experiences: Honor guard at Angelo Tsuolapoulas funeral in Cambridge, England.

Civilian activities include carpenter, fisherman and owner of a bed and breakfast. He is married to Virginia N. Brewer and has four children: Barry, Marcia, Joanne and Joni; eight grandchildren; and five great-grandchildren.

ERNEST EMIL BROWN, BM1/c, born

July 7, 1920, in Lincoln, RI. Enlisted in the service Nov. 12, 1942, with active duty beginning Jan. 3, 1943, Providence, RI. Boot camp, 81st NCB, Co. B, 7th Plt.

CBMU-505: Upolu, British Samoa, 14

months; Solomon's, Florida Island, 10 months; Saipan four months.

On August 28 granted emergency leave. His brother was killed in B-24 crash July 22, 1945, Langley Field, VA. Took six weeks to get the bad news.

Flew from Saipan to Pearl Harbor on APB-2Y. From Pearl Harbor to San Pedro as passenger aboard the USS battleship *New York*. It was the first group ferried stateside.

Awarded the American Area Medal, Asiatic-Pacific Campaign Medal and WWII Victory Medal. Discharged Nov. 1, 1945, at Fargo Bldg., Boston, MA.

He has three children, nine grandchildren and five great-grandchildren. He and his wife have visited the lower 48 states and have crossed country eight times (round trips) visiting former shipmates. Retired since 1982.

FRANKLIN D. BROWN, MM3/c, drafted Oct. 4, 1944; took boot training at Great Lakes, IL; from there to Camp Endicott at Davisville, RI; then on to Port Hueneme, CA, to join the first Seabee Truck Bn., the 139th NCB.

After advanced training they boarded the good ship *Cape Perpetua* and went off to Okinawa to do their part in WWII. In 1945 they went to Guam to link up with the 134th NCB to head to San Francisco, CA, and then on to Bainbridge, MD, to be discharged June 23, 1946.

Married Betty Lou in 1950 and has two children and three grandchildren. Worked in construction and drove a trailer. Now retired after driving a bus in public transportation for 35 years. Active in veteran's organizations and presently commander of the American Legion Post.

JOE W. BROWN, inducted into the service at Ft. McClellan, AL, in October 1943. Military locations and stations were Camp Peary, Williamsburg, VA, 1943-44, 31st Spec. NCB, Saipan, Marianas Islands, 1944-46.

Discharged at NAS New Orleans, LA, in May 1946 as SKD2/c. Brown is a retired accountant, Maxwell AFB, AL.

JOHN O. BROWN, EOCS, USN (Ret.), enlisted in the Seabees at Altoona, PA, in 1943. Trained NCTC Camp Peary, VA. Shipped out at Port Hueneme, CA, to Pearl Harbor with 301st MCB, further to Guam and Okinawa.

Discharged at Sampson, NY, in January

1946. Re-enlisted USNR-R in 1947. Called to active duty in 1952, NAS Oceana, VA, and Harbor Defense Unit, Little Creek, VA.

Re-enlisted USN in 1955, NAV School Port Hueneme, CA, NAVSTA Guam, MCB 11, NTC Bainbridge, MD, NAVCRUITSTA Pittsburgh, PA. Re-enlisted in 1961, MCB 11, MCB Three, NAVSTA Adak, AK. Re-enlisted in 1964, MCB Four, NAS Sigonella, Sicily, MCB Seven.

Awards/medals include: Good Conduct Medal w/4 Bronze Stars, Asiatic-Pacific Campaign Medal w/Bronze Star, WWII Victory Medal, National Defense Service Medal w/ Bronze Star, Vietnam Service Medal w/3 Bronze Stars FMF Combat Insignia, Navy Expert Rifle Medal, Navy Unit Commendation Ribbon Bar w/Bronze Star, Meritorious Unit Commendation Ribbon w/Bronze Star, RVN Meritorious Unit Citation (Gallantry Cross Medal Color w/Palm), RVN Meritorious Unit Citation (Civil Action Medal, First Class Color w/Palm), RVN Medal w/1960 Device. Released to inactive duty, Davisville, RI, in April 1970.

Relocated to Lititz, PA. Retired Pennsylvania Railroad, freight conductor. Fully retired in 1986. Life member Navy Seabee Veterans of America Island X-13 Florida, VFW and American Legion.

Married 58 years to "Goldie" and has three children: Patricia, John and Robert; five grandchildren; and four great-grandchildren.

ROBERT A. BRUNS, MM2/c (T) (CB), inducted into the service Dec. 23, 1942, at Davisville, RI. Vessels and stations included USNCTC, Davisville, RI, 75th Nav. Construction Bn., USNAAS, Arcata, CA, ABRD, Port Hueneme, CA.

Military locations and stations were French New Caledonia, Guadalcanal, Bougainville, Russell Island, New Guinea and Philippine (South Pacific).

Awarded the Victory Ribbon, American Area Ribbon, Asiatic-Pacific Ribbon w/3 stars, Philippine Liberation Ribbon and Good Conduct Ribbon. Discharged Jan. 21, 1946, at Great Lakes, Chicago.

Memorable experiences: Getting inducted

into the Seabees Christmas Eve and landing in South Pacific, New Caledonia.

Married June 3, 1950, to Martha Walters, and has two sons and five grandchildren. Has lived in Hagerstown since 1947. Life member of Seabees, Island X-3, Cleveland, OH.

Went into business (construction) in May 1951 (basements, open ditches for counties, etc.). Semi-retired in 1995. Has had two strokes, can walk and talk). Son Mike is now president.

H. HOYT BRYSON, enlisted in Navy Seabees, in Atlanta, GA, 1943. Early training at Camp Peary, VA, then to U.S. Marines, 4th Div., Camp Pendleton, CA.

Shipped out of Frisco to Pontoon Assembly Det. #3 in New Guinea; a number of men were in Leyte invasion in October 1944. Went back to New Guinea and 16 of them were transferred to PAD-4 on Samar in the Philippines on their way to China, but war was over and left Samar in November 1945.

Awarded the Asiatic-Pacific Combat Medal. Discharged Dec. 13, 1945, at Charleston, SC.

Since discharge has been in Iron Worker's Union. Worked in Iran, Turkey, South America, Trinidad, U.S. Virgin Islands, plus many places in the U.S. on dam construction. Retired in 1979 from Iron Works Local #33, Rochester, NY.

Life member Navy Seabee Veterans of America, No. 975, Island X-8, Tonawanda, NY. Married to Inez Bryson and has three children: Carolyn, Karyn and David and three grandchildren.

JAMES BUREL, CE1/c, enlisted at Muskegon, MI. Trained at Great Lakes in June 1954. Served aboard USS *Everglades* and USS *Robert A. Owens* through December 1957.

Enlisted in 1968 in Seabees and trained as a DPPO at Gulfport and Davisville where attached to MCB the Great 58. Entered into Vietnam Chu Lai in February 1969 at Camp Shields. Assigned to base maintenance projects and shared in bringing 440 to Vietnam. Then served with civic action and helped build high school for Vietnamese on Cu Lao Re Island.

Received Combat Action Navy Achievement w/Combat V and the Vietnamese Cross of Gallantry Bronze Star. Honorably discharged.

Married Shirley King in May 1973 and

has four daughters and nine grandchildren. Continued in Naval Reserve and returned to work at Dow Chemical, Midland, MI, as electrician. Retired Navy service and Dow Chemical in 1996. Joined Navy Seabee Veterans of America Island X-17 as life member where he acts as a go-for when needed.

ALAN EUGENE BURNS, S1/c, 127th NCB, inducted into the service July 27, 1943, at Grand Central Palace, New York City, NY.

Military locations and stations were Camp Peary, VA; Gulfport, MS; Port Hueneme, CA; Wailuku, Maui, HI; Manicani Island, Philippine Islands; Yokosuka, Japan CBMU-602; Treasure Island, CA; Pier #92, New York City, NY; and Brooklyn Navy Yard, New York.

Awarded the American Theater Medal, Asiatic-Pacific Medal, Philippine Liberation Ribbon and Victory Medal. Discharged April 5, 1946, at Lido Beach, Long Island, NY.

After discharge he spent five years at various jobs and 40 years as a bartender. A Bronxite for 40 years, he moved to Jersey for 25 years. Retired in 1991 to Henderson, NV. After four years of retirement, fishing every day, got bored and got a job as a security guard at a government facility. Feeling good for 74 years. Now living in Bould City, NV.

His wife, Eileen, is deceased. He has three children: Stephen, Richard and Susan; and four grandchildren: Steven, Stacey, Nicky and Stephanie.

MARTIN JAMES CALLAWAY, enlisted in the USN June 3, 1952, on a "kiddie cruise." Boot camp at Great Lakes, AE School at NAS

Jacksonville. Spent rest of hitch at NAS North Island. RAD July 21, 1955. Attended one and one-half semesters of teacher's college before enlisting in USAF. Spent four years working on F-86 Ds and Ls before being discharged in October 1959.

Remained a civilian for 13 years while he became a master plumber. Enlisted in the Naval Reserve as a UT2/c in September 1972. Assigned to RNMCB 25 out of Great Lakes. Performed ACDUTRA at Camp Pendleton, Gulfport, Quantico, Crane Weapons Center and Great Lakes.

Recalled to active duty in April 1984 as a canvasser-recruiter. In 1990 assigned as zone supervisor in Minneapolis for Naval Reserve Recruiting Command Det. 2. Retired in July 1995 as UTC.

Life member of Seabee Veterans of America. Earned Naval Commendation, Air Force Outstanding Unit, Naval Unit Commendation, Air Force and Naval Good Conduct,

Recruiting Service, Marksman and National Defense medals.

Married to Mary for 43 years. Has five children and six grandchildren.

CHARLES THOMAS CARTER, BM2/c, V-6(T), born March 18, 1923, in Seattle, WA. Enlisted in the USN Jan. 14, 1943, at Seattle. Military locations and stations included Constr. Bn. USNCTC, Williamsburg, VA; Seventh Spec. Naval Constr. Bn.; 36th Spec. U.S. Naval Constr. Bn.; PSC, USNB, Bremerton, WA; Dutch Harbor and Okinawa. Worked in rope and cable area.

Awarded the Asiatic-Pacific Area Campaign Medal w/star, American Area Campaign Medal, Good Conduct Medal and WWII Victory Medal.

Married Nov. 6, 1949, to Jane H. Watt of Bellingham, WA. Has two children, Jeffery Lynn and Susanne Marie. Worked for King County Maintenance, Highline School Dist. #401 as transportation supervisor, motion picture operator and Highline Maintenance Dept. supervisor. Loved fishing, hunting and traveling to Alaska in his own vessel *Nor'wester.* Carter passed away in 1996.

HUMBERTO NAPOLEON CATALA, inducted into the service at West Palm Beach, FL, in August 1962. Military locations and stations were Port Hueneme and Camp Pendleton, CA; Okinawa; Southeast Asia; MCB-9 and MCB-5.

Catala was awarded the Unit Citation and Armed Forces Expeditionary Medal. Received discharge certificate in August 1967 at Tampa, FL.

Civilian employment as ITT-Hartford, construction technical consultant. Retired after 29 years. Spent prior five years as field engineer, A.P. Green Div. U.S. Gypsum. He is now an engineering-construction consultant. Catala is married to Sybil and has three children: Paul, Marta and Mary; and one grandchild, Emerson. He is a member of Island X-11, Tampa, FL.

WALTER MARK "BUD" CHISSUS, born March 3, 1923, in Southfield, MI. Inducted into the service Dec. 26, 1941, at Detroit, MI. Military locations and stations were WWII destroyer in Pacific and carrier in Korea. Joined Seabees in August 1952.

He was awarded the Navy Commendation

for Korea. Retired in March 1983 as a chief builder.

Memorable experience was meeting new people.

He is married to Joyce and has eight children. Chissus is now retired and is a motor home jockey traveling states.

ALBERT J. CHOMOR, born May 9, 1926, in Sharon, PA. Enlisted in the Navy at Great Lakes Naval Training Base in September 1944. He served in the 5th Spec. and 29th NCB units.

Initially shipped to New Guinea, then to the Philippine Islands of Leyte, Luzon and Samar building landing strips and boat docks. From there he was sent to Guam and finally to Truk Island to build air landing strips.

After his discharge as MM3/c at Bainbridge, MD, in May 1946 he returned home to Sharon and married "Norma Jean" Feb. 5, 1949. The couple has five children and nine grandchildren. He is a member of Navy Seabee Veterans of America, past master of Masonic Lodge #250 and a retired United Steel worker.

RONALD CHRISEY, enlisted in the USN at Kingston, NY, in 1953. Trained at Bainbridge, MD, then Port Hueneme, CA. Shipped out to Kwajalein with Det. Able, MCB-10, then to Guam, MCB-10, main battalion.

From there to Adak with MCB-9. Back to Kwajalein NAS until separation in 1957 at Treasure Island, CA. Served in the Ready Reserves until discharged in 1961 as CM2/c.

After discharge, continued working as a heavy equipment mechanic for 20 years, at which time, he entered the Civil Service market and worked as building maintenance coordinator for 22 years and retired.

Married to Bev, the couple has three children and four grandchildren. As a life member of the Navy Seabee Veteran's of America, Chrisey has held the office of vice commander, historian, Island X-9, Kingston, NY. Bev is Island auxiliary treasurer and state department historian.

FRED C. CLARKSTON, MOMM3/c, born Jan. 12, 1925, in Londonderry, OH, and attended school in Ohio. Went into the Seabees June 17, 1943, and trained at Camp Peary, VA. Was assigned to the 111th Nav. Constr. Bn. and in January 1944 boarded the *Mauritania* to go to England where they prepared for D-Day.

Was involved in D-Day by transporting men and equipment from LSTs to Omaha Beach. On Jan. 15, 1945, sailed from Boston to Hawaii via the Panama Canal. Docked at Pearl Harbor Feb. 6, 1945, and left on February 11 to go to Calicoan Island. Assisted the Aussies in the invasion of Borneo. On Aug. 14, 1945, was on the way to Japan when the war ended.

In October 1945 the 111th Bn. disbanded and then was assigned to the 96th Nav. Constr. Bn. and sent to Manchuria where they built an airfield. Was discharged March 4, 1946.

Married "Ruth" June 2, 1946, and has three children, nine grandchildren and one great-grandchild. They settled in Pearl River, NY and love to travel.

Active in the Naurashank Masonic Lodge #723, Nauraushaun Chapter #434, OES, Masonic War Veterans of the state of New York and Navy Seabee Veterans of America, Inc.

MARC P. CLINCH, enlisted in the USN at Great Lakes, IL, in 1981. Trained at CBC, Gulfport, MS, and affiliated with NMCB-133. Completed four deployments to Greece, Cuba, Japan and Spain.

After discharge in 1986 he affiliated with the Seabee Reserves while attending college. His first reserve assignment was with Det. 0127 in Manchester, NH. After completing college, he relocated to Florida and affiliated with NMCB-14 where he continues to serve as a steelworker senior chief (Seabee Combat Warfare). He is a senior construction manager and associate with an Orlando based engineering and construction firm.

Married to Pamela, the couple has two children, Jena and Kensey. Clinch is a member of Island X-4, Florida.

CHARLIE C. COCHRAN, CM3/c, inducted into the service April 15, 1970, at Atlanta, GA. Served with NMCB-71/SBT-7107. Military locations and stations were Gulfport, MS (boot), Co. #173; Little Creek, VA; Davisville, RI; Gito, Cuba; Rosevelt Roads, PR; and Mytho, South Vietnam.

Awarded the 45 Marksman Award, Vietnam Campaign Medal and Unit Citation SBT-7107. Discharged Oct. 15, 1972, at Davisville, RI.

Cochran is owner of Competition Carrier Service, Macon, GA. He has been married to Sandra for 29 years and has one child, Jay (23 years old). He is a life member of Navy Seabee Veterans of America.

ANTHONY COFRANCESCO, enlisted in the USN at Paterson, NJ, in 1944. Trained at Davisville, RI, then shipped out of Gulfport, MS, to Hawaii.

Initially shipped to Guam, 301st NCB, then to Saipan and Tinian. Transferred to 597th CBMU then on to Okinawa.

After discharged as EM2/c, he went to school and was an engineer for 20 years. He later opened his own private school of drafting and design in New Jersey. He eventually moved to New Port Richey, FL, and started a consulting firm from which he is now retired.

Married to Lil, the couple has two children and one grandchild. As a member of the Navy Seabee Veterans of America, Cofrancesco has held the office of vice commander, commander and executive committeeman, Island X-17 Florida.

ROY E. COMBES JR., enlisted in the U.S. Navy Seabees in August 1942. From Richmond, IN, he trained at Camp Allen, VA; Camp Bradford, VA; and Gulfport, MS. He shipped out of Port Hueneme, CA, to New Caledonia, Guadalcanal and the island of Tulogy. He was back home by November 1943 with a medical discharge.

Unable to continue his trade of interior decorating due to his war injury, he returned

to business college and spent the next 38 years in the wholesale food industry. Among many of his food industry achievements was the development of the Poly Bag Frozen Foods, used widely today.

He is currently president of the 26th Bn. Seabees; life member of American Legion, VFW and Island X8-New York. His family consists of his wife, Dorothy; seven children; eight grandchildren and nine great-grandchildren.

NORMAN EDWARD COOPER, worked as a welder in Evansville, IN and was making LSTs when he enlisted in the Navy Seabees, Oct. 5, 1943. Trained at Camp Peary, VA, and was reclassified from fireman first class to SF3/c. After boot camp was sent to Port Hueneme, CA, and put in CBMU-586. Left Port Hueneme April 5, 1944, for Bougainville, Solomon Islands and arrived there May 4, 1944.

Left for the Philippine Islands Aug. 13, 1945, and arrived at Calicoan Samar Sept. 2, 1945, and was put in the 75th Bn. On September 15 was sent to Jinamoc Island near Tacloban, Leyte to relieve the 88th Bn. On Nov. 16, 1945, was advanced from SF3/c to SF2/c. On Dec. 1, 1945, left Jinamoc Island to return to Calicoan.

On Dec. 7, 1945, was transferred to 93rd Bn. On Dec. 18, 1945, left Calicoan for Tubaboa Naval Receiving Station and on Dec. 21, 1945, got on (APA-190) USS *Pickens* and arrived at the Golden Gate Jan. 7, 1946. Was discharged May 16, 1946, at St. Louis NAS. Awards include the Asiatic-Pacific w/star, American Area and Victory Medal.

Cooper is a life member of Seabee Veterans of America X5 of Ft. Lauderdale. Retired as mold maker from Owens Illinois Glass Co., Alton, IL, after 30 years. Moved to Florida in 1986 and is happy to be living there. He is married to Ruth and has two children, Alan and Linda, and two grandchildren, Mark and Brian Cooper.

CHARLES COUSINS, Coxswain, inducted into the service June 2, 1943, at New York, NY. Military locations and stations were Camp Peary, USNCTC, Williamsburg, VA;

Camp Pendleton MFTC, Oceanside, CA; 38th Marine Repl. Bn., Oahu, HI; 13th Spec, Naval Constr. Bn., Oahu, HI; and Guam.

Awarded the Asiatic-Pacific Campaign Ribbon w/Bronze Star, American Campaign Medal, WWII Victory Medal, Honorable Service Button and Navy Honorable Discharge Button. Discharged Dec. 19, 1945, at Lido Beach, NY.

Memorable experiences: While stationed at Camp Pendleton in 1943, he participated in the making of the movie *The Fighting Seabees*. He played three parts: a civilian construction worker, a Seabee and a Japanese soldier. The invasion of Guam was memorable. They were delayed at sea, the days of the actual invasion and the experiences following.

After discharged tried various occupations in and around New York (carpenter, plumber, machinist and a few others). In 1956 he headed west for California where he landed a position with Hughes Aircraft Co. After 29 years with Hughes he retired as a program manager. Married to Rita since 1971.

EDWIN M. CRENSHAW, CE1/c (SCW), born Nov. 9, 1950, in Orlando, FL. Graduated from Colonial High and enlisted in the Navy in 1968. Attended boot as one of the first companies (075) to go through NTC Orlando. His first choice out of boot was to be a Seabee. However, the Navy had other ideas and he ended up an aviation electrician.

Made three tours to Vietnam with VA-196 out of Whidbey Island, WA. Discharged off active duty in 1973 and went to work for the Orlando Utilities Commission of which he retired after 26 years in 1999 as a manager of the Revenue Protection Dept. Went into the Navy Reserves in 1978, this time as a Seabee, a construction electrician, in NMCB-14 and CBHU-14, retiring in 1997 after 24 years of total service.

Graduated from Columbia College with BA degree in criminal justice. Active in the Navy Seabee Veterans of America having held positions up to commander of Island X-4 Orlando and presently serving as executive vice commander of the DOFL Navy Seabee Veterans of America.

Married for 30 years to Pauline who is an active member of the Navy Seabee Veterans of America Auxiliary. Two grown children, Shane and Heather. Will live in Young Harris, GA, after retiring in 1999.

PAUL LEO CREPEAU, enlisted in the Navy Seabees at Providence, RI, July 17, 1942. Trained at Camp Allen, VA. Shipped to Davisville, RI, attached to 28th Bn. Nov. 9, 1942. Shipped to Navy Fuel and Salvage De-

pot, Iceland Dec. 23, 1942. Shipped to 28th USN-CD Camp Massey, Iceland April 23, 1943 (air base).

Transferred to 1040 Det. CB Unit May 17, 1944. Overseas with 1040 Det. Algeria, North Africa May 10, 1944. Departed via 40-18 May 13, 1944, to Bizerte, Tunisia, May 17, 1944, for causeway training. Temporary duty via LST-1010 June 28, 1944, and further duty.

Participated in allied invasion of Southern France Aug. 5, 1944, D-Day. Went to shore on LST-1010. Departed 8th Army of invasion launching platoons causeways. Returned to Bizerte Africa on LST-1010. Completed duty on LST-1010 Sept. 28, 1944, to regular duties AATB, Bizerte, Africa.

Returned to States via LST to New York, NY, to Davisville, RI, July 4, 1945. Transferred to Davisville Station USNCTC for duty Aug. 23, 1945. Shipped to Boston, MA, Dec. 15, 1945, for discharge. Served USN Seabees three years, five months, one day.

After discharged trained under GI Bill of Rights, automotive repairs. Retired as service director of a Chevrolet dealer in Florida.

ORVILLE CRITCHLEY, CM1/c, born Nov. 6, 1921, in Roslyn, WA. Moved to Tacoma, WA, area where eventually his apprenticeship in ship building began. Enlisted in USNR, Seattle, WA, then a short time later called to active duty, going to Camp Peary, VA, for basic training, Port Hueneme, CA, for as-

signment to 7th Spec. Bn. for service in the Aleutian Chain-Dutch Harbor to Adak 17 months. Back to Port Hueneme, assigned to 36th Spec. Bn., eventually to Okinawa. Returning home to pursue his shipbuilding career that lasted for 40 years.

Memorable experiences: Raising a bear on Adak and being the first Seabee unit to land on East Coast of Okinawa.

Awarded the Asiatic-Pacific Area Campaign Medal w/star, American Area Campaign Medal, WWII Victory Medal and Seabee Insignia.

Activities: Church related, Scouts to become a Silver Beaver, Toastmaster activities, "old" life member VFW National Home and Spanaway Historical Society. He has been married for 54 years and has three children and two grandchildren.

ROBERT A. CROWELL, PO3/c, enlisted in the Navy Seabees at Allentown, PA, in June 1943. Completed basic and advanced training at Camp Peary, Williamsburg, VA. Additional training followed at Port Hueneme, CA. Commissioned in the 105th NCB. Shipped out aboard SS *Sea Devil* in December 1943. Served in New Guinea and participated in the invasion of the Philippines.

Authorized to wear the Philippine Liberation Ribbon w/2 Bronze Stars, American Campaign Medal, Asiatic-Pacific Campaign Medal w/Bronze Star, WWII Victory Medal, Philip-

pine Presidential Unit Citation - Foreign and Honorable Service Lapel Button.

After discharge as shipfitter second class, returned to hometown of Easton, PA, and went into the plumbing business.

Married former Anna Borowski in April 1941. They have two daughters, Lorraine and Constance. They continue to reside in Easton. Life member of Navy Seabee Veterans of America Island X-4 Louisiana.

JAMES S. CUNNINGHAM, DKC, born in Ashland, MO, May 4, 1925, and joined the USN in 1943 at St. Louis, MO. Attended boot camp and Storekeeper School at Farragut, ID, before being assigned to USS *Uvalde* (AKA-88) and on board when commissioned. Served in South Pacific during 1944-45-46 in New Guinea, Philippines and Okinawa area.

Authorized to wear two Bronze Battle Stars and Philippine Liberation Ribbon w/star and other miscellaneous ribbons. Released to inactive duty in 1946 and recalled in 1951 to active status with MCB-6 which was commissioned at Norfolk. Advanced to CPO in Newfoundland while serving with MCB-6 and aboard the USS *Benewah* (APB-35).

Released to inactive duty in late 1952 and discharged from Reserve in 1958. Served in management and executive positions with oil cooperative in Columbia, MO, and retired in 1990. Married in 1947 and he and his wife, Alva, have one daughter and one granddaughter. Member of several veteran and Masonic organizations including the Shrine.

EUGENE P. CZERNIAWSKI, EON3/c, USN, MCB-4, born Oct. 31, 1946, in St. Clair, MI. Inducted into the service Dec. 2, 1965, at Detroit, MI. Military locations and stations were Great Lakes NTC; Port Hueneme, CA; Camp Hoover, RVN, Hill 1937 (1967) and Camp Evans, RVN, LZ Sally (1968).

Awarded the RVN Meritorious Unit Commendation Gallantry Cross, Meritorious Unit Commendation Ribbon, Republic of Vietnam Meritorious Unit Commendation Civil Actions Ribbon, Navy Unit Commendation Ribbon w/ Bronze Star, Vietnam Service Medal w/FMF Insignia, two Bronze Stars and five Campaign Stars and Navy Unit Commendation Ribbon w/Bronze Star. Discharged Jan. 22, 1969, at Port Hueneme, CA.

He is married to Darlene and has one daughter, Kristina and one son, Casey. Employed as millwright/welder. Member of Vietnam Veterans of America, Veterans of the Vietnam War, Inc., Vietnam Era Seabees and Seabee Veterans of America. Current activities include hunting and farming.

FRANK J. DARSILLO, WT3/c, born July 23, 1927, in Brooklyn, NY. He attended school in Brooklyn and enlisted in the Seabees in February 1945 just after his 17th birthday. He trained at Davisville, RI, and was then shipped to Guam where he was stationed until the war ended. As a water tender third class he served with the CBMU-506, Constr. Bn. #103.

He was discharged in August 1946 but was recalled to active duty in February 1951 during the Korean Campaign and sent back to Guam until his discharge in October of that same year. He worked for the New York City Dept. of Sanitation for 27 years and then as an assistant engineman for the U.S. Postal Service for five years.

Darsillo has been married for 47 years. He and Toni have five children and seven grandchildren. He presently resides in Dingmans Ferry, PA, and spends the winter months in Deerfield Beach, FL.

CHARLES A. DEROMA, enlisted in the USN in September 1942 and celebrated his 21st birthday with the 30th Bn. in (boot camp) Virginia. After a 30 day leave home to Boston, he reported to Davisville, RI, and was sent to Keflavik, Iceland with the 28th NCB as a heavy equipment operator to build a bomber and fighter airfield that is now used by Icelandic Airways.

Returned to the States and was put in Station Force, Davisville, RI, for a year before he volunteered with the 83rd NCB for duty in Hawaii. 30 days later they were sent to the Philippines for a year and then to China.

He was discharged Jan. 27, 1946, as MM2/c, USNR. Recipient of WWII Victory Medal, Asiatic-Pacific Area Medal, Philippine Liberation Ribbon and Good Conduct Medal.

In 1946 he started his heavy equipment and construction business in Boston. Now at 77 years plus, he's still active with his son, buying and selling construction equipment and trucks. Married Shirley Dec. 7, 1963. They have two children, Tracey and Charles Jr. They have two grandchildren, so far, Tyler and Remy.

As a life member of the Navy Seabee Veterans of America, he says that through his business life, he has benefited and owes a lot of his success to the knowledge obtained from his fellow mates and officers in the Navy Constr. Bn. Occasionally he attends a reunion meeting with the mates of the 28th NCB.

Civilian activities: Italian American Club, Historical Construction Equipment Assoc., American Truck Historical Society (past president of New England Chapter and past vice president of Granite State Chapter) and Antique Truck Club of America.

HARRY FRANKLIN DERR JR., CM3/c, attended Dalton High School, Dalton, PA. Entered the USN in 1954. After boot camp at Bainbridge, MD, he was stationed in Washington, D.C. when he transferred to MCB #1. Military locations and stations were Port Lyaudy, French Morocco, Guantanamo, Cuba, Roosevelt Roads, PR, Davisville, RI; and Antarctica (Operation Deep Freeze II).

Awarded the Good Conduct Medal. He was discharged Sept. 15, 1958, at Brooklyn, NY.

A member of Dalton and Factoryville Fire companies. He held many offices in the fire company and was also an instructor in Fire Schools. He is a diver on Scott Township Dive Rescue, Montdale, PA. Member of the Factoryville Planning Commission. Director of Public Works for Abington Township, Waverly, PA. Pennsylvania certified water and sewer plant operator.

Member of the Factoryville F&AM Lodge #341; Lackawanna Royal Arch Chapter #185; Melita-Coeur-de-Lion Commandery #17; Irem Remple AAONMS; Endless Mt. Antique Assoc.; Seabee Veterans of America; and the Factoryville Methodist Church.

Past president and past master of travel of a Masonic family camping group and organizer of local chapter Susquehanna Valley #43.

On the way to the South Pole the ship, the USS *Arneb*, was caught in an ice crush. A large hole in the side had to be repaired. At Antarctica they built bases at McMurdo Sound, Knox Coast and Cape Adare.

Married Allean in June 1956 and has three children: Jacqueline A. (Bisch), Howard H. (Ret., USN) and Kenneth F. (Ret. USAF); and six grandchildren: Lacey and Michael Bisch, Erika and Alyssa Derr, Grant Palmer and Ashley Derr.

RAYMOND BERNARD DIERKES, SF2/c, inducted into the service at the Federal Building, St. Louis, MO, April 16, 1943. Military locations and stations were Camp Peary, Williamsburg, VA, April 23, 1943; Camp Endicott, Davisville, RI, June 6, 1943; Roseneath, Scotland, Sept. 23, 1943; (Vicaridge) Plymouth, England, Nov. 25, 1943; Queen Victoria Hospital, Netley, England, Jan. 18, 1944; (Peel Bank) Isle of Wight, April 29, 1944.

Trained for the Secret Mulberry Floating Harbor, May 13, 1944; participated in the invasion of Normandy, France, June 5-August 3, 1944; Tilbury, England, Aug. 10, 1944; Tignmounth, England, October 13, 1944; returned to the USA Oct. 25, 1944; Camp Endicott, Port Hueneme, CA, Jan. 27, 1945-

June 4, 1945; arrived at Okinawa July 14, 1945; debarked Nov. 15, 1945.

Awarded the EAME Medal w/star, Commendation Medal for work on the Secret Mulberry Operation, Asian Occupation Medal, Asiatic-Pacific Campaign Medal, U.S. WWII Freedom Medal, French Liberte Medal, French Jubilee Freedom Medal and the Golden Dragon was awarded by Cmdr. Guest (crossing Equator).

Civilian activities: In June 1946 became licensed journeyman plumber. October 1963 joined the Contractor Plumbers Assoc. In February 1958 became licensed master contracting plumber. Joined American Society of Sanitary Engrs. in May 1970 and is still active. In April 1984 became president of the Missouri Assoc. of Plumbing, Heating and Cooling Contractors Assoc. Retired from business in 1995 at age 72. Active in bowling and golf. Held every office in the 97th/108th Seabee Organization since 1949, currently president and missed only four reunions in the 50 reunions from past years.

Married Virginia Ahrens in 1948, celebrating 51 years of marriage; two daughters, Barbara Thomas and Nancy Hermen; five grandchildren: John, Steve and Jaclyn Thomas and Barbara and Dennis Hermen.

JAMES C. Di PIETRO, SW3/c, born Oct. 7, 1936, in Richmond Hill, Queens, New York City. Attended schools in Ozone Park and Richmond Hill, NY. Learned the iron trades from his father, Charles, who owned Di Pietro Ironworks. Studied music at the Gene Krupa School of Drumming in Manhattan.

Enlisted in the USN in 1958, Brooklyn Navy Yard. Basic training at Great Lakes Naval Training Facility in Illinois. Assigned to Mobile Constr. Bn. #7. Tour of duty in Grand Turk, Caicos and San Salvador, British West Indies and Davisville, RI, where he was a drummer in the Seabee band. While on Grand Turk he wrote the "Ironworkers Column" for the Seabee newspaper. He was discharged in 1960.

Retired from Chevron Oil Co. where he worked as a pipe welder, welding inspector and welding instructor, he currently resides in Napa

Valley, CA, where he enjoys stamp collecting, writing, gardening, the study of history, traveling and wrought iron projects. His three daughters: Deanne, Denise and Dina live in the Sacramento, CA, area. He is a life member of the National Seabee Veterans of America, Island X-7.

BEN J. DORFENKEL, MM3/c, inducted
into the service May 31, 1944, at Chicago, IL. Military locations and stations were Guam, Saipan, Tinian and Yokosuka.

Awarded the Asiatic-Pacific Medal w/ Bronze Star, American Area Medal and Victory Medal. Discharged at Great Lakes, IL, Jan. 17, 1946.

Memorable experiences: Was on Tinian with the A-bomb. Trivia - Inducted in Area #38; lived at 3838 West End; served in 38th NCB.

After discharge he went to school with an education subsistence allowance of $90 per month and became an optometrist.

He is married to Mary Ann and has two children, Donna and Alan, and four grandchildren: Ben, Jason, Joshua and Holly.

RICHARD TAYLOR DOWNES, born
July 27, 1923, in Boston, MA. Enlisted in the USNR July 7, 1942, at Providence, RI, as HA2/c. Boot camp at Newport, RI, July-August 1942. Hospital Corps training September-November 1942, Newport Naval Hospital. 70th NCB, Davisville, RI, December 1942 and North Africa February-December 1943.

Married Ethel Louise Kennedy Aug. 11, 1944, at Providence, RI.

Then served with 70th at Oahu, HI, October-December 1944; Guam, Marianas, January-February 1945; Iwo Jima, February-March 1945; and Guam, Saipan, Philippines, Japan, April-September 1945. Decommissioned Guam in October 1945. Discharged Nov. 26, 1945, Boston, MA, as PhM1/c.

Has three sons, three grandchildren and three great-grandchildren. Received AB degree in 1949 at Brown University, Providence, RI, with majors in biology and economics. Employment in hotel management, 1949-65 in Massachusetts, New York and Florida; labor market analyst, state of Florida, Aug. 1, 1966, Jacksonville; public health statistician, state of Florida, Nov. 1, 1967, Jacksonville; retired as Vital Records administrator, state of Florida, July 1, 1989, Jacksonville. Downes is a member of Seabee Veterans of America, Island X-9 Florida, Jacksonville.

JAMES "JIM" DRAGISH JR., enlisted
in the USN at Philadelphia, PA, Jan. 13, 1943. Trained at Camp Peary, VA, with the 89th Bn. Then shipped out of Port Hueneme, CA, to

Auckland New Zealand in 1943 as CBMU-501.

They crossed the Pacific Ocean without a convoy escort; 501 was the first maintenance unit formed in WWII. In 1944 their unit was assigned to the Russell Islands. His most unusual job there was on a grave detail, removing bodies from the naval grave yard to be shipped off the island. When war ended sent to Philadelphia Navy Yard then to NTC in Bainbridge, MD, for discharge as a MM3/c Jan. 11, 1946.

Married his wife, Alice, Aug. 31, 1946. They have two great sons and four terrific grandchildren. He is a life member Seabee Veterans of America and chaplain for Island X-76 Pennsylvania and continues to look forward to the CBMU-501 reunions.

ROBERT T. "BOB" DUNN, inducted into
the service in 1943, NRS, Newark, NJ. Military locations and stations were CB, NTCT, Williamsburg, VA; 13th NCB, Camp Parks, CA; RS, TI, San Pedro, CA; RS, New York, NY; Permanent Shore Patrol 3rd ND; PSC Lido Beach, Long Island, NY.

Awarded the American Theater Medal, Victory Medal and Asiatic-Pacific Medal. Discharged in 1946 at PSC Lido Beach, Long Island, NY.

Experiences: Demolition School, Camp Parks, CA; Detached Svc., 13th NCB; Med. Dept., Camp Parks, CA, Hawaii, Tinian; and Water Purification Unit, Okinawa.

Served as Honor Guard for returning war dead, Newark, NJ. Member VFW, Navy Seabee Veterans of America, Island II, Tampa, FL, chaplain, charter and life member. Received BS degree at Seton Hall University; Graduate degree at New York University. Career in sales, marketing and advertising with several national companies. Retired as vice president.

Married to Julia and has five children: Eileen, Maureen, Roberta (Bonnie), Sheila and Robert, and five grandchildren.

EARL R. DUPRIEST JR., born May 2,
1918, in Savannah, GA. Graduated from Brookland Cayce High School and attended

Porter Military Academy and Clemson University. His first construction job was as an oiler on dragline in June 1936. Married Catherine Elizabeth Sox Aug. 17, 1940.

Volunteered for service in February 1942 as coxswain. Called to report in on March 15, 1942. Reported to Camp Allen, Norfolk, VA, in April 1942 and assigned to 20th U.S. Naval Constr. Bn., two weeks boot camp. Reported to Camp Bradford and Norfolk, VA, for advanced training for two weeks. Then to Port Hueneme, CA, for further training (one week) and Treasure Island, CA, (one week) drawing supplies and "getting shots."

Boarded USS *President Coolidge* two weeks to New Caledonia. Disembarked *Coolidge* to Stevedore at New Caledonia. *Coolidge* proceeded to Espiritu Santos, New Hebrides, ran into one of our mines and sunk there, only two lives lost. The 20th USNCB was broken up and parts went to several locations in the South Pacific. His part went to Australia, then to New Guinea, Guadalcanal, Bougainville, Russell Islands and New Britain.

After approximately two years they returned to Brisbane, Australia for a break. Then back to the U.S. for replacements. After 45 days they returned to California, stationed at Camp Parks. Boarded USS *McCauley* for Pearl Harbor, Saipan, Tinian. Boarded LSTs at Saipan for Okinawa. Landed D-Day on East Shore. There they built a Navy base airport and repaired various places in need of repair. In between working as stevedores and whatever.

They remained on Okinawa until the war ended. He left for Tokyo and boarded the USS *Kershaw* to the U.S. He was discharged Oct. 25, 1945, at Charleston, SC. After this he and his wife started a family. Their first child was a boy, Earl R. DuPriest III.

He was back in construction following gas and oil line construction all over the U.S. until daughter, Molly Catherine, was born. Then he decided to go into the construction business as a contractor and his children could go to school in their home state. They were blessed with another son, Steve Craig. Steve was about 5 when they lost his mother in 1965. He and his sons have continued in the construction business. His oldest son has a business in Beaufort, SC. His youngest son is carrying the family business on. His daughter is an attorney in Columbia and Mt. Pleasant, SC.

McCauley is just a laid back old "Seabee" and enjoys every second of his life. Visiting and rehashing memories of active days in the Seabees with old friends and former shipmates, and hoping that the Legend of the Seabees will never end. He is a grandfather and a great-grandfather - five grandchildren (three boys and two girls) and three great-grandchildren (two boys and one girl).

PETER A. DURANTE, MM1/c, enlisted in the service July 23, 1943, in New York City. Military locations and stations were Camp Peary, VA (boot camp); 119th NCB, Davisville, RI; Quoddy Village, ME; Port Hueneme, CA; Milne Bay, New Guinea; Hollandia, Manila; Cavite, Guam; and Seattle, USA.

Awarded the Pacific Victory Medal. Honorably discharged in March 1946 at Lido Beach, Long Island.

Memorable experiences: The 119th built 7th Fleet HQ and Communication Center in Hollandia, 7th Fleet tank farms surveyed for roads in New Guinea, built receiving hospital at Oro Bay, New Guinea, cleared wreckage in Manila, Cavite Naval Base.

Took course in architecture and building construction at Pratt Institute, Brooklyn, NY. Worked for hospital architect Katz, Waisman in New York City. Went into real estate and insurance. Durante is widowed and has three children: Peter Jr., Donna and Laurie; and two grandchildren, Arthur and Grace.

GEORGE F. ELLENBERGER, born Oct. 1, 1920, in Pendleton, OR. Inducted into the service July 21, 1943, at Seattle, WA. Military locations and stations were Camps Peary and Parks, Midway Island, Philippines and Samar.

Discharged in November 1945 at Bremerton, WA. Memorable experiences: four years comm. X1 Wash. and state comm. three years.

He is married to Donna and has three sons and two grandchildren. He is now retired and enjoys fixing shoes and fishing. Ellenberger is a member of 123rd and 93rd Bns.

ROBERT O. ELLIS, born March 5, 1923. Drafted from Illinois farm by Army in 1943, Signal Hvy. Constr. Bn. Learned about Seabees in Hawaii, Marianas and Okinawa. Waited for Japan invasion.

After discharge found a Seabee reserve unit in Peoria. Then went to Korea. Requested two years duty and stayed for 17. Went to Subic

Bay instead of Korea where MCB-3, 5, 9, 11 were moving a mountain, building a naval air station. This was a five year job. Stella made a good Seabee wife. His uniforms were always ready.

Shore duty is no cruise, like NAS Twin Cities. Not secure until no snow in paths of planes. Retired after 20 years in 1968 (EO1). What a happy day when he got into Civil Service. Still with and for military another 18-1/2 years.

Ellis still attends Seabee Birthday Balls and Old Outfit Reunions whenever possible. His family includes grandchildren and great-grandchildren scattered from Little Rock to Chattanooga. He is a life member of American Legion and VFW.

BILLY E. ERICKSON, CM3, inducted into the service in July 1946 at Great Lakes, IL. Military locations and stations were Port Hueneme, CA; Sangley Pt.; Philippines; Yakutat, AL; and maneuvers in Adak, AK.

He was awarded the Good Conduct Medal and discharged in July 1950 at Seattle, WA.

Memorable experiences: He never drove until the Filipinos taught him to drive. They also taught him automotive repair skills. After his discharge he worked as a mechanic at several places. In 1957 he opened his own repair shop in Bloomington, IL. He enjoyed the Seabees very much.

Erickson is married to Christine and has three children: Barbara, Richard and Connie; and six grandchildren: Janelle, Thad, Chad, Scott, Stacey and Andrew. He is a member of Island X4, Peoria, IL.

MELVIN J. ETTERS JR., MM3/c, born July 11, 1927, in Coraopolis, PA. Inducted into the Seabees March 24, 1944, at NTC, Sampson, NY. Military locations and stations were USN Personnel Separation Center, Bainbridge, MD; NTC, Sampson, NY; NCTC, Davisville, RI; CBRD, Camp Parks, CA; Base Fray, HI; CBMU-541, 58th NCB, Okinawa.

Etters was awarded the Pacific Theater Ribbon, American Theater Ribbon and Victory Medal. He was discharged July 7, 1946, at USN Personnel Separation Center, Bainbridge, MD, MM3/c.

He is married to Lucille and has one son, James K. (USN, Ret) and two daughters, Susan and Karen. He retired from J&L Steel as

controls and instrument technician. Etters is a past member of CB Div. 4-4, USNRTC Neville Islands, Pittsburgh, PA, construction electrician's mate second class.

LAWRENCE DAVID FAIRBAIRN JR., EOC, born Feb. 29, 1924, in Pullman, WA. Inducted into the service July 22, 1943, at Portland, OR. Military locations and stations were USNTC, Farragut, ID, NCB 25th, 30th NCB, 109th NCB, CBMU-1507, 103rd NCB, CBMU-1804, ACB-1, U.S. Naval Schools Command, Port Heuneme, CA, USNAS Adak, AK, Antarctic support activity, McMurdo Sound, Antarctic, Naval Recruiting Office, Ukiah, CA.

Memorable experiences: Liberation of Guam with 25th NCB and being the 72nd person to sign log book at South Pole Station.

Awarded the American Theater Medal, WWII Victory Medal, Asiatic-Pacific Medal, Good Conduct Medal (5), Navy Occupation Medal, Korean Service Medal, UN Service Ribbon, K-10 Star, Korean Service Medal, National Defense Service Medal, Asia Clasp, Armed Forces Expeditionary Medal, Antarctic Service Medal and Vietnam Service Ribbon. Fairbairn was discharged July 1, 1966, at NRS Treasure Island, San Francisco, CA.

He is married to Helen. After retiring from the Seabees he entered into a second career with U.S. Forest Services. Served as a consultant for 10 years in watershed conservation work. At present time enjoying retirement and working around his five acre homesite near Eugene, OR.

DONALD LAWRENCE FERGUSON, enlisted in the USN at Cincinnati, OH, in 1952. Basic training at Great Lakes Naval Training Center, then three months at Class A Seabee School at Port Hueneme, CA. Two years at Yokosuka Naval Base in Japan working with CEC on blueprints and specifications for Armed Forces construction projects, climbed Mt. Fuji, and earned the Korean Service Medal as they were direct support to the Korean War. One year at Subic Bay, Philippine Islands, building power lines and helping build an airfield and aircraft carrier pier with MCB-5.

Discharged as construction electrician first class, CE-1 in 1956. Married and has four children and six grandchildren. Commander of the VFW Post 3438 for four years in Dayton, OH. Forty-two years with the Dayton Power and Light Company, now retired and writing books (novel about the USS *Leyte*), active in the Unitarian Church and the VFW Post, and senior vice commander of Navy Seabee Veterans of America Island X-7, Dayton, OH.

WARREN J. FERLANDY III, BU2/c, born Jan. 8, 1944, in Oakland, CA. Inducted into the service April 20, 1964, at New Orleans, LA. Military locations and stations: Training at Port Hueneme and Camp Pendleton, CA; Chu Lai, Vietnam; and Da Nang, Vietnam.

Memorable experiences: Charter member Island X-3, Picayune, MS, elected vice commander. Island established in 1998.

Awarded the Fleet Marine Force Combat Operations Insignia, Vietnam Service Medal w/3 Bronze Stars, Vietnam Campaign Medal and National Defense Service Medal. Released from active duty and transferred to Naval Reserve. Discharged from USNR April 19, 1970.

Married Kay Mitchell May 15, 1976, and living a great life. For 25 years he operated and owned cabinet and renovation shop. Now project manager for Abry Brothers, Inc. (established 1849, house raising/shoring contractor in New Orleans, LA).

HARRY E. FIELDER, CM2/c, enlisted in the USN at Los Angeles, CA, in July 1944. Boot camp training at San Diego Naval Training Center. Shipped in a draft of 12 others to Hawaii and from there on to Saipan on a merchant ship. During this 30 day zig zag trip one of the 12 peeked at their orders and found they were in the Seabees, they didn't really know much about the Seabees at that time but later found it was the best duty one could have at time of war.

The 12 of them were shipped on to Tinian from Saipan and were assigned to the 18th Seabee Bn. as replacements for the older men that had enlisted during the early days of the war and had been overseas for as long as three years and more. When the 18th went back to the States for deactivation some of them were transferred to the 38th Bn. and traveled to Japan and back to Guam. He was then transferred to the 109th Bn. on Guam and remained there for about nine months until shipped home to San Francisco and on to Los Angeles and discharged at San Pedro, CA.

After discharged as CM2/c, went to work as a carpenter for the city of Los Angeles, Public Buildings Dept. Left the city of Los Angeles as a construction cost estimator and then went on to work for Hughes Aircraft Co. Retired from Hughes in August 1985 as a major construction project manager.

Married Pat on Oct. 25, 1946 and they have a daughter, Beverly; a son, Michael; and two grandsons, Chris and Ben Hodges. They just celebrated their 53rd Wedding Anniversary.

He is a member of Navy Seabee Veterans of America and secretary/treasurer of Island X-1 Las Vegas, NV.

He enjoys retirement life very much with many hobbies. His most enjoyable hobby is amateur radio since 1959 with the call sign "WA6GLB."

WARREN FLADING, SW3/c, born Jan. 26, 1930, in Buffalo, NY. Enlisted in Buffalo, NY, in 1951, received basic training in Newport, RI.

He was sent to Port Hueneme to attend S.W. instructions. Upon graduation he reported for duty on Kwajalein in CBD-1506. While there he operated heavy equipment, became an instructor for crane operations. After a one year tour he was sent to Korea at K-3 CBMU-101. He ran grader and bulldozer to help provide a 500 ft. extension of the airstrip for the Marines (MAG-33). After 18 months in Korea he spent six months at Port Hueneme in Ship's Company. After discharge he became an operating engineer for 31 years until retirement.

Married Ann in 1954 and has three children and eight grandchildren. Moved to Florida in 1990. They are both active in the Navy Seabee Veterans of America and Navy Seabee Veterans of America Auxiliary. He has been treasurer, vice commander and currently island chaplain.

BOBBY FLETCHER, born March 17, 1931, at Carlsbad, NM. Enlisted in the USN in August 1950 and retired from USN in October 1977 with rate BUCS(E-8).

Tours of duty: Amchitka Aleutian MCB-3; Kwajalein CBD-1509; Guam MCB-10; Yokosuka, Japan ACB-1; Yokosuka, Japan PWC; New Iberia, LA, NAS PWD; Okinawa (two tours) MCB-9; Kodiak, AK, MCB-9; Da Nang and Thoung Duc, Vietnam MCB-9; Oppama, Japan NAVORDFAC; Da Nang and Chu Lai, Vietnam NSA; Naples, Italy MCB-10; Rota, Spain MCB-1; Port Hueneme, CA, 31st NCR; and Adak, AK, NAVSECGRUACT.

Awards/Medals received: Navy Commendation w/Combat V, Navy Achievement, Combat Action, Navy Unit Commendation w/3 Bronze Stars, Navy Meritorious Unit, Good Conduct (six awards), National Defense w/ Bronze Star, Vietnam Service w/1 Silver and 1 Bronze Star, RVN Gallantry Cross w/Palm, RVN Civic Action w/Palm and RVN Campaign.

Employed by Los Robles Regional Medical Center in Thousand Oaks, CA, from March 1978-July 1993 as director of engineering, maintenance and security departments. Also as the safety officer.

Relocated to Las Vegas, NV, in November 1993. Married to Kazuyo Noma from Osaka, Japan. They have two daughters. Enjoying retired life golfing, fishing and playing poker.

ROLLAND K. FLICKER, enlisted in the Navy Seabees at Albany, NY, July 3, 1943. Trained at Camp Peary, Williamsburg, VA, where the 115th was formed. Shipped out of Davisville, RI, to Gamadodo on Milne Bay, New Guinea. Then on to Olongapo, at Subic Bay.

After discharge at Subic Bay joined the Merchant Marines for a short time. Worked at various electronic firms then started a TV sales/ service business. Retired from that and worked for Social and Mental Health Agencies until second retirement.

Married Sally M. Glock Aug. 18, 1988, and has stepson, Paul. Life time member of Navy Seabee Veterans of America and member of X-10 in Albany, NY.

ROBERT HENRY FLOOD, Shipfitter third class, born April 28, 1922. Inducted into the service at Fargo Building, Nov. 24, 1942, Boston, MA.

Military locations and stations were 77th NCB formed in Camp Peary, VA; commissioned in Davisville, RI; Port Hueneme, CA; Guadalcanal; Vella La Vella; Bougainville; Emirau; Brisbane, Australia; Sangley Point, Philippine Islands. Discharged Jan. 6, 1946, at Fargo Building, Boston, MA.

Married to Virginia for 49-1/2 years and has three daughters. Remarried to Phyllis for six years. He has 25 grandchildren. Worked in appliance business and radio/tv repair. Now retired and traveling all states in their RV. Member of Navy Seabee Veterans of America Island X-4, Stoughton, MA. He is also active in Masonic Lodge.

DELBERT D. GILLIHAN, MM2/c (T)(CB), V6, USNR, born May 29, 1916, in Portland, OR. Inducted into the service Jan. 12, 1943, at NRS Portland, OR. Military locations and stations were Norfolk, VA; Aleutian Islands (16 months); and island of Okinawa.

Memorable experiences: Was in a typhoon at Okinawa in 1945 and had to eat "Spam" three times a day for about two weeks.

Awarded the Good Conduct Medal, American Area Campaign Medal and WWII Victory Medal. Discharged Nov. 22, 1945, at Bremerton, WA.

He is married to Alice and has one son, three grandchildren and seven great-grandchildren. Gillihan retired in 1978 and now enjoys bowling and hiking.

HARRY JAMES GLASS, CE1/c, born Jan. 9, 1936, in Syracuse, NY. Enlisted July 7, 1954, completed basic training at Bainbridge, MD. Served at communication stations in Imperial Beach, CA; San Diego, CA; and NAS Sangley Point, Philippines. Separated in 1958 as TE2/c.

After working as an electrical draftsman, he re-enlisted in 1960. Served as RM2/c on USS Lake Champlain (CVS-39) and at NAVCOMMSTA, Long Beach, CA. Discharged in 1964.

For 30 years he was an electrical designer of building systems for Syracuse area engineers. Married to JoAnn, they have five children and six grandchildren.

In 1982-83 he served two years as a sergeant in the Army Reserve Combat Engrs., completing active duty at Camp Edwards, MA.

He enlisted in the Reserve Seabees in 1984, serving in NMCB-13, 21 and 27. Active duty stations included NAS Brunswick, ME; Westover AFB, MA; Fort Jackson, SC; NCBC Gulfport, MS; Fort Benning, GA; NCBC Davisville, RI; Camp Lejeune, NC; NCHB Cheatham Annex, NOB Norfolk, NAB Little Creek, VA.

A life member of the Navy Seabee Veterans of America, Island X-19, he was recruited by present national commander, Jack Brandt. Glass retired from the Navy Jan. 9, 1996, at age 60.

His awards include three National Defense Service Medals for Korea, Vietnam and Desert Storm; also the Armed Forces Expeditionary Medal for the Cuban Missile Crisis. He is a member of several military organizations.

Moving to Tidioute, PA, in 1992 he worked for the borough maintenance department and for a general contractor, retiring in 1998.

RONALD D. GLASSER, BU2/c, born Sept. 9, 1930, near Polk, NE. Graduated from Clarks High School, class of 1948. Enlisted in USN in 1951 with basic training at San Diego, followed by Seabee Builders' School, Port Hueneme, CA, then to Davisville Det. CBD-1523.

Glasser was among the 120 then sent to Brooklyn Navy Yard and on to Guantanamo Bay, Cuba. Davisville, RI, served as home base with two tours of duty each to Cuba and Port Lyautey, French Morocco. Served in MCB-1, 7 and 8.

After discharge in 1955 continued education at UNL and Milford Trade School. Married Dorothy in 1957, has one daughter and two grandchildren. Semi-retired after 45 years in production agriculture.

He and Dorothy have traveled extensively throughout Europe, Asia, Africa and Central America, always with a camera. The Glassers' travelogues are shown throughout the area.

Active in Clarks United Methodist Church, Masonic Lodge AF&AM, York Rite of Free Masonry and Order of the Eastern Star. Member of Merrick County Historical Society, American Legion, Merrick County Hospital Board of Directors and Litzenberg Foundation Chairman. Life member of Navy Seabee Veterans of America from MCB-7 Island at Large and the NRA.

LOUIS GOLDFARB, *photos only, no bio submitted*

RALPH K. GOODMAN, joined the USN in 1944. Training USNB Great Lakes, IL. Shipped out in December 1944 to 7th Fleet duty, USNSD Subic Bay, Philippine Island.

Transferred for three months to 24th Seabees as a storekeeper, off loading cargo to

service the fleet and build the NSD at Subic Bay, transferred back to NSD and sent to Iwo Jima on hospital ship, Solace, to take on wounded, sent back to NSD Subic for short period of time, transferred to USS Pensacola (CA-24) for training and the two "atomic bomb" tests at Bikini Atoll. Served as crew member on USS Atlanta and USS Iowa (BB-61).

Discharged in August 1947. Recalled to active duty from 1950-52 during Korean War. Awarded the Asiatic-Pacific Medal w/star, Philippine Liberation Medal w/star, WWII Victory Medal, American Defense Service Medal, National Defense Service Medal, American Campaign Medal, Korean Service Medal and Presidential Unit Citation (Harry Truman).

Retired from U.S. Postal Service in 1987. Now lives in Toney, AL (40 years). Likes to (and does) travel. He and wife Helen have one son, Mike; one daughter, Kitty; and one grandson, Nick.

ELMER F. GOODWIN, born Nov. 20, 1911, in Chelsea, VT, enlisted in the Seabees in November 1942 as a SF3/c, at Los Angeles. Boot camp at Camp Peary, assigned to the 92nd NCB, on to Camp Endicott and Port Hueneme, then to Hawaii until July 1944. Leaving Hawaii stopping at Eniwetok waiting for the invasion of Tinian, was there until November 1945, then back to the States by the way of Seattle.

Discharged at Long Beach, Dec. 7, 1945. He received all the usual medals and awards.

He worked at the Bellflower Post Office for 33 years, retiring in November 1971. During this time he was in a Seabee Reserve Unit, retiring in November 1971 as a senior chief. He and his wife, Etta, have two sons and three grandchildren. One son is a Navy CEC captain and a grandson is in the Naval Academy. He has been a member of the Seabee Veterans of America for many years.

JAMES EARL GORDON, MM3/c, born in Winesap, WA, June 13, 1922. Inducted into the service in November 1942 at Wenatchee, WA. Military locations and stations were Camp Peary, Camp Endicott and ETO.

Most of the Seabees were in the Pacific during WWII. Their 69th Bn. was in the Atlantic. Their first mission was in Newfoundland building a naval repair station for ships going and coming from Europe. Then to England to prepare for the invasion of France at Omaha Beach. Building the barges that were sunk to make a breakwater. Repaired damage done by the huge storm so supplies could keep moving. As Germans retreated, they took over unloading supplies for the Army.

Returned to England then they followed

the Army into Bremen and Bremerhaven and occupied this section of Germany until the end of the war. Discharged in November 1945 at Seattle, WA.

His 26 year civilian career was at McNeil Island Federal Penitentiary where he served in many capacities, retiring in 1972. Gordon is married and has four children. He is now retired and has many hobbies.

FREDERICK LINWOOD GORMAN,
SC2/c, entered the USN July 28, 1942, just after his 19th birthday. Hometown: Wilmington, NC. Assigned to the 20th U.S. Naval Constr. Bn., Co. B and later transferred to HQ Co. as a cook. After a period of advanced training he was sent to the Embarkation Center.

On or about Oct. 20, 1942, the ship, USS *President Coolidge*, landed at Noumea, New Caledonia. For a year or more the unit was assigned the duty of stevedoring work which consisted of unloading ships and shipping much needed materials for the forces. Engaged in the various island campaigns, the *Coolidge* was sunk later on as a result of a mine off the New Hebrides Islands.

Returned to the States in October 1944. Having had duties at various installations he was separated from the Navy in January 1946. Awarded the American Area Medal, Asiatic-Pacific Campaign Medal and WWII Victory Medal.

Memorable experiences: The 20th Bn. succeeded in building forward area bases enabling their aircraft to render crippling blows to such enemy strongholds like Truk and Rabaul. He had the honor to be at a ceremony at which time Father Frederic P. Gehring was decorated with the Legion of Merit. Gorman is proud to have been a part of a wonderful organization like the Seabees.

Married Lena Croce Oct. 6, 1948 and has a daughter Betty. He retired from the USAF after completing a total of 20 years of active military service and currently resides in San Antonio, TX.

JAMES L. GRISWOLD, CMG2/c, born
Nov. 23, 1931, in Midland, MI. Inducted into the service in December 1950. Military locations and stations were Midway Island, Det. 1503, and Cubi Point, Philippines MOB-9. Discharged in December 1954.

Griswold is married to Patricia. He is now retired.

KENNETH D. GRUBB, Carpenter's Mate
2/c, inducted into the service May 10, 1943, at Camp Peary, VA. Military locations and stations were Camp Peary, VA; Camp Endicott, RI; Camp Holliday, MS; Camp Mugu, CA; Camp Mohnlua, Oahu, T.H.; Camp Kingbee, Saipan; Camp Ryan, Okinawa. Discharged Nov. 28, 1945, at Sampson, NY.

Memorable experiences: While on Saipan they went through many air raids. One, two, as many as three in one night. On Saturday night, Dec. 30, 1944, the Japanese were practically on top of their camp. He grabbed for his gas mask, but could not find his shoes. Then Shorty Lamotte said "Grubb, you have them

on." Grubb said, "Shorty, don't you say a word." Well! The next issue of their battalion paper, *Bolts and Bullets*, splashed in big headlines across the front page were the words "Grubb Grubbs For His G.I. Brogans." Needless to say it took a long time to live that one down.

He kept a daily diary from the time he left the States until he returned home.

Civilian activities as a building contractor, residential and commercial, in Sebring, FL. Retired in 1988, but stays very busy in volunteer work.

Married to Ruth and has two children, Dale Grubb and Cynthia Condran, and two grandchildren, Matthew and Madison Grubb.

GORDON COOPER "GUS" GUSTAFSON, SF3/c, born Nov. 16, 1924, in Tacoma, WA. Inducted into the service June 11, 1943, at NRS Seattle, WA. Military locations and stations were "CBMU-518," Camp Peary, VA; ABD Gulfport, MS; Guadalcanal, British Solomon Islands; Camp Parks, CA; Terminal Island

His half of CBMU-518 was transported to Guadalcanal aboard USS LST-124. He was in the 6th Plt. of 518. CBMU-518 embarked ABD Gulfport, MS, Nov. 4, 1943. Arrived Guadalcanal, British Solomon Islands 99 days later on Feb. 10, 1944. Spent 18 months there. Embarked Guadalcanal aboard USS *President Monroe* (AP-104) Aug. 11, 1945. Arrived San Francisco, CA, two weeks later on Aug. 25, 1945.

Memorable experiences: Terminal Island Navy Yard aboard the USS YR-23.

Awarded the American Theater Medal, Asiatic-Pacific Theater Medal and WWII Victory Medal. Discharged March 20, 1946, at NOB Terminal Island, San Pedro, CA.

Married and has two daughters, two grandchildren and one great-grandchild. He is 74 years old and a retired boilermaker. He worked steel construction for many years, then took a maintenance boilermaker job in a local pulp and paper mill for 27 years, "St. Regis" which became "Simpson Tacoma Kraft."

His memberships include Masonic Lodge, Clover Lodge #91, Tacoma, WA, F&AM; VFW Post #969, Tacoma, WA (life member), American Legion Post #138, Tacoma, WA; National Rifle Assoc.; Boilermakers International Union Local #568, Tacoma, WA (retired), Navy League of USA; and Rocky Mountain Elk Foundation, Missoula, MT.

Remember "Stuebonville, OH" and "Wieston, WV," fellas (4.0 + liberty towns)?

WILLIAM HERBERT GUYER, enlisted
in the USN at Philadelphia in January 1942 as

a QM2/c. Trained at Camp Bradford, VA, and transferred to Gulfport, MS, where he skippered a work barge involved in creating a camouflaged runway on Cat Island in the Gulf of Mexico.

Shipped out of Gulfport to Trinidad, British West Indies, 83rd CB Bn., where he skippered the CB ocean work vessel *Dudley* and was a naval functional and survival swimming instructor.

Then shipped to Camp Endicott, Davisville, RI; was assigned to the advance base depot at Goose Point, RI, and was chief in charge of the Seamanship and Navigation School.

Was discharged as chief boatswain mate at Boston, MA, in November 1945, and returned to work for the Bell Telephone Co. of Pennsylvania in management from which he is now retired after 48 years. Currently lives in Langhorne, PA, where he is married to "Ruth" and has five children and eight grandchildren.

Currently a member of Navy Seabee Veterans of America Island X-76 Pennsylvania, and Quaker City Yacht Club of Philadelphia and a licensed U.S. Coast Guard, ocean sailing and mechanically operated vessels since 1939. Past president of the Kiwanis Club of Lincoln Hwy. and past commodore of two sailing clubs and a member of Boy Scouts and Sea Scouts of America for 38 years. American Red Cross Water Safety Aquatic instructor many years. United States Power Sqdn. member since 1952.

JOHN LYMAN HALL, AKC, USN (Ret.),
born in Stokes County, NC. Enlisted in Washington, D.C. Rodman (surveyor) S1/c, shipped to Camp Allen Norfolk, VA, April 24, 1942. Shipped to NAS Quonset Point, RI, training in Q Hut construction. Leaving Rhode Island by troop train for San Francisco, CA. In Fifth Naval Constr. Bn., HQ Co.

Embarked on *Lureline* for Honolulu, HI. Arriving month of the Battle of Midway June 15, 1942, embarking from Pearl Harbor aboard the USS *Wright* for Midway Island 1,285 miles north by east Hawaiian Islands. They immediately surveyed and completed the second air field at Midway before Thanksgiving same fall. After finishing cutting through the native flora to establish grades, Surveyor Richards, Kettelson and Hall separated.

Appointed to yeoman and assigned to HQ office work in a building the Japanese left standing with windows intact. The *SeaBreeze News Letter* listed several men after physical at Pearl Harbor to NTS, San Diego, CA, to become assigned to Naval Officer Procurement, Bureau of Naval Personnel, after spending July 1, 1943-March 5, 1944 in Class V-12 Unit Gustavus Adolphus College.

His next station was Pre-Midshipman School, Asbury Park, NJ, and later USNRMS Cornell University and several weeks in an accelerated training curriculum. He separated to Davisville, RI CB Det. 1047 and 128 YSNCB (pontoon). Before embarking he was assigned to Naval Record Management Center, Philadelphia, PA, Navy Yard. And his rate was changed to archivist third class.

After graduating from Gustavus Adolphus College in 1948, he was an attendance supervisor, Levittown Public Schools, Levittown, NY, for 23 years and now is living in Pinehurst, NC. He has one son, Dr. J.L. Hall, Chester Springs, PA; one daughter, Mrs. Bonnie Stillwell, Tenby, Wales, United Kingdom; and six grandchildren. His first wife deceased May 4, 1983. His present wife, Charlotte Hon Palmer, and he were married Jan. 11, 1990.

ROBERT G. HALL, born Jan. 12, 1926, in Manly, IA. Enlisted in August 1943 at Louisville, KY. Boot camp at Camp Peary, VA. Assigned to Co. D, Plt. 6, 133rd NCB when formed. Training at Endicott, RI; Gulfport, MS; Port Hueneme, CA.

First overseas assignment NAS Honolulu, TH. In October 1944 shipped to Maui for training with 4th Marine Div. The 133rd NCB was assigned to 23rd and 25th Regimental Combat teams. D-Day, Feb. 19, 1945, at Iwo Jima Plt. 6 landed on Blue 1. Spent seven months on Iwo Jima. Discharged in April 1946.

Now retired from General Electric Appliance Park, Louisville, KY. Has four children and eight grandchildren. Very proud to have been part of history on Iwo Jima with Seabees and Marines. Life member of Navy Seabee Veterans of America. and 4th Marine Div. Assoc.

HENRY W. "HARBI" HARBINSON SR., enlisted at Philadelphia, PA, in 1946 with basic training in Bainbridge, MD, and then was shipped to Port Hueneme, CA. After Refrigeration School in 1947 he was shipped to Adak, AK, 124th NCB. Early in 1948 he returned to Port Hueneme for advanced construction electrician training. He shipped out later in 1948 to Guam 103rd NCB and then off again to Saipan and Tinian to CBD-1504. He stayed 18 months and five days.

He returned to the States in 1950 and was assigned to the Amphib. Base 104th NCB at Coronado, CA. He was discharged CECN May 31, 1950, San Diego, only 26 days before Korea, and he returned home to New Jersey.

Henry W. Harbinson Sr. was born and raised in Camden County, South Jersey. He finished high school, married Kitty Dimter, RN, MS.ED and raised a family of eight children and now 16 grandchildren. He worked for Mobil and U.S. Steel. The family moved to Hollywood, FL, in 1967.

In Florida he worked for Pan Am and Eastern Airlines as an airframe and power plant mechanic. He finished college, Barry University, with a BS degree, had a real estate company and is now retired. He was elected to the Broward County School Board in 1974, served one term. Presently active with the Seabee Veterans of America as executive officer of Island X-5, Ft. Lauderdale, FL, and the American Legion Post 400. He has his condo on the beach. "Yea, Harbi."

JOHN RAE HARDING, born April 15, 1923, in Newark, NJ. Inactive duty began Nov. 30, 1942, with active duty Jan. 3, 1943. Military locations and stations were NCTC Williamsburg, VA; ABD Port Hueneme, CA; NCBRG, Camp Pendleton, Oceanside, CA; 5th Det., 2nd CB, Pontoon Assoc. Det. 1; U.S. Mobile Hosp. #7 BBRD Camp Parks, CA; NCTC Quoddy Village, ME; NCTC, Davisville, RI.

Was on boxing team while at Williamsburg, VA, and an ensign pon. wanted him to stay and be on the team. Had about five fights at Camp Peary winning all before he left with the outfit. While he was at Camp Pendleton had a few bouts and won all. Also fought at the Hollywood Bowl Arena while on liberty.

When in American Samoa he boxed a Marine named Joe Chesall for light heavyweight champ of South Pacific also winning a decision. After leaving service he boxed professional in Boston, Detroit, Florida, California and Canada.

Awarded the American Area Medal, Asiatic-Pacific Medal and WWII Victory Medal (but never received any of them). Discharged Nov. 15, 1945, at Fargo Bldg., Boston, MA, with rank of machinist's mate third class.

He is married to Marilyn. Harding lost two wives to cancer. Current activities include golf, fishing and dancing. Worked 33 years for Shell Oil Co. in Florida and retired to golf and fishing. Belongs to Island X-5 out of Ft. Lauderdale, FL.

DWIGHT D. "HARRY" HARRINGTON, enlisted at Montpelier, VT, in 1972. Trained at Port Hueneme as an engineering aid, stationed with NMCB 40 at Davisville. Present when Davisville was closed. Made deployments to Rota, Spain; Okinawa; and Puerto Rico.

Discharged as an EA3/c and later re-enlisted with RNMCB 27 at Burlington, VT. Served two years then joined the Vermont Air National Guard in 1982. He is currently superintendent of the carpenter shop for the 158th Civil Engr. Sqdn. holding the rank of master sergeant.

His Seabee training landed him a job as a civil engineering technician for Dufresne-Henry, Inc. in Vermont after a college education in surveying. His job is mostly computer drafting and surveying. Married to Bernadette in 1976. Now serving as commander of Island X-1, White River Jct., VT since 1996.

CARL L. HATLEY, BU1/c, born Jan. 16, 1949, in Cabarrus County, Concord, NC. Inducted into the service Oct. 23, 1968, MCB 133, Gulfport, MS and discharged Oct. 14, 1970.

Re-enlisted Sept. 15, 1975, RNMCB 24. Military locations and stations were Gulfport, MS; Guam; Vietnam; Saudi Arabia; and Desert Storm.

Memorable experiences: Attending reunion in Charlotte, NC, and meeting new friends.

Awarded the Navy "E", National Defense Service Medal, Expert Pistol, Marksman Rifle and Combat Action Ribbon. Discharged second time on Jan. 1, 1994.

Married to Julie and has one daughter, Jodie and two grandchildren, Jake and Hannah. Member Island X-24.

ERNEST "BRUNO" HAUER, BU2/c, born Aug. 20, 1934, in Paterson, NJ. Inducted into the service in March 1957 at Brooklyn, NY. Military locations and stations were Brooklyn Administration, Brooklyn, NY; Barbados, West Indies; and San Salvador, Bahamas.

Awarded the Letter of Commendation from commanding officer. Discharged in April 1959 at Jacksonville NAS, Jacksonville, FL.

He has been married to Patricia for 42 years and has one daughter, Kathy; one son, Jim, who took over his construction company in 1991; and three grandchildren. He is now retired! Works on their two antique cars and recently acquired 19' O'Day sailboat.

GEORGE C. HAWK, SWS1/c, inducted at Omaha, NE, in 1944. Military locations and stations were Great Lakes, IL; Port Hueneme, CA (CB training); Attu, AK; Saipan

(Marianas); Amchitka, AK; Philippines; Korea; and Adak, AK.

Awarded the WWII Victory Medal, Asiatic-Pacific Campaign Medal, Marine Combat Ribbon w/3 stars awarded to Navy personnel, Korean Presidential Unit Citation, American Presidential Unit Citation and others. Discharged in Seattle, WA, in 1954.

He is now retired and an active member of Navy Seabee Veterans of America, Island X-9. Hawk is married to Joanne (Chief) and has five children: Lynda, Marcy, Kathleen, Teresa and Andrew, five granddaughters and seven grandsons.

BILL HEINE, Rear Adm., began his Navy career with his admission to the U.S. Naval Academy in June 1958 where he earned the Navy N as a member of the varsity sailing team and graduated June 6, 1962, as ensign, Civil Engr. Corps, USN. He served at NAS New York and Subic Bay, Philippines prior to joining Naval Mobile Constr. Bn. 62 in 1967.

He deployed to Da Nang, Vietnam in 1968 and to Dong Ha, Vietnam in 1969. He received the Bronze Star w/Combat V for service as the battalion's operations officer. He then reported to commander construction battalions Pacific at Pearl Harbor where he served until September 1972, at which time he affiliated with the USNR. In 1983 he took command of the 9th Reserve Naval Constr. In 1987 he became the chief of staff Reserve Naval Constr. Force and First Naval Constr. Bde.

In 1990 he was promoted to rear admiral USNR. Assignments included Reserve Div. Naval Facilities Engineering Command and director Reserve Naval Contingency Engineering Programs. In September 1993 he received his second star and reported as the commander 2nd Naval Constr. Bde. with responsibility of the 9,000 active duty and reserve Seabees of the Navy's Atlantic Fleet until his retirement in October 1995.

In addition to his Navy duties RAdm. Heine is the founder and president of American Constructors Inc. in Austin, TX.

JAMES DANIEL HILGERS, BUL2/c, born Feb. 25, 1947, in Mauston, WI. Inducted into the service July 29, 1965, at Great Lakes, IL. Military locations and stations were boot camp at Great Lakes, IL; Builders "A" School, Port Hueneme, CA; home port, Davisville, RI; military training at Camp Lejeune, NC; and

two eight month tours to Da Nang and Hoi An, South Vietnam.

Military experiences: He is presently on his second year as commander, Island X-19, Syracuse, NY, and enjoys recruiting at the State Fair and air shows.

Awarded the National Defense Service Medal, Vietnamese Campaign Medal, Vietnam Service Medal w/Fleet Marine Force Combat Operations Insignia and three Bronze Stars. Discharged Aug. 28, 1968, at Davisville, RI.

He is married to Carol Marie. He is a life member of Seabee Veterans of America (currently commander) and VFW. He belongs to the American Legion and the Vietnam Era Seabees. He is on the Board of Directors, Chapter 103, Vietnam Veterans of America and also on the Board of Directors, Vietnam Veterans Foundation of Central New York. Hilgers enjoys fishing and stock car racing.

NORMAN W. HILL, BKR3/c, born May 5, 1925, in Calais, ME. Graduate of Calais Academy in 1942. Enlisted in the Seabees in August 1943. Boot at Camp Peary, VA and advance training at Camp Parks, CA.

Deployed to Moanalua Ridge, Oahu in March 1944. Worked at concrete batching plant for six months. Assigned to galley as baker striker, promoted third class in summer of 1945. Shipped to Boston for further assignment. 10 weeks at Portland Receiving Station. Discharged in May 1946.

Joined Navy Seabee Veterans of America in 1967. Elected national vice commander at Toledo in 1989. Elected national commander, Sarasota, in 1990. Served two years. A great experience to serve as national commander during 50th Anniversary of Seabees. He is secretary of Seacoast Island X-1, New Hampshire.

Married Jean in 1948, deceased in 1993. Has one daughter, Ginny (an RN); two sons, Scott (a graphic artist) and Steve (a builder); and two granddaughters. Belongs to American Legion, VFW and volunteer Scouter many years. Retired from food service in 1988. Has a small yard care service in the summers and spends the winter in Florida.

JOHN P. HOWARD, BU2/c, inducted into the service at Albany, NY, in October 1950. Military locations and stations were Davisville, RI; Pt. Lyautey, French Morocco; Guantanamo Bay, Cuba; Bermuda; MCB #1, CBO-1521.

Awarded the Good Conduct Medal and Korean War Medal. Discharged at Boston, MA, in August 1954.

Memorable experiences: All duty stations and Seabees he worked with, especially LST trip to Bermuda in January 1954 from Davisville, six days. What a ride!

Howard is a retired banker. He is married to Jean and has four children: John, Jackie, Judy and James.

WILLIAM IVAN HOY, born Aug. 21, 1915, in Grottoes, VA. Attended Lees-McRae College, 1933-34; BA degree from Hampden-Sydney College in 1936, DD degree in 1997; BD degree at Union Theological Seminary in 1942; STM, Biblical Seminary, New York in 1949; and PhD degree at University of Edinburgh in 1952. Married Wilma J. Lambert April 29, 1945, and has two children, Doris Lambert Hoy Bezanilla and Martha Virginia.

Civilian employment as high school teacher in Virginia, 1936-39; interim pastor, Asheboro, NC, Presbyterian Church, 1948, 1952-53; assistant professor, Bible, Guilford College, 1947-48; assistant prof. of religion, University of Miami from 1953, professor from 1963-81, chairman department of religion from 1958-79 and professor of religion emeritus, 1981-.

Cons. World Countries Christian Education, Lima, Peru, 1971. Moderator, Presbytery of Everglades, 1960-61, stated clk., 1968-73, 1978-79; interim stated clk. Presbytery of Tropical Florida, 1991-93; moderator Synod of Florida, 1985-86; president, Greater Miami Ministerial Assoc., 1964, 1980-82; member, board of Christian Education Presbyterian Church U.S., 1969-73, member, General Assembly Mission Board, 1978-88; board of directors, Met. Fellowship Chs., 1970, vice president, 1972-73, executive secretary, 1974-76, member Task Force on World Hunger, 1978-81; trustee Davidson College, 1975-87, trustee South Florida Center Theological Studies, 1985-96; participant professional international conferences, Barcelona, Lausanne, Rome, Sydney, Goettingen, others and three White House conferences for religious leaders.

Served to commander USNR, ret. Decorated Purple Heart; awarded keys of cities of Miami Beach (twice) and Coral Gables, 1987; named to Honorable Order of Kentucky Colonels. Fellow Social Science Study Religion; member International Assoc. Historians Religion, Soc. Bibl. Lit., American Academy Religion, American Soc. Ch. History, Studiorum Novi Testamenti Societas, Scottish Ch. History Soc., Religious Research Assoc., International Conference Sociology of Religion, American Oriental Society, International Sociol. Assoc., Reserve Officers Assoc. (past national chaplain, national councilman 1965-66, president Florida department 1965-66, vice president for Navy Dept. Florida), Seabee Veterans of America, Iron Arrow, American Legion, Rotary (president South Miami Club 1991-92,

Paul Harris fellow [2]), Phi Kappa Phi, Omicron Delta Kappa (province department, member general council 1971-76.

Distinguished Service Key 1976, Robert L. Morlan Faculty Sec. national award 1990), Lambda Chi Alpha Alumni Hall of Fame, 1996, Alpha Psi Omega, Theta Delta, Omega. Co-author: *History of the Chaplains Corps, USN*, Volume 6; also articles and book reviews in various publications. Resides in Miami, FL. "It is better to fail at a worthy cause than to succeed at an unworthy one."

WALLACE FRANK HUFTILL, CECS (Ret.), enlisted in the USN at Dubuque, IA, in 1965. Was son of Fred J. Huftill a WWII Seabee veteran assigned to the 99th CB and brother to Warren W. Huftill, also a Seabee veteran of the Korean Conflict. Trained in San Diego, Port Hueneme, Gulfport, Davisville and many overseas locations.

Two deployments to Vietnam with MCB-53, two deployments with NMCB-40 and plankowner of Project Raindeer Station on Diego Garcia. Was first resident Seabee at the U.S. Liaison office in Peking, China, while assigned to U.S. Naval Support Unit, Washington, D.C.! Tour of duty at NAS South Weymouth and a two year tour at USNS Guantanamo Bay, Cuba with deployments with NMCB-74. Shore duty at Service Schools Command, Orlando then again deployed with NMCB-3, returning to NTS Orlando for final tour and retirement in 1989.

Married to Christine Gervais of Woonsocket, RI, they have three daughters and three grandchildren. A life member of Navy Seabee Veterans of America, Island X-4 in Orlando, FL.

C. CUTLER HUMISTON, Machinist Repair first class, born Nov. 24, 1916, in Berwyn, IL. Inducted into the service July 14, 1943, at Chicago, IL. Military locations and stations were Milne Bay, New Guinea; Isabela DeBasilano, Philippine Islands; Camp Peary, VA; Endicott, RI; Gulfport, MS; and Olongapo Subic Bay Philippine Islands. Served with 118th NCB, 11th NCB and 115th NCB.

Memorable experiences: Served in WWII at above locations. Recalled Aug. 30, 1950, for Korean Conflict, now pure Navy, Reserve Fleet, Green Cove Springs, FL.

Awarded the Asiatic-Pacific Ribbon, Philippine Liberation Ribbon and WWII Victory Medal. Discharged Nov. 13, 1951, at Great Lakes NS, IL.

Married March 27, 1948, to Jean Francombe PHM1/c, and has three children. He has been a widower since Aug. 4, 1998. Humiston has had third hip replacement, then

a stroke in the hospital. He retired from Electro-Motive Div. GMC as foreman machinery repair after 38 years of service. Past commander, Hinsdale Post 250 American Legion; Chef DeGare Passe 40 et 8, DuPage Voiture 263; past commander, USCB Auxiliary 9WR-10-8.

JAMES R. HUTTON, CM3/c, born April 6, 1925, in Chicago. Inducted into the service July 15, 1943, at Chicago, IL. Military locations and stations were Camp Peary, VA (boot camp and advanced camp); Camp Parks, CA; Port Hueneme, CA; Gamadodo New Guinea; Hollandia, New Guinea; Samar Islands, Philippines; and Truk Islands. Discharged Jan. 15, 1946, at Great Lakes, IL.

Married to Shirley and has two children and four grandchildren. Civilian employment as captain, Chicago Police Dept. Retired after 36 years of service. Member Island X-2, Chicago, IL.

ALZEBRA C. "A.C." JENKINS, Coxswain, born Aug. 6, 1922, in Gallatin, Cherokee County, TX. Sworn in Oct. 27, 1942, with active duty beginning Dec. 20, 1942, at Dallas, TX. Military locations and stations were Camp Allen, Norfolk, VA, for processing shots and issue of uniforms, set up 201 personnel file; next, Camp Bradford for boot; next, Camp Peary for advanced; next, Camp Rousseau, CA (Port Hueneme) to prepare for and embark to Pacific, then Dumbea Valley, New Caledonia and Guadalcanal, Solomon Islands.

Memorable experiences: In late 1991 initiated procedure of locating all members of 4th Spc. Bn. resulting in first nationwide reunion at Las Vegas, NV, in September 1992. Elected secretary-treasurer/newsletter editor/reunion arranger, serving through Oct. 25, 1998.

Awarded the Asiatic-Pacific Campaign Medal w/Bronze Battle Star. Discharged Oct. 30, 1945, at Camp Wallace, TX. Army service during Korean Conflict. Separated as first lieutenant (QMC) in 1952.

He married Rachel E. Partlow Dec. 25, 1946. They have two children, Jan E. (b. Sept. 7, 1955) and A.C. III (b. Dec. 25, 1955), four grandchildren and four great-grandchildren. After service separation resumed employment at Heat & Frost Insulator, then elected four terms as clerk, State District Court. On Aug. 17, 1998, went from semi to fully retired after 44 years in life, property and casualty insurance business. As independent agent, sold agency March 5, 1984, having bought four agencies from 1962-80. Semi-retired at age 61, although he still manages his own real estate rental units. Still blessed with good health at age 76, no major health problems, maintaining fitness regimen of 30 years duration.

LENNO C. JOHNSTON, born June 18, 1918, in northeast Oklahoma. Attended high school and college in Tahlequah, graduating from college in 1941.

Rosemari Harris tricked him into saying "I Do" March 22, 1940. He and Rosemari had two children, Loren, who served in the Navy during the Vietnam fiasco, now living in California and Vicki, a school librarian living in

Alaska. The "I Do" lasted until July 31, 1995, when Rosemari lost her battle with cancer.

His military duty started in February 1942 at Ft. Leonard Wood, MO, with the Army Engr. Corps and was discharged with honors in June 1942. In July 1942 he enlisted in the USN Seabees with training at Camp Peary, Camp Endicott, Camp Parks and Port Hueneme. His tours of duty in the Eniwetok Atoll of the Marshall Islands. Back to Hawaii for a period of time, then to Okinawa arriving there about the time of Japan's surrender.

After obtaining his master's degree from Tulsa University he spent 31 years in the field of education, from teacher to superintendent from which he retired in 1978.

His work with the Navy Seabee Veterans of America included two years as national commander and six years as national chaplain. With the exception of one year since 1982 he has served as the reunion coordinator and newsletter editor.

He presently resides in Shelton, WA, but will be moving to Oroville, CA.

FRANKLIN E. "ED" JONES, UTC, USN (Ret.), born Oct. 4, 1928. Inducted into the service at Nashville, TN, in 1945. Started with the 124th NCB and served in Korea and Vietnam (two tours). Awarded 16 medals (too many to list separately). Discharged at Port Hueneme in 1966 and transferred to Fleet Reserve. Retired in 1976.

Elected national commander in 1996 and served two terms. Married to Gloria with five children and seven grandsons. He is now working with the Navy Seabee Veterans of America.

JOHN V. KANE III, Civil Engr. Corps, USNR (Ret.), commissioned a line officer, USN upon graduation in 1961, bachelor of architecture, Illinois Institute of Technology, Chicago. Capt. Kane served active duty aboard ship, USS *Oklahoma City* (CLG-5) and USS *Taconic* (AGC-17).

Accepting a reserve commission upon release from active duty in 1964 he joined the Naval Reserve Program in 1965 with NRCB 3-12, Poughkeepsie, NY. Change of designator to Civil Engineer Corps in 1968 and various reserve construction battalion and facilities management staff and command assignments culminated with Capt. Kane's final assignment as inspector general, national staff, Reserve Div., Naval Facilities Engineering

Command, Alexandria, VA. Subsequently he retired from the Naval Reserve in 1991.

A licensed architect in New York, with certification by the National Council of Architectural Registration Boards, Capt. Kane is architect partner of Hayward and Pakan Associates., Engineers Architects Surveyors, Poughkeepsie, NY. Professional and military association activities include membership in NYS Association of Architects/American Institute of Architects, various Historic Preservation Societies, Poughkeepsie Rotary, Naval Reserve Assoc., Fleet Reserve Assoc. and Navy Seabee Veterans of America, Island X-6 New York.

Natives of Buffalo, NY, Capt. Kane and his wife, Dorothy (Peck), have resided in the Poughkeepsie/Mid-Hudson region of New York since 1965, and have two children, Michael and Maureen.

PAUL KAPLAN, inducted into the service in December 1942. Military locations and stations were Camp Marks, Pleasanton, CA, Guadalcanal, Tulagi, Emerau, New Zealand and Okinawa. Discharged in November 1945 at Camp Shoemaker.

He worked for an insurance company as a sales agent for 27 years. Now retired and plays golf. Kaplan is married and has two daughters.

RAYMOND MILLER KARAM, MM2/c, born Sept. 3, 1916, in Shelton, CT. Inducted into the service Sept. 3, 1943, at Brooklyn, NY. Military locations and stations were Banika, Solomon Islands; Guam; USNRS New York; Constr. Bn., Williamsburg, VA; ABD Rec. Barracks, Gulfport, MS; Pontoon Assembly Det. #2; U.S. Fleet Hospital 110; and USNR T.I. San Pedro, CA.

Awarded the American Theater Ribbon, Asiatic-Pacific Ribbon, Victory Medal, Presidential Unit Citation Ribbon (4), Navy Unit Commendation, Reserve Special Commendation, Good Conduct Medal, National Defense Medal and Sea Cadet Corps Medal. 100% attendance in the Reserves. Discharged Feb. 3, 1946, at Lido Beach, Long Island, NY. Enlisted in the Reserves May 2, 1947, at Phoenix, AZ, and retired in 1977 at Detroit, MI, as lieutenant junior grade, honorary commission.

Married Lucy and has five children and 10 grandchildren. Was Sea Cadet Corps instructor and recruiter (five years) at Brohead NRS, Detroit, MI.

WALTER AUGUST KAUFMANN, born Oct. 26, 1921, in Detroit, MI. Inducted into the service Nov. 5, 1942, at Detroit, MI. Service (vessels and stations served on) were Constr. Bns. USNCTC, NOB Magruader, VA; Spec. Bn. #1; 2nd Spec. USN, Constr. Bn.

Awarded the American Area Medal, Asiatic-Pacific Medal, Victory Medal and Good Conduct Medal. Discharged Dec. 19, 1945, at USN Personnel Separation Center, Great Lakes, IL.

Memorable experiences: Work - sweat - sweat - work - work, primarily unloading and loading ships.

Civilian employment as owner of Kaufmann Construction Co. He is active in the

Lutheran Church Mo. Synod, The Bible League, Habitat for Humanity and Rotary Club. Married to Margaret and has three children: Ken, Tim and Chuck; seven grandchildren; and one great-grandchild.

KENNETH KELLY, CM3/c, born Aug. 21, 1925, in Coopersville, MI. Inducted into the service Aug. 2, 1943, at Grand Rapids, MI. Served in 127th, 78th and 82nd Bns. Boot camp at Camp Peary, VA and advance training at Gulfport, MS. Shipped out at New Orleans on New Year's Day in 1944 for Pacific War Zone. He joined the 78th at Los Negros Island in the Admiralty Group March 30, 1944. He served in it while he spent nine months in the Admiralties, five months in New Caledonia and four months on Okinawa where he was decommissioned in September 1945. He then transferred into the 82nd and spent two months with it until he returned to the States in November 1945 arriving in San Francisco on Thanksgiving Day 1945. After a 30 day leave he was assigned as on shore patrol riding trains between Chicago and Buffalo. While doing this he was stationed in Chicago and met his future wife. They were married in September 1946 one week before he enrolled at Michigan State studying to become a civil engineer.

Memorable experiences: Living and working with older, experienced construction men.

Awarded the American Theater Medal, Asiatic-Pacific Campaign Medal w/2 Battle Stars and the WWII Victory Medal. Discharged March 14, 1946, at Great Lakes, IL.

He and his wife, Ruth, of 52 years have three sons and seven grandchildren. After graduating as a civil engineer from Michigan State he worked as one for two years designing and building roads for County Road Commissions and then he moved into industrial work where he spent 10 more years working as an engineer and salesman. In 1963 he and his wife started a business selling, manufacturing and installing overhead cranes, hoists and monorail equipment. They have since turned the business over to their sons who run it but he continues to work with them as an engineer. While attending Michigan State he joined the Naval Reserve, obtained a commis-

sion as a line office and now is a retired lieutenant commander. He is a life member of the American Legion (and past commander) VFW, Seabee Veterans of America, Retired Officer's Assoc., Naval Reserve Assoc., 78th Seabee WWII Assoc. (where he's co-president), Seabee Veterans of American Island X-11 Jamestown, NY, and a regular member of U.S. Naval Institute.

ROBERT L. KEMP, BUC, born Oct. 12, 1941, in Turlock, CA. Inducted into the service in Houston, TX, March 25, 1959. Military locations and stations were USNTC San Diego, CA; BUA/B School, Port Hueneme, CA; MCB-3, HED SUPPACT Taipei; NAS Dallas, TX; MCB-121 NS Greece; and MCB-5 NAVSCON Inst., Port Hueneme, CA.

Awarded the Expert Rifleman/Pistol, Navy Unit Commendation, Vietnamese Gallantry Cross, Combat Action Ribbon, Good Conduct Awards, National Defense Medal, Armed Forces Expeditionary Medal and Vietnam Service Medal. Discharged Oct. 15, 1977, at Port Hueneme, CA.

Married to Alis July 2, 1966, and has four children and nine grandchildren. Current activities include golf and fishing.

JAMES D. KEMPKES, born Dec. 8, 1924, in Everett, WA, to CWO Matthew and Helen Kempkes. His father was a veteran of the Spanish-American War, WWI and WWII. His mother was a dietitian at a Navy hospital.

Raised in Pella, IA, trained with V-12 Unit at Northwest Missouri State Teachers College and at Midshipmen Schools at Notre Dame, IN and Davisville, RI. Joined the 27th Spec. Bn. at Tinian, then on to Okinawa. Transferred to the 36th Spec., then to the 3rd Spec., both units also on Okinawa. Completed duty with CBD #1108 at Red Hill, Oahu, HI. Released to inactive duty in 1946. Discharged as lieutenant (j.g.) CEC in 1953.

Returned to Central College, Pella, IA, for bachelor's degree. Graduated from Drake University Law School and passed Iowa Bar Exam. Employed in Trust Div., Norwest Bank Des Moines (now Wells Fargo) for 36 years. Retired in 1986.

Still living in Des Moines. In 1998 celebrated Golden Wedding Anniversary with wife, Marian. Has four sons living in Des Moines with their families. Recently attended a "mini-reunion" with Tom Wattle and Leland Graber, both from the 27th Spec. and Bob Kem, from the 3rd Spec. Currently a member of Island X-2 in Chicago.

STEWART "STU" KERR, born in Dickson City, PA, Dec. 23, 1934. After gradu-

ation from Dickson City High School in 1952, he joined the Navy and completed boot camp at the Naval Training Center, Bainbridge, MD. Following boot camp he was assigned to the USS *Siboney* (CVE-112) in "B" Div.

In mid-1953 he was transferred to the USS *Hornet* (CVA-12) as part of the recommissioning crew at the Brooklyn Navy Yard. Kerr served in "B" Div. No. 3 Fireroom and the Boiler Repair Gang until November 1955.

Following his discharge from the Navy Kerr took advantage of the Korean GI Bill and completed his mechanical engineering at Johnson Technical Institute. During that time he enlisted in the Naval Constr. Force Reserve "Seabees." Shortly after joining the Seabees he was promoted to chief petty officer. Later he applied for the Civil Engineering Corp (CEC) Warrant Officer Program and of 2200+ that applied for this program, he was one of 48 that was selected.

During the years with the Naval Constr. Forces he served in many billets in the various Naval Constr. Bns., Constr. Regts., the First Naval Constr. Bde. and the Mine Inshore Underwater Unit #1.

He holds the following awards/medals: Presidential Unit Citation, Navy Good Conduct, China Service, Japanese Occupation, National Defense, Naval Reserve Medal, Korean Medal, United Nations Medal, Armed Forces Reserve Medal, Navy Expert Pistol and Navy Expert Rifle.

Kerr retired as a chief warrant officer (CWO-4) in November 1985.

In civilian life he is a senior engineering officer in the Engineering Div. of FM Global. In this capacity he is involved with boilers, pressure vessels, turbine/generators, gas turbines, all types of mechanical and electrical equipment, as well as, high pressure piping.

He is a member of the American Society of Military Engineers, American Society of Safety Engineers, Technical Assoc. of the Pulp & Paper Industry, The Black Liquor Recovery Boiler Advisory Committee, The National Board of Boiler & Pressure Vessel Inspectors, National Assoc. of Power Engineers, has Boiler & Pressure Commissions in various states, American Legion, Reserve Officers Assoc., National Assoc. of Uniformed Services, Navy Seabee Veterans of America, Island X-4, Kingsbury Lodge #466 F&AM, and the Keystone Consistory.

Kerr was a certified state instructor in fire technology for the state of Pennsylvania, a former fire chief, fire training officer and chief engineer in a volunteer fire department.

He married his wife, Joan, June 8, 1957, and they have a daughter, Lisa and a son, Eric. Lisa and her husband, Dean, have triplet sons: Spencer, Logan and Garrett, born in 1993. Eric and his wife have a son, Evan, born in 1996.

EDWARD KESS, S1/c, born Feb. 7, 1923, in Elizabeth, NJ. Inducted into the service May 29, 1944, at Newark, NJ. Military locations and stations were Milne Bay, New Guinea; Leyte-Samar, Philippines; and Portsmith, VA.

Awarded the Asiatic-Pacific Campaign Medal and Philippine Liberation Medal. Kess was discharged Aug. 14, 1945, at Portsmith, VA.

MELVIN "COOKIE" KOCH, MM1/c, enlisted in the Seabees after high school graduation in 1943 at age 18. Boot camp at Camp Peary, VA, then to Gulfport, MS, and the SS *Afoundria* to the South Pacific. Assigned to 35th Bn. then 5th Regt. on Manus Island (Admiralties). After rest in New Caledonia, flown to Hawaiian Islands to ship out for the invasion of Okinawa. Discharged in April 1946.

Went into building business plus real estate broker and appraiser. Still active in business plus raising Arabian horses. He is a life member of Island-5 and the VFW Post 2940, both in West Seneca, NY. He and his wife, Shirley, have been married 51 years and have three children.

He is still in touch with several old war buddies, has had lots of visits together and sadly attended funerals for some. They turned out to be some of the best friends he ever had. He lives in West Valley, NY.

HERBERT FREDERICK KORTZ, Chief Bldr., born May 2, 1918, in Dunn County, WI. Enlisted in the Seabees Oct. 13, 1943. Took boot training Oct. 18-Dec. 30, 1943, at Camp Peary, VA. Then to Gulfport, MS. At Camp Holliday from Jan. 1-Feb. 9, 1944. Arrived at Port Hueneme, CA, Feb. 13-May 1, 1944. Arrived at Maui, HI, May 11, 1944. Left Maui May 1, 1945. Arrived in the Philippines May 24, 1945. At Tabbaboo, Samar, Calican and Manicani. Left Manicani for Japan Sept. 28, 1945. Went ashore Oct. 16, 1945, at Yokosuka Japan. Left Japan Nov. 5, 1945.

Arrived at Treasure Island, CA, Thanksgiving day Nov. 22, 1945. Arrived in Minneapolis, MN, Dec. 6, 1945, and was honorably discharged. He was with the 127th Seabee Bn. Enlisted in the Navy Seabee Reserve from April 1954-April 1962. In eight years he was honorably discharged as a chief bldr.

He worked as a carpenter on the island of Maui and the Philippines. When he arrived home he joined the Carpenters Union as a third year apprentice. Went to Vocational School in Eau Clair, WI. In one year he was advanced to a journeyman carpenter. He received his 50th Year Gold Card Feb. 6, 1996. He retired at age 62. For a hobby he builds wheel chair ramps for handicapped people. He has built 232 ramps for a total length of 6,869 feet.

The 127th Bn. won a commendation for its work in the Philippines when the war in the Pacific was blazing to its climax. Formed in September 1943 the 127th NCB was on its way five months later. Members of the unit worked for a year on housing and dock facilities there, standing 12 hours shifts. The 127th went to the Philippines in May 1945 and was assigned a harbor project with a tough construction schedule. Members of the unit met a bittered construction schedule all along the line. A feat which won the commendation.

Kortz is a life time member of VFW 7051 and member of the Navy Seabee Veterans of America Island X-1 of Minnesota. He has been married 58 years as of Dec. 2, 1998, and has one son, two granddaughters and one great-granddaughter.

ROBERT CARL KRAMER, enlisted in the USN in Portsmouth, OH, immediately following Pearl Harbor, having been married the previous August to Jean Aeh. Finally sent to boot camp in Camp Allen, VA, and trained with the 22nd NCB. Moved to Camp Bradford after three weeks for advanced training, and then shipped to Port Hueneme, en route to Dutch Harbor, to join the 4th NCB. Returned to the States in October 1943. Christmas day 1943 shipped out of San Francisco for Pearl Harbor. After six months of building, finally went to Guam for 10 months. On to Okinawa where they remained. He came home aboard the *Shangri La*, as ships company, and discharged from Great Lakes Oct. 19, 1945.

He and Jean have two daughters, Lynn King and Kaye Osborne, of whom they are very proud. He is retired from Goodyear Atomic Corp. and a life member (#100) of the Seabee Veterans of America.

LEO L. KUBIET, MM3/c, inducted into the service Oct. 15, 1942, at Camp Bradford, VA. Joined the 59th NCB at Dam Neck, VA, for basic training. Shipped out of Port Hueneme, CA, destined for Honolulu, HI, and subsequently to Hilo, HI. In June 1944 shipped out to Guam, service there for 16 months. Discharged Jan. 6, 1946, at Bainbridge, MD.

Memorable experiences: Exploring caves on Guam looking for hidden Japanese soldiers or souvenirs. Had a very scary experience during a typhoon while on the USS *Rudyard Bay*, a baby carrier, on their return to Honolulu.

Attended college under GI Bill. Entered the newspaper business with the *Detroit News* in 1950. Later moved to *St. Petersburg Times*, St. Petersburg, FL, serving in several executive advertising/marketing positions. Retired as senior vice president in April 1989. Married Jean Metz in September 1946 while in college. They have two sons, Lawrence and Martin; and five grandchildren: Kurt, Mike, Chris, Alexander and Nicholas.

KENNETH CARL LAIRD, inducted into the USN Dec. 2, 1942, at Charleston, WV. Released to inactive duty Dec. 3, 1942. Recalled to active duty Jan. 2, 1943, to NCTC Camp Peary, VA. Jan. 3, 1943, Constr. Bn. USNCTC, Williamsburg, VA. From USNRS Charleston, WV, to J.G. Ware, captain, USN (HPD) with rate S2/c, V-6. April 1, 1943, transferred to ABD Hueneme, CA, FFT. Date aboard April

6, 1943, Port Hueneme. April 6, 1943, transferred to Base Maint. Unit 504 for duty. CO R.C. McNamara, lieutenant CEC-U(S)USNR. Rate changed to S1/c Sept. 16, 1943. Sailed May 1, 1943, from U.S. limits, Wallis Island Air Base. U.S. Naval Hospital May 14, 1944. May 17, 1944, USNS Tutuila Samoa. June 22 USNH Oakland, CA, by USS *Cape Esperance*. Aug. 8, 1944, granted 45 days leave to expire at 0800 Sept. 22, 1944, at USNH Philadelphia, PA. March 5, 1945, NCTC Davisville, RI, for duty. May 17, 1945, to Co. NCTC, Davisville, RI. May 28 ABRB, Port Hueneme, CA. June 4, 1945, 19th USN Constr. Bn. June 12, 1945, sailed aboard USS *Heywood* (APA-6). Arrived Pearl Harbor June 18, 1945. July 22, 1945, crossed 180th Meridian. June 25, 1945, arrived Eniwetok. Sailed July 10, 1945. Arrived Ulithi July 20, 1945. Arrived Okinawa Shima Nov. 2, 1945. Transferred to West Coast FFT for separation Nov. 26, 1945.

Awarded the WWII Victory Medal, American Campaign Medal, Asiatic-Pacific Campaign Medal, Navy Occupation Service Medal and Asia Honorable Service Pin. Honorably discharged Nov. 28, 1945, at Bainbridge, MD, conduct 4.0.

Memorable experiences: Okinawa the night war was declared over. The ships and thousands went wild firing all kinds of weapons everywhere. He was deeper in fox hole than had ever been. Also three different typhoons.

Civilian activities included concrete road work at 16, lumberman at 18, worked as clerk in store, Broughtons Dairy Plant #2, Pepsi Cola Bottling Plant, gas station attendant, high voltage lineman. He married Garnetta Fay Harden Dec. 14, 1941. She passed away Oct. 5, 1997. They have five children: Connie, Sandra, Shelia, Debra and Kenneth; seven grandchildren: Chris, Ginger, Jason, Adam, Ashley, Garret and Rose Anna; and one great-grandson, Jearamy.

JOHN D. LAW, SF3/c (CB), inducted into the service June 27, 1945. Naval training at Great Lakes, IL, Co. 926, volunteered for the CB after eight weeks and reported to Camp Parks, CA, and was on leave after boot when Japan surrendered.

Left Camp Parks on October 12 and sent to Treasure Island for three days then boarded the U.S. *Baxter* and issued foul weather gear for occupation on Japan. MacArthur didn't want any CBs, his engineers could do more than the CBs so on to Guam for about 10 days, then on an LCI for Saipan where he spent about 10 months with the I-21st Bn. which was awarded a Presidential Unit Citation. They were on the *Baxter* for 30 days and just a salt water shower. He did get to go ashore while they were in Tokyo Bay to pick up some rifles for ships company and the guys that loaded them from boxcars sitting on a siding close to shore. They were in Tokyo Bay for six days refueling, etc. January 1, he made seaman first and on Jan. 2, 1946, made SF3/c.

He volunteered for the Navy June 16, 1945, seven days before his 18th birthday and on June 16, 1946, his name appeared on the list to leave Saipan. Boarded the U.S. *Samuel Chase* and headed for Pearl, everyone west of the Mississippi got off for seven days and then got on the USS *Lubbock* for the trip to California. July 14 they docked in Frisco and passing under the Golden Gate Bridge was a pleasure. Had leave where he got a tattoo on July 15 and back to Treasure Island on the 16th, then on a troop train. While on Saipan he drove a truck and worked on a garbage dump just 300 feet from Suicide Cliff where the natives jumped to their death when they heard the U.S. soldiers and Marines were landing.

Law was married in 1953 to Darlene McPherson and has three sons: David, Tomas and James; and five grandchildren: Stepanie, William, Colby, Amy and Kaylee.

JOSEPH T. LESH JR., CET3/c, born Nov. 30, 1944, in Detroit, MI. Inducted into the service in May 1963 at Bremerton, WA, USNR. Active duty in November 1964 at Port Hueneme, CA. Military locations and stations were Class "A" Electrical School, Co. B, MCB-5, Port Hueneme, CA, from September 1965-June 1966; Camp Hoover, Vietnam (Da Nang).

Memorable experiences: Being in communication in Vietnam (radio/telephone operator).

Awarded the Vietnam Service Medal and National Defense Service Medal. Discharged from active duty in November 1966, Port Hueneme, CA, and from USNR in May 1969.

Married to Cindy for 28 years. Spent four years as electrical apprentice (IBEW) and 25 years as journeyman electrical. Electronic technician at Hood Canal Bridge in Washington state. Current activities include black powder shooting, gold panning and union activities.

JOHN ALFRED LEWIS, EM3/c, born Sept. 9, 1923, in Indianapolis, IN. Inducted into the service Dec. 15, 1942, at Indianapolis, IN. Military locations and stations were boot camp at Camp Peary, VA, in April 1943; advanced combat training, Camp Endicott, Davisville, RI; advanced training, Camp Holliday, Gulfport, MS; embarkation, Camp Rousseau, Port Hueneme, CA; Red Hill and Iroquois Pt., T.H.; Tarawa, Gilbert Islands; Guam, Marshalls, Treasure Island, port entry in 1945.

Awarded the WWII Victory Medal, Asiatic-Pacific Theater Medal w/star for Tarawa and American Defense Medal. Discharged Feb. 5, 1946, at Great Lakes Naval Separation Center, Great Lakes, IL.

Memorable experiences: Played in several Seabee battalion bands, 98th NCB and 34th SPNCB. Most memorable was Tarawa landing experience in November 1943. Stevedoring on Guam. Saw USS *Indianapolis* at Guam three days before she went down July 31, 1945. Pearl Harbor west lock explosions (1944) where the 98th NCB equipment was destroyed preventing their Saipan invasion voyage via LSTs.

Married with three children and three grandchildren. After discharge attended Indiana University earning AB degree in 1948 and MA degree in 1949. Was teaching assistant at University of Illinois, Urbana, IL, 1949-50; teacher of English, Morton High School and Junior College, Cook County, IL, 1950-61; retired from Indianapolis Technical High School in 1985.

Life member Navy Seabee Veterans of America, Island X-2, Indianapolis, IN, member of American Legion, Indiana Post 34, 40/8 Voiture 145, Indianapolis. Member Grand Band Duke University, Indiana, 40/8, sax-clarinet and Indianapolis Symphonic Band, clarinet. Helped organize the 98th NCB Veterans Assoc. in 1994. Has since served as secretary/treasurer of 98th for past five years. Does volunteer work for local fire department, Washington Township, and Nora-Northside Community Council Boards of Directors. Served as secretary of White River Yacht Club, Indianapolis, IN, for three years.

ROBERT W. LEWIS, PO3/c, born March 8, 1947, in Pittsburgh, PA. Inducted into the service July 20, 1966, at Philadelphia Naval Yard. Home base at Gulfport, MS, MCB 133. First tour Camp Faulkner, Da Nang Vietnam and second tour Hue, Phu Bai Vietnam.

Memorable experiences: A lifelong friendship with Vic Lovell, a fellow Seabee.

Awarded the National Defense Medal, Vietnam Service Medal, Vietnam Campaign Medal and Fleet Marine Combat Insignia. Discharged July 18, 1968, at naval station in Long Beach, CA.

Married for 31 years to Rose and has three children and two grandchildren. Current activities: City of Pittsburgh fire fighter, DJ and antiques.

JOHN A. LITCH, Coxswain, born Dec. 13, 1919, in Detroit, MI. Inducted into the service Nov. 2, 1943, at Detroit, MI. Military locations and stations were CB USNOTC Win., VA; N. Gunnery Ctr., Dam Neck, VA; 28th Spec. NCB Port Hueneme, CA; Moanalua Ridge, Oahu, HI; USNH Navy #10, 35th Spec. NCB Pearl Harbor, HI; CB Maint. U., Aiea Hts., HI; USNH St. Albans, Long Island, NY; CBMU-522.

Memorable experiences: Securing beach at Port Hueneme, CA; stevedore action at Pearl Harbor, HI; Aiea Height, HI; Panama Canal; Long Island, NY; USS *Enterprise*.

Awarded the Seabee Combat Warfare Badge, American Campaign Medal, Disabled Veteran of WWII, Asiatic-Pacific Campaign Medal, 50th Anniversary of WWII Medal, 50th Anniversary of Victory in Pacific and Distinguished Service Medal. Discharged Jan. 9, 1946, U.S. Naval Hospital, St. Albans, Long Island, NY.

Married with two sons and three daughters. Retired after 25 years at Army Tank Auto Ctr., seven years with Chrysler Missile Command. Service officer for Veterans of Foreign Wars, Disabled Veterans of America volunteer at Det. Veterans medical Center, Knights of Columbus 4th degree Honor Guard, Macomb County Veteran Ritual Team, Retirees bowling team and American Legion member.

On duty in Pearl Harbor on Ship X he sustained multiple injuries and hearing in right ear. He was carried off ship in a coma. Transported to base hospital at Aiea Heights. After intracartial injury operation he regained consciousness and medical treatment for back and left shoulder. After four months he was released for limited duty (no combat action). Returned to U.S. on USS *Enterprise* (CV-6) to USN hospital, St. Albans, Long Island, NY.

AMOS JUDSON "MAC" MACCREERY JR., BUL3/c, enlisted in the Naval Reserve in February 1953 at Poughkeepsie, NY. In February 1955 transferred NRCB 3-12. Entered active duty in July 1957 serving with NMCB-7 in Barbados, British West Indies. Here they constructed base taken over by Nav Fac 505 where he finished active duty. Was separated in July 1959, Navy Receiving Station, Brooklyn, NY, and transferred to NRCB 3-12 inactive duty status until his discharge in February 1961.

MacCreery is a charter member of Island X-9, Kingston, NY. Civilian employment in automotive repair and general building construction. He ran his own auto repair shop until he retired in 1996. Does volunteer work for civic organizations. Member Ulster County Civil War Roundtable.

Married to Sandra "Sandy" and has five children: Steven, W. Scott, Patti, Linda and Michael; and seven grandchildren: Jacqueline, Shaun, Andrew J., Nicholas, Sydney, Andrew C. and Matthew.

WILFRED D. "BUD" MACGIFFERT, born in Greenport (Columbia County), NY. Graduated from Hudson High School. Joined Seabees in August 1943. Attended boot training at Camp Peary, VA. They became the 133rd NCB trained at Rhode Island, MS; Port Hueneme, CA. Shipped to Oahu, HI, and worked and trained. Joined up with 4th Marines on Maui. Sent to Iwo invasion. Some of the 133rd were sent to Peleliu, as well as to the Iwo invasion.

The 133rd landed on Iwo D-Day. Their outfit suffered more casualties than any Seabee battalion during WWII. They stayed on Iwo after it was secured and built it into a small city. The air strip was said to be the longest in the Pacific. Was discharged in March 1946. They were awarded a Unit Commendation for their part on Iwo. Awarded the Navy Commendation Medal, American Theater Medal, Victory Medal, Asiatic-Pacific

Medal w/2 stars and Sharp Shooter Medal. He was a MoM2/c.

Memorable experiences: Pipe line and pile driving jobs in Honolulu. Landed on D-Day on Iwo with the 4th Marine Div. They were shelled real bad when they landed on Iwo as well as many of the days during the operations. When he first landed they were pinned down at the water's edge. He had his rifle laid across his leg when an artillery shell landed near him. A large piece of steel hit his rifle stock taking a large chunk out of it. That rifle saved his leg.

The 133rd stayed on Iwo for approximately seven months after the invasion. When the war ended they went to Guam, then on to Seattle, WA. All the East Coast Seabees traveled by train back home.

He and his brother owned and operated a garage business for 40 years. His first wife died in 1968 leaving two sons, Robert and Paul. Remarried in 1973 to Constance and has three stepchildren: Joe, John and Mary Ann. They now have six grandchildren together.

He is a life member of Island X-5 of Ft. Lauderdale, FL. Reunions held with Seabee Units of Iwo invasion, also Navy Corpsmen 3rd, 4th and 5th Marine Div. each year in different cities. They have attended the Atlanta, GA; Pensacola, FL; Mobile, AL; New Orleans and Biloxi, MS reunions.

ANDREW F. MACKEY, BUH3/c, inducted into the service Dec. 20, 1962, at Boston, MA. He went to Great Lakes, IL, for basic training, then to Port Hueneme, CA, for Builder "A" School. Then joined MCB-4 in Argentina, Newfoundland in August 1963. After returning to Davisville, RI, the battalion went to Camp Lejeune for training. He then deployed with a detachment to Quantico, VA, then to Vieques, PR. In January 1965 the battalion went to Rota, Spain. Later MCB-4 Unit went to Camp Lejeune again, was transferred to Port Hueneme, CA, and then to Chu Lai, Republic of Vietnam. He was discharged from the Portsmouth, NH Naval Hospital June 23, 1966.

Memorable experiences: He attended the 1st Annual Seabee Jamboree in Laconia, NH, in May 1998, and the 2nd Annual Seabee Jamboree in West Warwick, RI, in June 1999. While in Rhode Island he attended the dedication of the refurbished "Seabee" statue at Davisville, and met several men he had not seen in over 30 years.

He has been a survey party chief for 30 years. He is a member of the American Legion and is presently secretary of Island X-4, New Hampshire. He married his wife, June, on June 15, 1968, and they have three children: Jane, Susan and Andy W.

ROBERT F. MAGUIRE JR., EM1/c, 140th NCB, Co. D, Pt. 3, inducted into the service Oct. 6, 1943, and honorably discharged Jan. 7, 1946. While in the Seabees he received WWII Victory Medal and the Asiatic-Pacific Theater Medal.

He did his boot training at Camp Peary, VA. His advance training at Davisville, RI. Then a bazaar thing happened. 140th, a new battalion, was sent to Camp Parks, CA, to be among all the veteran battalions returning from South Pacific and Aleutian Islands for rest and relaxation.

They were then shipped to Port Hueneme for embarkation to the Admiralty Islands for 19 months. They left the Admiralties in late November 1945.

Returned to civilian life and worked as electrician, member of IBEW Local 103. Retired from Massachusetts Bay Transportation Authority after 27 years of service as chief inspector - instructor of signal and communications. Spent the next 21 years as a consulting engineer on the design procurement and installation of signal and communication systems for railroad and rapid transit systems.

WILLIAM MALONE, enlisted in 1943 at Boston, MA. Trained at Camp Peary, VA. Bureau of Ordinance, Washington, D.C., Camp Lejeune Marine Base, NC, Port Hueneme instructor military training area. 41st NCB Guam HQ Co. under Lt. Orville Christenson. 41st NCB commended for their excellence in carrying out their construction assignments. May 6, 1945, 41st defeats the Naval Air Base 2-1 in a 21 inning game. Pitchers Stan Juscen 41st NCB, Johnny Rigney of NAB former White Sox hurler. Discharged in 1945.

In 1948 returned to Guam with the Pacific Island Engrs. for the reconstruction of Guam and all Naval facilities. navy permitted his wife, Lucy, to join him. All that was left of the 41st NCB Camp was the church and it was converted to a fire station. Officer in charge of Guam construction was Capt. William Sihler who also was base commander at Port Hueneme in 1943. Cmdr. E.E. Gibson, who served with the 18th NCB in WWII relieved Capt. Sihler. Completed his Guam reconstruction contract in 1952.

Joined Holmes and Narver engineers and constructors who had the contract to design and construct the facilities for the testing of the Atomic bomb in the Marshall Islands, Eniwetok, Bikini, Johnston Island, Amchitaka and Nevada test site. Many Seabees know these islands well. Retired after 18 years with Holmes and Narver.

Looking back, those yesterdays of life with the Seabees, reconstruction of Guam, overseas testing of the Atomic Bomb and U.S. are rich in memories. Currently resides in Las Vegas, NV. His wife passed away in 1997.

PAUL A. MARGUGLIO, EA1/c, inducted into the service July 10, 1982, PEBD. Military locations and stations were Camp Lejeune NCB, Navac London, England, 29 Palms, MCB Guantanamo, Roosevelt Roads, Philadelphia Naval Base, Gulfport, MS, Eglin AFB, Port Hueneme, NAS Jacksonville, McGuire AFB, Ft. Dix.

He has been awarded the Expert Rifle, Expert Pistol, Armed Forces Reserve, Overseas Service, Humanitarian Service, National Defense, Meritorious Service (5) and Navy-Marine Corps Achievement (6), SCWS career counselor. Marguglio is still active in the service.

Memorable experiences: Air America, July 1963-August 1964.

Civilian activities include Lockheed Martin, Information Systems, Orlando, FL (Hill AFB and Kirkland AFB) and Lockheed Martin Missile Systems. He has two children, Paul Jr. and Dane Leigh, and one grandchild, Dane Lee.

RICHARD W. MAYER, born Jan. 20, 1925, served in the USN Seabees from Dec. 20, 1942-March 31, 1946. His promotions were S2/c, S1/c and CM3/c. He was stationed at Williamsburg, VA; Ft. Pierce, FL; Camp Parks, CA; overseas; Treasure Island, CA; and Lido Beach, Long Island. Combat duty at Marshall Islands, Eniwetok, Marianas Islands, Saipan, Tinian, Ryukyu Islands, Okinawa, Chichi Jima and Ha Ha Jima.

The citations and awards he received were as follows: American Theater, Asiatic-Pacific Theater, Good Conduct and Victory Medal.

He enlisted Dec. 20, 1942, in New York City. Called for duty in April 1943. Discharged at Lido Beach March 3, 1946.

He and his wife, Marie, have a son who is an engineer and works for "Bectel" in Boston. One daughter, Marie, and Alice, our veterinarian. Bill has two girls, one is studying in Germany (art work and German). The other is a sophomore. Marie has two children, one boy, Bud, who is graduating Cornell this year and a

daughter, Marie, sophomore at Boston College. They have a 22 ft. Escape and travel around the USA and Canada. They love the Navy and always will! *Submitted by Marie A. Mayer, wife.*

RONALD B. MAXON, BUR3/c, inducted into the service Oct. 16, 1961, at Great Lakes, Chicago. Military locations and stations were boot camp at Great Lakes; "A" School, Port Hueneme, CA; PWD, Argentina, Newfoundland; MCB-8, Davisville, RI; Det. Echo, Marathon, Greece, MCB-8 transferred to CINPAC in September 1965; to Da Nang, South Vietnam, Camp Faulkner.

Awarded the Vietnam Service Medal and National Defense Service Medal. Discharged Feb. 3, 1966, at Treasure Island, San Francisco, CA.

Memorable experience: His entire Seabee experience has been deeply imprinted on his memory. Many names have faded but the experiences are still bright.

Worked construction as carpenter and millwright for 14 years. He has worked for what is now Ameren CIPs for the past 19 years as a mechanical maintenance repairman.

Enjoys camping, traveling and hunting (both gun and archery). Member VFW Post 4325, American Legion Post 2910, Masonic Lodge 664, Scottish Rite, Ainad Shrine Temple and IBEW Local 702. He is married to Marcea Maxon and has five children: Lyn, Katrina, Jeremy, Matthew and Allison; and five grandchildren: Alis, Donald, Kayla, Justin and Christian.

RUSSELL A. "RUSS" MAZZEO, Cdr., born May 16, 1937, in Waterbury, CT, received a BS degree from Central Connecticut State University, 1960; MS degree from Syracuse University, 1963.

Enlisted June 1, 1954, in the USNR, Seabee Reserve Div. 3-22, as a CR. His military locations and stations: USNRTC, Bainbridge, MD; CBC, Davisville, RI; CBC, Gulfport, MS; NMCB Det. Guantanamo Bay, Cuba; EFD, Philadelphia, PA; EFD MED, Naples. Served with CB Div. 3-22; NMCB-13; 21st RNCR; 7th RNCR; NREFD North; NRFHCBTZ 2D.

He was awarded the Seabee Combat Warfare Medal - Officer, Meritorious Unit Commendation Medal, Reserve Special Commendation Ribbon, Armed Forces Reserve Medal w/2 Hourglasses, National Defense Service Medal and Expert Rifleman Medal.

Achieved the rank of CDR Jan. 1, 1984, retired to retired list July 1, 1994. His memorable experiences: received direct commission to LTJG Oct. 1, 1968; mobilization officer for

7th RNCR during Mobilization Exercise in which NMCB-12, 13 and 27 were successfully "mobilized" to and from Camp Lejeune, NC, during their annual two weeks AT.

Mazzeo has never married. Employed as senior research scientist by Uniroyal Chemical Co., Inc. Member of the American Chemical Society, Rubber Div. of ACS, BPO Elks Lodge No. 967, Connecticut Rubber Group, National Association for Uniformed Services and Lakewood Social Club. Mazzeo is a life member of Navy Seabee Veterans of America, Island X-5, Fort Lauderdale, FL.

JOSEPH F. MCCARTHY, SKD3/c, inducted into the service April 17, 1943, at New York City. Military locations and stations were boot camp at Camp Peary, VA. Assigned to 98th NCB. Went to Davisville, RI, for advanced training. To Gulfport, MS, in August 1943. To Port Hueneme, CA. Shipped out to Hawaii Oct. 19, 1943. To Tarawa Nov. 26, 1943.

Awarded the Good Conduct Medal and Asiatic-Pacific Theater Medal. Discharged April 18, 1946, at Lido Beach Separation Center, NY.

Memorable experiences: While on Tarawa Atoll in 1943-44 experienced 26 night raids by Japanese bombers. They only hit island once. Very little damage. Went back to Hawaii via Abemama Atoll, Gilbert Islands. Arrived Hawaii April 1, 1944. Went to Sasebo Japan Sept. 22, 1945, for occupation duty. Came home on leave Dec. 22, 1945.

Worked for city of New York 33 years in clerical-administrative duties. Retired April 6, 1983. Still likes to ski and play golf. Never married. He lives with his brother.

HOWARD L. MCLARNEY, CD2/c, served in the military in 1943 during WWII and in 1953 during the Korean War. Military locations and stations were Great Lakes; Williamsburg, VA; Port Hueneme; Attu Island; Okinawa; Korea K-3, K-6, K-9.

Awarded the American Campaign Medal, Asiatic Campaign Medal, Victory Medal, National Defense Service Medal, Expert Pistol Medal, Good Conduct Medal, Korea Defense Medal and other still pending.

After he was discharged in November 1945 a group of Seabees from the Chicago area got together along with Capt. Howard P. Potter at Great Lakes and got the Seabees started. In the spring of 1948 they had a get together to get the first National Convention started and in the fall at the La Salle Hotel they held the first National Convention which was his privilege to take part in. When they got started Mr. Mathison, who was the hotel manager, told them that they were short a little over $400. With the help of Al Landsman, who was connected with the Stage and Actors Guild, got a stag show for the men and a stage show with dancers and a magic act for the ladies. They sold tickets and when the end of the evening came and they paid the bill to Mr. Mathison they had $216 to the good. Three years later he was called back into service. For the next 23 months he was in MCB-1 in Korea. Got connected with Island X-2 and became a life time member.

McLarney married Irene May 10, 1941. They have two children, Geraldine and Kathleen, four grandchildren and six great-grandchildren.

JOHN LELAND MCMILLIN SR., inducted into the service Nov. 9, 1943, at Cleveland, OH. Military locations and stations were Camp Peary, VA; Camp Endicott, RI; Port Hueneme, CA; Pearl Harbor, HI; and Great Lakes, IL.

Awarded the Asiatic-Pacific Area Campaign Medal, Victory Medal and American Area Campaign Medal. Discharged April 14, 1946, at Chicago, IL.

He and his wife, Gayle, have been married for 53 years. They have three children: John, Barbara and Kelly; and five grandchildren: Blair, Sander, Hilliary, Sean and Robin Rachel. He retired from automobile sales and management at age 56. He was a charter member of the 35th Spec. Bn. McMillin is a member of Island X-8, Youngstown, OH.

WALTER MCNAUGHTON, was inducted into the service Dec. 21, 1942. Took boot training at Camp Bradford, VA. After boot training, placed in Replacement, then from there on KP duty at Camp Peary, VA, for 90 days. After that he was in Replacement and went to Davisville, RI on security patrol for 12 months. Then into Maint. Unit 611.

Shipped out to North Africa and Southern France. Came back to the States. After his 30 day leave he went back on KP in charge of preparing the menu for the cooks. Then in the last part of September 1945 went to New Orleans, LA, and received his discharge Oct. 1, 1945.

He came home and married Clossie M. Murphy Burton. She had one daughter and two sons. He went to work doing mill work, cabinets and doors for about 20 years or more. Also worked at the Louisiana Amo. Served about five years. Then he retired and worked the yard and garden. He likes to fish and watch ball games and visits around with the neighbors.

He enjoyed being in the Navy Seabees. If he were to do it over he would go back in the Seabees. He regrets that he did not stay in for 20 or 30 years. He and his wife have one daughter. He also has three grandchildren, two great-grandchildren and a great number of step-grandchildren and step-great-grandchildren. McNaughton is a member of Navy Seabee Veterans of America, Inc., Island 6, Shreveport, LA.

WILLIAM A. MERTZEIS, born April 25, 1928, in Homestead, PA. Enlisted in the service June 18, 1945, and served with the Navy Seabees. Military station was in the Pacific. Discharged Aug. 18, 1946, with rank of CM3/c.

Mertzeis is married to Elizabeth and has three children: William L., Terry L. and Scott T., and eight grandchildren. Current activities include camping.

BERNARD L. MEYER, BUCA, inducted into the service May 25, 1972, at Philadelphia, PA. Military locations and stations were RTC Great lakes, CBC Gulfport, MS, NMCB-74 Gulfport, MS and Diego Garcia, Guam.

Meyer was awarded the National Defense Service Medal. Discharged Feb. 6, 1975, at Gulfport, MS.

Memorable experiences: The stories and meeting new people. He is the youngest member in Island X-1.

After discharge he went to work with the Federal Government and worked there for 25 years before taking an early retirement. He worked as boiler and AC plant operator. Now works for Porter Medical Center in Vermont. Meyer is married to Cindy Anne and has one son, Andrew J. He belongs to a Vietnam Era Veterans Group out of Bethel, VT, and goes to all kinds of meetings.

CLIFFORD W. MINER, SF1/c, was working as maintenance welder for Scintilla Maganato at Sidney, NY, at time of Pearl Harbor. He was 33 years old and having had five uncles and a grandfather in Civil War he felt patriotic. He enlisted at Binghamton, NY, and took his exam at Albany, NY. Was sworn in Seabees in early 1943 and sent home on inactive duty until called to service. After about three months he left Albany, NY, for Camp Peary, VA. After boot camp was sent to Camp Endicott, RI, for more training and was assigned to Proving Ground at Davisville, RI.

Lived at Wild Acres. After several months at Proving Grounds working with pontoons and steel work, was called to ship out to South Pacific with the newly formed 1023 CB Det. and was sent to Gunnery School 20mm.

He believes they were the first troop ship to leave Davisville Docks, USS *Santa Monica*, 1800 men (9th Spec. Seabees and several companies of Marines). They sailed into New York Harbor and joined a convoy of 40 ships, four ships wide and 10 long. Once in the convoy Lt. Sanborn assigned them to armed guard and they did 20mm anti-aircraft duty until they reached New Caledonia in South Pacific.

They sailed down the East Coast to Panama Canal to Balboa on west side. Went aboard supply ship *Cape Briton* and across the Pacific alone to New Caledonia, the staging area of South Pacific. Next stop Brisbane, Australia. Two weeks to transfer supplies across city and on to Casens where they built a pontoon dry dock. They used men from various CB Bns.

From Casens, Australia to Milne Bay, Papua, New Guinea, Lodovia Mission where they built another dry dock and many pontoon barges and docks of all descriptions. Long hours and hard work. Sometime in the late 1944s Lt. Sanborn was called back to the States and they were attached to Pontoon Assembly Det. #3 at Gornadoia, New Guinea.

Later with PAD-3 they had an assembly factory. Flat steel was shipped from Australia they welded it into pontoons. There they built many causeways for LST invasion craft.

Having had both ear drums perforated and a fungus infection he ended up in Army Hospital at Woga-Woga and was given orders to return to U.S. In States in May 1945 #3 air priority which was not very good. Made it home in New York state on rehabilitation for 30 days and was home when they dropped the Atomic Bomb. Returned after 30 days to Pier 92, New York City and was sent to St. Albans Hospital on Long Island. Was medically discharged in late 1945.

Awarded the Good Conduct Medal, Asiatic-Pacific Campaign Medal and Seabee Insignia. Discharged Oct. 9, 1945, USNH St. Albans, NY.

Civilian activities as mink rancher, farmer, railroader, lumber jack, welder and iron worker. He is married to Marilla. He has a life membership in Navy Seabee Veterans of America Island X-5 and is very proud to have been a Seabee in the South Pacific during WWII which he considers to be the last good war?

WILLIAM R. MOORE, EOC, born March 10, 1926, in Waterbury, CT. Enlisted NRS Portland, ME, in June 1943. Trained at

Williamsburg, VA. Advanced training Davisville, RI, 104th NCB, shipped out of Gulfport for Milne Bay, New Guinea, Los Negros, Admiralty Islands and Tacloban, Philippine Islands.

Transferred to 83rd NCB in Tanggu, China; 103rd NCB, Guam, MI; and then Point Barrow, AK. Shore duty Chincoteague, VA. MCB-2 Cubi Point, Philippine Islands and MCB-10 Guam. Shore duty NAS Brunswick, ME, and ONI Atsugi, Japan. Shore duty NAS Miramar, CA. Retired to Australia for 10 years.

Married to Connie and they have seven children and 19 grandchildren. Member of International Chief Petty Officer Assoc., FRA and Navy Seabee Veterans of America, Island X-14, Florida.

JAMES CLYDE MORGAN, BM2/c, enlisted in Springfield, MA. Military locations and stations were Solomons Islands, MD; Davisville, MD; Camp Peary, VA; Guam; and Philippines.

Awarded the American Defense Medal, American Victory Medal and Philippine Liberation Medal. Discharged at Sampson Naval Station, Ithica, NY.

Memorable experiences: This actually begins in 1923 while going through boot training at Newport, RI. They were told that there were two names that they were not called unless they were one: these names being: SOB and CS. If you can't handle the caller normally, use a coffee bowl or a squilge handle; we will back you up!

In 1943 while in NCB-128, Iroquois Point, HI, a man from Newport News, VA, named Allen called Morgan a SOB and he came off his bunk. Allen hit Morgan with the base of a shell that was used as a candle holder.

Time went on and he took the examination for BM1/c. Being congratulated later, but told that the rank would not be given on account of his not having a 4.0 record.

Returning to Guam it was seen that Allen had the First Class Crow. They embarked on the USS *Pennsylvania* taking 23 days to make the trip to Bremerton, WA. He searched everywhere for Allen, with every intention of giving him the Deep Six, but he was not found. Neither was he on the troop train that took them to Sampson, NY, for discharge!

There's not the slightest doubt that Allen was held back in Guam by Commander Husband, suspecting Morgan's intentions!

Civilian activities as chief storekeeper Tuberculosis Hospital. Several shipping and receiving jobs. Was interviewed July 27, 1998, as second oldest living Seabee in the nation.

His wife is deceased. There were no children.

DAVID ANGUS MORRISON, born Oct. 26, 1916, in Great Falls, MT, to Daniel MacDougal and Annie Mae Zink MacDougal of Nova Scotia, Canada, deceased. He attended school in Lewistown, MT, and was president of his senior class, played football and participated in the Glee Club, Opera and Thespians. He graduated in June 1935.

Was an electric welder at Puget Sound Navy Yard, Bremerton, WA, 1938-42. Pearl Harbor, Dec. 8, 1941-August 1942. Joined USN, Sept. 2, 1942. Boot camp at Camp Allen and Camp Peary, Norfolk, VA, 34th all Black Stevedore Bn.

Attached to Navy Pontoon Assembly Det. #1, November 1942, Gulfport, MS. Boarded USS *George Clymer* in December 1942, Norfolk, VA. Through Panama Canal, Dec. 24, 1942. Became shellback Dec. 30, 1942. Landed in Noumea, New Caledonia Jan. 1, 1943.

Moved up to Bienka Island in the Russell Islands. Built PAD #2 Jan. 30, 1943. Completed first pontoon Jan. 31, 1944.

Received 30 day leave to Lewistown, MT, in December 1944. Reported back to Camp Parks, Livermore, CA. Met and married Elizabeth Irene Colley Feb. 10, 1945. Returned to PAD #5, Los Negros, Admiralty Islands March 1, 1945.

War ended in August 1945 and was shipped back to San Pedro, CA, on a slow moving liberty ship. Picked up his wife in Oakland, CA, and they went to PSNY, Bremerton, WA, where he was a chief petty officer, received his honorable discharge as chief ship fitter, 4.0 rating, Nov. 12, 1945.

Awarded the Asiatic-Pacific Area Campaign Medal, American Area Campaign Medal, Good Conduct Medal, Special Commendation and WWII Victory Medal.

They returned to Lewistown, MT, in December 1945 where they raised one son, Michael Daniel and two daughters, Cheryl Lee Garrett and Jocqueline Ann. Today they have four grandsons, a great-grandson and a great-granddaughter.

SAMUEL T. MURPHY, enlisted in the USN at Jacksonville, IL, in 1945, took basic and advanced training at Great Lakes, IL, and Camp Parks, CA. He was first in 41st NCB and then 121st NCB. Sent to Japan and then to Guam to repair bombed roads, then transferred to Saipan as a bulldozer operator where they covered Japanese tanks, trucks and jeeps left behind by Japan's troops. Served out rest of enlistment at the Marine Supply Office where he issued supplies to all units of service.

Awarded Victory Ribbon, American Area Ribbon and Asiatic-Pacific Ribbon. Ended ser-

vice as a SK3/c. Returned home to farm and founded Murphy Bro. Fertilizer and Chemicals. Retired in 1992. Married to Shirley, has two daughters, two step daughters, one stepson, two grandchildren and four step grandchildren.

Active now in Legion, VFW, Moose, Elks, Masons and Shrine.

SQUIRREL MURPHY, BU1/c (SCW), inducted into the service March 1, 1966. Trained at Great Lakes then Gulfport, MS. Served with Brownwater Navy in Vietnam on coastal and riverine operations. Then served two more years in Vietnam with MCB-121. The second tour was with the battalion doing construction. He was involved in taking back Hue during the

TET Offensive in 1968. The third tour he spent with the Civic Action Program. He worked with CORDS, CRS, USAID, 24 COPPH and MACV and 101st to name a few. After active duty he joined the Reserves with NMCB-23, NMCB-20 until decommissioned then transferred to NMCB-24 where he now is serving as the training PO and special military instructor.

He has many awards including Expert Pistol, Rifle, 60mm and 50 cal. He has been awarded the Navy Achievement three times, the Vietnamese Meritorious Unit Citation for Civil Action w/Palm, Vietnam Unit Citation Gallantry Cross w/Palm, Navy Unit Citation, President's Unit Citation, Vietnam Service w/ 4 Bronze Stars and the Fleet Marine Emblem, National Defense w/Bronze Star, the Battle E, Vietnam Campaign and the Silver Star for Gallantry in Action. He was in the documentary film *50 Years of the Navy Seabees*.

He lives with his wife, Linda, and his 13 year old daughter, Megan, on a farm in southern Indiana near Hardinsburg. He just retired from teaching this year. He is a life member of the Naval Enlisted Reserve Assoc., charter life member of Veterans of the Vietnam War and life member of Navy Seabee Veterans of America, Island X-1 of Indiana. Treasure of Indiana.

He loves outdoors and farming. His family are members of Valeene Christian Church where he is serving as elder. He and Linda enjoy teaching Bible School. Their daughter, Megan, raises chickens and registered quarter horses. He has a Seabee picnic the last Saturday of August each year. All Seabees welcome.

PHILLIP J. NEWMAN, PhM1/c, enlisted in the USN July 17, 1941, at the Fargo Bldg., Boston, MA, at 21. After boot camp at the Newport, RI Naval  Base and graduating from Hospital Corps School and Dental School, he did a tour of duty at the Naval Hospital in Newport, RI, in November 1941. On July 17, 1942, he was one of the first PhM assigned to the new Sampson Naval Training Base in Geneva, NY, for a tour of duty.

In September 1943 he was transferred to Camp Peary in Williamsburg, VA, to be assigned as a PhM3/c dental technician to the 133rd NCB, commissioned Sept. 17, 1943, and became known as "The Rainmaker Bn." In September 1943 the 133rd went to Camp Endicott, RI, then in November 1943 they went to Camp Holliday in Gulfport, MS, then on to Port Hueneme, CA, in February 1944, all for advanced training.

The 133rd left Hueneme in April 1944 arriving at the NAS Honolulu, HI, in May 1944. Completing their construction assignments they were sent to the Isle of Maui where they joined the 4th Marine Div. for jungle training. Boarding ships, soon after, they headed north and on Feb. 19, 1945, they began the invasion of Iwo Jima, Japan, where they manned a beach evacuation station after they lost their two medical doctors, dentist and chaplain, to a Japanese mortar. The war ended in August 1945 and after eight months on Iwo Jima he was shipped back to the Fargo Bldg., Boston, MA, for honorable discharge.

After discharge he entered the field of finance and banking, working up to management positions. The last 16 years he worked at local credit unions; then he retired. He is married to Pat and they have four children and three grandchildren. He is a member of the Sampson WWII Veterans Assoc., the Survivors of Iwo Jima, and the Seabee Veterans of America.

DONALD E. NICHOLSON, SF3/c, USN, enlisted in the service Feb. 3, 1943, at Broad Street, New York City. Military locations and stations were Camp Lejeune, NC; Camp Pendleton, CA; Marshall Islands, Matiana Islands-Saipan, Tinian.

He was awarded the Navy Presidential Unit Citation, Asiatic-Pacific Medal w/3 Battle Stars, Korea w/US Army, Bronze Star w/OLC and Korean Service Medal w/4 Battle Stars. Discharged Feb. 5, 1946, at Lido Beach, Long Island, NY. Highest rank held: Army, Korea, Major, AUS (Ret).

Memorable experiences in NSVA: assaults on Namur Island, Saipan and Tinian; living in shanty town on Tinian and seeing the B-29s land on an airfield constructed by the 121st NCB.

Civilian activities as president of Nicholson Sprinkler Corp.; president of Security Fire Protection Co., Ohio; and life member National Fire Protection Assoc. His first wife, Mary Sue Quigg, is deceased. His sec-

ond wife is Jane Esselman Hientjes. Nicholson has seven children and four grandchildren.

ANTONIO NOBREGA JR., CM3/c, inducted into the service July 6, 1944, at Boston, MA. Military locations and stations were Sampson, NY NTS; Camp Parks, CA; Guam; Okinawa; 301st NCB Engrs. Transferred one month to 103rd NCB in April 1946.

Awarded the American Theater Medal, Good Conduct Medal, Navy Unit Commendation Medal, Asiatic-Pacific Area w/Battle Star and WWII Victory Medal. Discharged June 14, 1946, at Boston, MA.

After discharge he graduated from business school, worked as bookkeeper for super market, salesman of beverages and retired from Equifax after 34 years as investigator. Widower of Louise. He has been married to Marcia for 12 years. Nobrega has three children: Dennis, Brian and Robert; and five grandchildren: Chad, Brian Jr., Mallory and Samantha Nobrega and Tammy Drew; and one great-grandchild, Brianna King. He is a member of Island X-3, Florida. Active in Boy Scouts of America 43 years as volunteer, past offices of cub master, troop committee, instructor, chairman of activities, camping, advancement, council advancement chairman, executive board member. Volunteer 12 years Charlton Memorial Hospital, Fall River, MA, as patient representative. He is also a VFW and Legion member.

JOSEPH FRANKLIN NOFFSINGER, Yeoman third class, inducted into the service Oct. 26, 1943, at Elkhart, IN. Military locations and stations were Constr. Bn. USNCTC Williamsburg, VA; USNTC Davisville, RI; 12th Naval Constr. Regt. Advance Base Construction Depot, Pearl Harbor, HI; and USNAV Barracks, Washington, D.C.

Awarded the Pacific Theater Ribbon, American Theater Ribbon and Victory Medal. Discharged May 17, 1946, at Bainbridge, MD.

Started his own business in 1953 as Elkhart Camera Center, Inc. Gross sales exceeded one million for a number of years. Average work week is still 50 hours. Having a wonderful time with the new technologies. Avid fan of Thomas Jefferson, he has one room in his house devoted to him, including a commissioned watercolor portrait. Married Esther P. Decker Oct. 4, 1960, and has two children, Joseph Paul and Jan Yrineo, seven grandchil-

dren and six great-grandchildren. Noffsinger is a lifetime member of Navy Seabee Veterans of America.

FRANK J. NOSEK, M2/c, enlisted Oct. 25, 1942, active duty Jan. 4, 1943, assigned to the 83rd USNCB. Trained at Camps Allen and Bradford. Also at Camp Holliday prior to 13 months duty in Trinidad. One accomplishment there was building the Maracas Rd., still in use today. More training at Quonset Point, Camp Parks, Port Hueneme and in Hawaii at Camp Red Hill. From there to the Philippines, Samar, and when the war ended they were sent to China. There he got to visit Tientsin and Peking and the Forbidden City. Also saw the early ravages of the Communist-Nationalist war. Discharged Jan. 26, 1946.

Went back to former employment at Western Electric Co. Retired after 41 years. Married 52 years with two daughters. At present he has been retired 17 years and donates time to repair and rebind books for county libraries and museum.

KENNETH EARL NOWNING, S1/c, born Nov. 9, 1916, in Sioux Rapids, IA. Inducted into the service Oct. 16, 1942, at NRS Des Moines, IA. Military locations and stations were Davisville, RI, 62nd Naval Constr. Bn., USNH Aiea Heights, TH, USH Oakland, CA. Discharged Feb. 15, 1945, at USNH Philadelphia, PA.

Married to C. Marie and has one son, Mark L. and one stepson, James A. Hinckley. Nowning is now in health care for Alzheimer's. His hobbies were flying, hiking and reading. He is a DAV.

WILLIAM ROBERT OSBORNE JR., MM3/c, inducted into the service in August 1944 at Manchester, NH. Boot camp at Sampson, NY. Transferred to Seabees and trained at Camp Parks, Pleasanton, CA, to Thermal, CA, to Port Hueneme, to Okinawa and China.

Awarded the Good Conduct Medal, Asiatic-Pacific Campaign Medal and American Theater Medal. Discharged at the Fargo Bldg., Boston, MA, in July 1946.

Memorable experiences: Served with CBMU-625 on Okinawa and 96th NCB in Tsingtao, China.

After service went back to high school and graduated in 1947 in Concord, NH. Moved to Connecticut in 1950, to California in 1952, and back to Connecticut in 1954. Retired in 1954 as caterpillar tractor dealer.

Married Elizabeth May Ferris Aug. 27, 1950. They have four children: Gary, Gregory, Jan and Judy; and eight grandchildren: Justin, Jason, Dan, Allison, Kyle, K.C., Katlyn and Samantha.

JOHN G. OWEN, MoMM3/c, enlisted in the USN in July 1942 at age 17. Went through boot camp with 31st Bn. in Davisville, RI. Afterwards he was assigned to the 53rd NCB.

Took Marine training at New River, NC. Shipped to California and later sailed to New Caledonia. Served at Guadalcanal and

Bougainville on D-Day. Back to Guadalcanal then Guam on D-Day.

After 26 months overseas shipped back to the States for 30 day leave, then back to Davisville, RI, then to California. War was over in couple of months. Shipped to Memphis, TN, for discharge. After discharge he worked for the railroad as locomotive engineer for 40 years. Retired from railroad in 1986.

Met and married Bonnie in 1958. She passed away in 1991.

Met and married Frances in 1996. They are enjoying their retirement years together.

THOMAS M. PAGLIA, SWCS, born Aug. 14, 1924, in Rochester, NY. Attended Mt. Carmel School; graduated Edison Technical and Industrial High School, two years Rochester Institute of Technology (mechanical and electrical engineering). Inducted into the service July 20, 1943. Original Seabee, retired after 40 years with eight and one-half years active duty and the rest reserve time. Training at Camp Peary, VA; CBMU-547; 138th Naval Constr. Bn.; Aleutian Island - Attu, Adak, Tanga; Island of Cuba; Davisville, RI; Quoddy Village, ME; Gulfport, MS; RNMCB-13; MCRTC-Rochester, NY; PC-1208; Rec. Station Brooklyn, NY; 3rd Naval HQ; CB Div. 3-13; LCS 3-1. Active duty 1943-46; 1949-52. Retired Aug. 14, 1984.

Retired from Monroe County Pure Waters as supervisor of electrical operations with 27 years. President of Electrical Installations, Inc., with a master electrician license.

Married to Cora, with four children, one stepdaughter, five grandsons, two step-grandsons, one granddaughter and one great-granddaughter.

Current activities: Membership in Island X, Buffalo, NY; Moose #113; American Legion; Police and Fire Square Club; life member, Orient Chapter #79, Royal Arch Masons Toronto, Canada; Damascus Shrine Temple; life member, Hiram Chapter #62, Royal Arch Masons; Rochester Consistory Scottish Rite; Monroe Masonic War Veterans; volunteer, VA Medical Center, Canandaigua, NY; and Executive Board, VA Medical Center, Canandaigua, NY.

Association recognition: Past master, Charlotte Lodge #1088, Rochester, NY; past grand lodge Masonic representative from state of Illinois to the state of New York; past thrice potent master, Scottish Rite, Rochester, NY; Masonic Service Award, Red Cap, Scottish Rite; past high priest, Hiram Chapter #62, Royal Arch Masons, state of New York, 1995 and 1997; Award of Recognition from the Board of Governors, Frank and Betty Paul, Scottish Rite Masons; Award of Appreciation from the Grand Lodge of Masons, state of New York; and upstate coordinator for the Grand Lodge, state of New York, for the Masonic Service Assoc. at the VA Medical Center, Canandaigua.

RICHARD A. PARKER, EQCM, USN (Ret), enlisted in Arizona in 1952. Duty stations were NRTC San Diego; NCBD-1509; NMCB-9; NMCB-3; NMCB (Special); NMCB-1; NAF Brown Field; NMCB-7; Antarctic Support Activities; CBC Port Hueneme; NMCB-40; NCBU-201; NMCB-1; NAVSCOLCONST Davisville; NMCB-1 (as command master chief); NAS Brunswick (as Seabee division officer); NMCB-3 (as command master chief); and RNMCB-12 (as drill site supervisor).

Awards include two Navy Achievement Medals, Combat Action Ribbon, three Navy Unit Commendations, two Meritorious Unit Commendations, seven Good Conduct Medals, Antarctica Service Medal and Vietnam Service Medal w/5 Campaign Stars and Fleet Marine Clasp. Transferred to Navy Retired List in 1982.

Married to the late Louise (Carty) Parker, he has six children and nine grandchildren.

A life member of the Navy Seabee Veterans of America and a charter member of Island X-1, Davisville, he was on the NCBC Davisville advisory committee for the Seabee 50th anniversary program in 1992. He was vice commander in 1994-95 and commander of Island X-1, Davisville from 1995 to the present time. As commander he signed the lease with the state of Rhode Island creating the Seabee Memorial Park, at the Chapel in the Pines at the former base at Davisville.

WILLIAM OVID PATRICK, joined Seabees in Waco, TX, July 26, 1942. Traveled by train to Davisville, RI. After boot camp training shipped to Bermuda with 31st USNCB. Worked 11 months and then back to Rhode Island. Joined 65th for a while and then 28th to Scotland and England. Spent weeks assembling Rino barges for invasion.  Traveled across channel by Rino barge and witnessed a Hell he will never forget. Thanks to the big battle ships' support, he is here today.

They were the second wave going in on bloody Omaha. They worked cleaning up beaches and getting equipment and troops on shore, setting up Navy HQ in Cherbourg and Le Havre. Then back to the States.

Shipped out from California to Okinawa. Worked endless hours hauling cargo. Received Presidential Citation. Went home on point system and was honorably discharged at Camp Wallace, TX, Oct. 30, 1945.

Life member at large #1776; active in Island X-1, Vermont; and Island X-1, Sea Coast; NH memorial; Navy Seabee Veterans of America.

His wife, Jean, passed away May 13, 1999. He has three children: Alan, Arnold and Ward; and two grandchildren, Alan D. and Ellen E. Active 40+ years as construction superintendent and general contractor building schools, hospitals and banks.

WILLIAM G. PETTUS, enlisted in the USN June 18, 1943. He was assigned to the 109th NCB after training at Camp Peary, Williamsburg, VA. After further training at Camp Endicott, RI, and Camp Parks, CA, he sailed from Port Hueneme, CA, on November 22 and arrived at Pearl Harbor on December 5. From there he sailed on January 22 to land with the second wave of Marines from the Fourth Div. in the invasion of Roi-Namur in the Marshall Islands.

On the night of February 12 Japanese bombers hit his tent area and detonated an adjacent ammunition dump in a humongous explosion that leveled Roi Island, killed many men including three from the 109th Bn., and wounded many more.

Pettus subsequently served on Guam in the construction of a submarine base until the end of the war. He was discharged March 22, 1946, with the rating of CM3/c. He was married March 22, 1947, to Arline Cash and they have one son, Bill Jr.

Pettus earned a BS degree in physics from Lynchburg College and a PhD degree in physics in 1956 from the University of Virginia where he served as instructor in physics and where he was elected to Phi Beta Kappa. He also served as instructor in physics at Lynchburg College for one year during this period. After receiving his PhD from University of Virginia, he worked in reactor physics and space nuclear power research at the Babcock & Wilcox Critical Experiment Laboratory in Lynchburg. He also participated in fusion research at the Princeton Plasma Physics Laboratory and was visiting professor of physics for one quarter at Virginia Polytechnic Institute and State University. He holds eight U.S. patents in various fields including a device currently under consideration at the University of Virginia Medical Center for brain tumor surgery and radiation therapy.

CHARLES WHITCOMB PHILLIPPE, M2/c(T), born Sept. 3, 1923, in Frankfort, IN. Enlisted in the Seabees Aug. 12, 1942, active duty Oct. 8, 1942. Basic training at Norfolk, VA. Shipped to Port Hueneme with 44th CB.

Sent overseas to New Hebrides then to Admiralties with 5th CR, New Caledonia Dec. 12, 1944, Pearl Harbor Jan. 10, 1945, assigned HQ COM CONST Troops invasion of Okinawa. Home on 30 day leave and Japan surrendered.

Spent the last three months as instructor on rifle range at Port Hueneme.

Awarded the Asiatic-Pacific Medal w/2 Bronze Stars, Victory Medal and Good Conduct Medal. Discharged at Great Lakes, IL, Dec. 22, 1945.

Went to work for General Tele. Co. March 5, 1945. Was promoted into management and held various positions in that capacity. Retired March 31, 1981.

Married Letha Cutler June 9, 1946, and has three children, eight grandchildren and one great-grandchild.

He was youth director of the Izaak Walton League and a past president; life member and past commander for two years of VFW; Elks member 42 years; Moose member 23 years; president, Men's Club United Methodist Church; and presently chaplain of Island 16 Seabees of America.

JACK E. PHILLIPS, entered the USN in July 1944, G Unit, Co. 547, Sampson NTC. Arrived Camp Parks, CA, in October 1944 for advanced training. Assigned to 36th NCB, Co. C in November and left San Francisco Feb. 2, 1945, aboard the *Cape Douglas*.

Arrival at Hawaii delayed by ship breakdowns; off loaded to Monaloa Ridge Camp on 28th. Left Honolulu on Dutch ship, *Tabinta*, March 9, off loading at Saipan on 23rd. After transferring to HQ Co., left Saipan on LST-820 landing at Gushikawa, Okinawa April 18. Participated in construction of Marine airstrip at Awashi. Weathered typhoons in September and October. Left 36th NCB and Okinawa in January 1946 onboard USS *Ticonderoga* arriving Seattle, WA. Separated from Navy at Sampson as Cox(T) Jan. 30, 1946.

Phillips is married to Mary F. Testani and they have six children and 10 grandchildren. He was employed at BNL as an engineer for 35 years. He is a member of 36th NCBA, SWW2VA and life member of Navy Seabee Veterans of America and VFW.

EDWARD B. PRICE, SF2/c, 92nd NCB, inducted in April 1943 at Houston, TX. Military locations and stations were Camp Peary, Camp Endicott via Port Hueneme to Red Hill, Oahu, HI, and Tinian Island, Marianas. Honorably discharged in December 1945 at Hitchcock, TX.

Attended Sam Houston State College (University), Huntsville, TX, and graduated with BBA degree in 1949. Met Peggy Jo Baynes, also a 1948 graduate Sam Houston State University, and they celebrated 50 years of married life May 25, 1998. They have three sons: Gary (1952-97), Joe (b. 1954) and Robert (b. 1956); wonderful daughters-in-law: Bobbi, Mary and Alexa; and four grandchildren: James, Bradley, Heather and Lauren.

Worked 37 years in oil industry (10 years in Tripoli, Libya). Retired from Mitchell Energy, Woodland, TX, in April 1986. Presently resides in Bellaire, TX.

Life member Navy Seabee Veterans of America, Island X-13, Pensacola, FL and member, CEC/Seabee Historical Foundation, Inc., Gulfport, MS.

Attended Seabee Museum opening in Gulfport and more recently, 50th Anniversary Navy Seabee Veterans of America National Convention and Reunion in August 1998 in Biloxi, MS.

RUSSELL NORMAN PRICE, SF2/c, enlisted in the Navy Seabees Jan. 4, 1943, in Philadelphia, PA. He was drill instructor at Davisville Station Force, RI, and he also was instructor of the rifle range Sun Valley, RI. While stationed there he attended Brown University in Providence, RI. He served with 129th Seabees in Honolulu, HI, and with 126th CB (armory, rigger and cable splicer).

He received the Pacific Theater Ribbon, Good Conduct Ribbon and Victory Ribbon. After service he became an ironworker with Local 451, Wilmington, DE, where he and his family settled. He successfully passed the National Competency test for welding in 1974. He was an ironworker apprentice training instructor. He attended DelTech Community College, Penn State University, Delaware State University and graduated from University of Delaware with a BS degree in vocational education. After 38 years as a structional ironworker he became a welding teacher at Howard High School in Wilmington, DE, and taught courses at Del Tech Community College, Stanton, DE. He was erection foreman on the bridge in Lisbon, Portugal.

He has been president Local 451 Credit Union and an elected board member of Local 451 Annuity. He has been a member of Civilian Military Training Corps, cross training teacher for skilled mechanics, a volunteer building schools in Vietnam. He has a library named after him in Baguio City, Philippines and he has made six trips around the world, three of them on container ships.

Married 52 years to Terri (McGlade) and they have five children: Leslie, Robin, Tina, Brian and Lisa; and eight grandchildren.

DONALD JOHN PRIOR, E-3, inducted into the service Nov. 15, 1960, NRSURDIV 1-36(M), Pawtucket, RI. Military locations and stations were Davisville, RI; Roosevelt Roads, PR; and Guantanamo Bay, Cuba. Discharged Nov. 14, 1966, USNR Div. 11-17, Long Beach, CA.

He entered the USNR when he was a high school senior and completed his basic training during their spring vacation at Great Lakes. After graduating from Wentworth in Boston he went active for two years with MCB-7 at Davisville, RI. While he was at Guantanamo manning the fence line, the Cuban soldiers constantly gave them problems. One night while on duty a Cuban soldier shot a flaming arrow over the fence and started a brush fire. While their fire crew was putting it out, the Cuban soldiers were laughing at their efforts.

Civilian activities: vice president of Anderson Nelson Engineering firm. Former chairman of Scottsdale Planning Commission; former vice mayor of the city of Scottsdale, AZ; current president of Papago Truckers, Preserve Military Bases; commander of Arizona Road Runner Island X.

Married to Barbara Ann (Peters) Prior and has three children: Liana, Eric and Alicia.

ERNEST PUIG, BM1/c, inducted into the service Oct. 6, 1943. Military locations and stations were NRS Sampson, NY; NCTC Williamsburg, VA; NTC Quoddy Village, ME; NCTC Davisville, RI; CBRD Camp Parks, CA; ABCD Pearl Harbor, HI; 301st NCB; and PSC Lido Beach, NY.

Awarded the Asiatic-Pacific Medal, American Theater Medal, Navy Unit Citation and Victory Medal. Discharged in March 1946 at Lido Beach, Long Island, NY.

Memorable experiences: Okinawa, sinking of tug, *Zephyr*, three typhoons, time aboard YM-20.

Civilian Activities: Operating Engineers Local 15, New York (1951) and excavating company from 1960-94. Married to Agnes and has three children: Ernest, William and Lisa; and eight grandchildren. Puig is a life member of Navy Seabee Veterans of America, Island X-2, Long Island, NY.

EARL L. PURSELL, Coxswain, inducted into the service Sept. 2, 1944, at USNTC Sampson, NY. Military locations and stations were 20th CB Constr. Bn. Unit #521, 79th CB, 135th CB and 14th CB.

Awarded the Pacific Theater Ribbon, American Theater Ribbon and Victory Medal. Discharged May 13, 1946.

Memorable experiences: One great outfit. They taught him a lot.

He is retired from Perkasie Power and Light. Married to Katherine B. and has three children: Rodney, Norene and Nadine; and four grandchildren: Gurney and Una Barett and Erik and Andy Pursell.

LAVERN PYLES JR., Cdr., CEC, USN (Ret), volunteered as an officer in the Navy Reserves in 1942. Upon receiving a BS degree in civil engineering from Clemson University assigned to Naval indoctrination at University

of Arizona. Assigned to duty for ship repair and overhaul operations at Philadelphia, New Orleans and Pearl Harbor.

Received a regular commission in the Navy Civil Engineer Corps in 1946. Served Public Works, ROCC and Bureau duties before assignment as operations officer of MCB-7. Led advanced party for battalion deployment to relieve MBC-4 at Port Lyautey, French Morocco. As a ringer, pitched for MCB-4 officer's ball team to beat the chief's 11 to 4.

Reassigned to MCB-6 with many deployed detachments from Shelburne Nova Scotia, Grand Turks to Rame, PR on Projects Caesar, Naval Hydrographic Research Projects Atlantic. As executive officer deployed to Antigua, British West Indies with initial detachment to construct the battalion camp and staging area at former WWII Army Cleveland Air Base.

Became commanding officer of Seabee training at Naval Schools, Construction (NavSCon) at Port Hueneme. Established ACDUTRA "Unit Training" for Seabee Reserve Units starting with NRCB Div. 11-10, San Bernardino and NRCB Divs. 11-5 and 11-19, Phoenix. Reserve units also participated in the Base Regimental Review Parades. This program later led to "Mobilization Reserve CB Battalion Training."

Retired in 1967. Worked as engineer-in-private practice as vice president of Total Engineering, Inc. Was elected as member of Commonwealth of Pennsylvania's House of Representatives and served as administrative officer in the Dept. of General Services' Public Works.

Was married to the late Evelyn Mae Vollmer of Philadelphia, has three children and four grandchildren; married to the late Audrey Fosdick Rinde-Thorsen of Long Island with three stepchildren.

He is a life member-at-large of Navy Seabee Veterans of America Island MCB-7.

RICHARD RADEI, EO1/c, inducted into the service in May 1979 at Hartford, CT. Military locations and stations were NMCB-12, Hartford, CT; 21st NCR, Davisville, RI; CRUITCOR VI, Norwich, CT; NMCB-5, Port Hueneme, CA; and 31st NCR, Port Hueneme, CA.

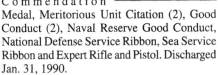

Awarded the Recruiting Badge w/3 Gold Wreaths, Navy Commendation Medal, Meritorious Unit Citation (2), Good Conduct (2), Naval Reserve Good Conduct, National Defense Service Ribbon, Sea Service Ribbon and Expert Rifle and Pistol. Discharged Jan. 31, 1990.

Memorable experiences: The monthly meetings of Navy Seabee Veterans of America, Island X-1, Davisville, RI, at Bickfords Restaurant in Warwick, RI, and sharing stories and experiences.

Civilian activities include graduating with honors from University of California, Santa Barbara; stock car racing; and doing volunteer work for Seabee Memorial Park at Davisville, RI.

Married Phyllis Sept. 21, 1974, and has four children: Julia, Clayton, Stephanie and Marilyn.

MELVIN D. "MEL" RAMIGE, USN Seabee, born Nov. 22, 1934, in Peoria, IL. Graduated from East Peoria High School in 1952, attended Bradley University and the University of Illinois. Married Rosemary in 1956 and has four children and four grandchildren.

Worked at Caterpillar for four years, did construction work for two years, then worked at Komatsu Dresser Co. for 32-1/2 years, retiring in 1995 as chief engineer, mechanical drive trucks.

Enlisted in the Navy Reserves in February 1953. Spent 31-1/2 years in Navy Seabee Reserves with RNMCB-25, made BUC in February 1964, BUCS in August 1969 and WO1/c in December 1969. Retired in October 1984 as CWO4/c.

Active in the Navy Seabee Veterans of America, serves as secretary, Island X-4, Peoria, IL; secretary, Dept. of Illinois; and National secretary since 1989. Previously served as Dept. of Illinois commander (1979-81), North Carolina District vice commander (1979-80), National vice commander at large (1980-81) and life membership chairman (1988-91).

CHARLES S. READDY, UT1/c, inducted into the service at Augusta, GA, in November 1952. Began active duty at Treasure Island, San Francisco, CA, in 1957. Military locations and stations: South Pacific (all over).

Readdy earned the usual medals. Discharged in 1960 at Augusta, GA.

He is married to Lynn and has two children, Debra Smith and Robert C., and three grandchildren: Amanda Smith and Aaron and Jenifer Readdy.

PAUL F. REGER, CM2/c, inducted into the service March 29, 1967, at Anchorage, AK. Military locations and stations were Port Hueneme, San Diego, Da Nang, Phu Loc and Kodiak.

Awarded the National Defense Service Medal, Vietnam Campaign Medal (two tours) and Southeast Asia Medal. Discharged Sept. 1, 1970, at Kodiak, AK.

Memorable experiences: TET Offensive 68, Da Nang (Freedom Hill), convoys to Phu Bai after TET, convoys to Liberty Bridge, building little yellow car at Phu Loc.

Civilian activities include being in the garage business for 15 years and commercial fishing (set net, west side of Cook Inlet), build-

ing and flying airplanes and owns and operates a sawmill.

He is married to Theresa and has three children: Dennis (30), Doug (24) and Richard (21).

JAMES SYLVESTER REYNOLDS, Coxswain third class, born Nov. 4, 1923, in Ozark, AL. Inducted into the service in October 1943 at Detroit, MI. Military locations and stations were Camp Peary, Williamsburg, VA; Port Hueneme, CA; Harbor Noumea; Milne Bay; Finschhafen in New Guinea; and finally, Admiralty Islands (Manus).

Awarded a service medal-ribbon for service in a war zone. Discharged Dec. 7, 1945, at Great Lakes, IL.

Memorable experiences: Loading/transferring needed cargo, meeting people from various states and seeing a ship blow up in the harbor of Manus Island.

Married 51 years with 7 children, 18 grandchildren and 10 great-grandchildren. Since moving from Michigan to Mulberry, FL, after 36 years of employment at Chrysler Corp., he now does voluntary work at a food bank, church related activities and is vice commander of Island X-2, Lakeland, FL. He enjoys swapping war stories (scuttlebutt) with the 1,141 men of Co. B, Manus Island. Would like to hear from them.

ALBERT G. RICHARDSON SR., EOCS (Ret), inducted into the service in January 1946. Military locations and stations were Det. 1516, Roosevelt Roads, PR; London, England; Port Lyutey, FM; Korea; Spain; and many other places. Retired in January 1976.

Civilian activities as business agent Local 545 IUOE, Syracuse, NY. Married to Ruth Egan Richardson and has two sons, Albert G. Jr. and Kevin M., and one grandson, Albert G. III.

EUGENE T. RICKER JR., born May 10, 1927, in Biddeford, ME. Inducted into the service July 28, 1944, at Boston, MA. Military locations included NCT Sampson, NY; trained at Davisville, RI; shipped to Hawaii; Okinawa with 81st NCB; Guam to 25th NCB; 109th NCB; and 133rd NCB.

Awarded the American Campaign Medal, Asiatic-Pacific Medal w/star, World War II Victory Medal and National Defense Service Medal. Discharged June 14, 1946, at Boston, MA.

After discharge as SF3/c went to school in St. Johns, Newfoundland and New Rochelle, NY. Re-entered USN in 1948. Served on USS *Pres. Hayes* (AP-20) until decommissioned in 1949. Shipped to Guam until 1950. After discharge from this tour of duty went to Butte, MT, and became an apprentice plumber and was certified as a journeyman plumber in 1955. At that time the opportunity to become a firefighter with the federal government was presented to him. He accepted the offer and became a firefighter at NAS Pensacola, FL (1955-65). Transferred to NAVWEPSTA, Charleston, SC, and became fire chief of NWS Charleston, SC (1965-80). Retired as fire chief in 1980.

Married to WWII veteran "Zee" Halford PM2/c, USN, in 1949 (from Butte, MT). Had three children, eight grandchildren and one great grandchild.

They live on a lake in upstate South Carolina and enjoy boating, fishing and traveling occasionally.

MELVIN "J" ROBERTS, CM3/c, born Feb. 15, 1927, in Corvalis, OR. Inducted into the USN Dec. 15, 1944, at Eugene, OR, later transferred to Seabees 86th and 103rd. Military locations and stations were San Diego, Camp Shoemaker, Okinawa, Guam, Eniwetok and Treasure Island.

Awarded the Asiatic-Pacific Campaign Medal. Discharged July 20, 1946, at Shoemaker, CA.

Memorable experiences: Went through the typhoon on Okinawa, built runways on Okinawa and put up the experimental test towers for the A Bomb.

Married to Leona in 1951 and has three children and two grandchildren. He was in the Reserves for eight years. Roberts is now retired and enjoys traveling.

JOHN ALDEN ROGERS, CM1/c, inducted into the service Nov. 25, 1942, recruiting station, Raleigh, NC. Military locations and stations were Camp Peary, VA; Camp Endicott, Davisville, RI; Camp Holladay, Gulfport, MS; and Camp Rousseau and Port Hueneme, CA.

Awarded the American and Asiatic Campaign Ribbons, one star for campaign in New Guinea, one star for Admiralty Islands Campaign and a third star for the Ryukyus engagement. Discharged Nov. 11, 1945, at Camp Pendleton, Norfolk, VA.

Memorable experiences: Became unable to drive, so didn't attend very many meetings, Island X-14, Leesburg, FL. The first printed materials from Seabee Veterans of America told of his battalion holding a reunion in Port Hueneme, CA. Got on the stick and attended.

Civilian activities include Masons, Rotary Club, active for years in Boy and Girl Scout work, aided in founding a new Methodist church, active there until hearing went bad.

Married Billie Jarve Vogler March 2, 1946, and has two children, Jarve Vogler and John Alden Jr., and four grandchildren: Christina Cabezas, John Alden III, Ramona Alden Cabezas and Elena Cabezas.

HARRY E. ROLLER, LCDR CEC, USNR (Ret), member of the 5th Det. Constr. Bn. of the Seabees. Destination: Wallis Island, 13° south of Equator on the international date line. This island was three miles by seven miles. Their job was to build one of the first airfields. He is now 86 years of age and resides in Mount Vernon, WA.

ROBERT J. ROMAN, born Dec. 15, 1942, at Barberton, OH. Inducted into the service Oct. 31, 1961, at San Diego, CA. Military locations and stations were Guantanamo Cuba, Argentina, Newfoundland, Rota Spain and Las Vegas, NV.

Awarded the Good Conduct Medal, Cuban Crisis Medal and Vietnam Campaign Medal. Discharged Feb. 28, 1968, at Las Vegas, NV. Memorable experience: Cuba crisis.

He is married to Charlotte Ann and has three children: Dr. Dan Roman, Denise Ann and Dawn Marie; and one grandson, Simon Robert. Current activities include crane operator for H.A. Selinsky Inc. (mover of heavy machinery), Local 18 Operating Engineers, Cleveland, OH. E-mail address is broman@akron5.neo.lrun.com.

RALPH T. ROWLAND, of Cheshire, CT, was born in Elizabeth, NJ, in 1920 and graduated from New Rochelle, NY, high school in 1937. Before WWII he studied engineering, then worked in construction and on design of YMS-class minesweepers. He enlisted in the Seabees in November 1942 as MM2/c, trained at Camp Peary, Davisville, Gulfport and Port Hueneme.

He served with the 78th Bn. in New Caledonia, New Guinea, the Admiralties and Okinawa. Promoted to chief in 1945. Married to Bernice since 1946; they have four children and eight grandchildren. Studied architecture and became an architect after the war, practiced 45 years and retired in 1997.

Long active in professional societies at state and national levels; also in various chambers of commerce, parish councils and local government. President of the original 78th Seabees Assoc. in 1953-55, now a life member of the successor organization. Wrote script for video history of the 78th Bn. produced in 1995. Life member of VFW. Member of Constitution Island X-6, Massachusetts.

JOSEPH "JOE RUBIN, Electrician's Mate 3/c, inducted into the service Oct. 25, 1943, at Providence, RI. Military locations and stations were USNCTC, Williamsburg, VA; Naval Constr. Bn. Training Center, Camp Lejeune, New River, NC; and 14th USNCB Camp Parks, CA.

Awarded the Victory Medal, American Area Medal and Asiatic-Pacific Campaign Medal. Discharged March 26, 1946.

Rubin is a member of Seabee Veterans of America, Island X-1, Las Vegas, NV. Married to Doris and has one daughter, Andrea Hannah.

MICHAEL ANGELO RUTIGLIANO, CM2/c, enlisted in the USN at New York City, Nov. 25, 1942. At Camp Peary, VA, boot with the 81st Bn. Sent to Davisville, RI, to school. Then into the 54th Bn., then to 103rd Bn. to Lido Beach, Long Island, NY. Arrived at Port Hueneme in October 1944. Departed Hueneme in December to Pearl Harbor. Left Pearl for Guam, arriving in December. Still on Guam when the war ended in 1945. Arrived in Frisco Dec. 2, 1945.

Awarded the Good Conduct Medal, Victory Medal, American Theater Medal and Asiatic-Pacific Campaign Medal. (Excellent work award while temporary duty with the 40th Naval Constr. Regt. on Guam). Discharged at Lido Beach, Long Island, NY, Dec. 15, 1945.

All the conventions in Florida and Biloxi, MS, were happy, memorable experiences for him and his wife.

He put in 26 years as a letter carrier, then retired. Went to St. Petersburg, FL, and spent 10 years as a city building inspector. Again retired. Married Shirley S. Sisson of Connecticut July 3, 1943, and has three children: Andrea, Bradley and Michelle; and two grandchildren, Christine and Andrew. He is now completely retired in Florida He is a member of X-8, Ft. Myers, FL.

GINO RICHARD SACCHETTI, CCM, inducted into the service Aug. 6, 1943, at Boston, MA. Military locations and stations were Camp Peary, Williamsburg, VA; Davisville, RI; shipped out of Davisville down East Coast to Panama Canal to Hawaii; then to Kwajalein Island, Marshall Islands.

Awarded the WWII Victory Medal, Asiatic-Pacific Theater Medal and American Theater Medal. Discharged in December 1945 at Fargo Bldg., Boston, MA.

Memorable experiences: They, the 141st CB Bn., were on their way to the invasion of Okinawa, while at sea with a great armada of ships and halfway to Okinawa they were pulled out and sailed to the island of Kwajalein-Marshall Islands to complete a B-29 bomber air strip. The island had then been secured. They set up a tent city for all of their troops, etc.

Civilian activities: Graduate of high school-vocational technical Wentworth Institute for architecture and design. After 25 years in the design build for retail and commercial interiors went into his own business of design build for retail and commercial interiors for the next 25 years. Now retired at 81. Married to Ethel T. Sacchetti and has three children: Richard, Arlene and Michael; 14 grandchildren; and 13 great-grandchildren.

ERNEST GERARD SALVAS, CM3/c, inducted into the service Dec. 5, 1944, at NRS New Haven, CT. Military locations and stations were NTS Sampson, NY; NCTC Davisville, RI; 126th NCB; 8th USNC Bde.; and 125th NCB.

Awarded the WWII Victory Medal, American Theater Medal, Asiatic-Pacific Theater Medal w/Bronze Star and Unit Commendation. Discharged June 18, 1946, at Boston, MA.

Memorable experiences: Went to boot camp at Sampson, NY, transferred to Davisville, shipped out of New Orleans to Hawaii. Then on to the Marshall Islands, Caroline Islands, finally reaching Okinawa and spending one year there.

After discharge went to trade school, later becoming a construction superintendent on the largest Native American Casino in the country. Life member Island 1, Rhode Island. Married to Theresa A. Salvas and has two children, Jacqueline and Linda, four grandsons and two granddaughters.

WILLIAM SCALES, Coxswain, born May 8, 1925, in Eagle Mills, AR. Inducted into the service Oct. 19, 1943, at Little Rock, AR. Military locations and stations were Camp Peary, VA; Camp Holliday, MS; Guadalcanal; Russell Islands; Florida and Tulagi; Kwajalein; Saipan; Eniwetok; Guam; Admiralty Islands; Leyte; New Guinea; Bougainville; Luzon; Samar; Ulithi; Oahu; and Port Hueneme, CA.

Awarded the Asiatic-Pacific Medal w/3 stars, American Theater Medal, Purple Heart, Philippine Liberation Medal w/2 stars and WWII Victory Medal. Discharged April 18, 1946, at Millington NAB, Memphis, TN.

Memorable experiences: Participated in assault landings on Guam, Leyte and Luzon as member of CBD-1039 (Causeways), later part of Co. A, 302nd NCB. Was scheduled to be in first unit ashore in invasion of Japan. Saved by the A Bomb.

After graduation from University of Arkansas in 1949, joined U.S. Army. Married Eleanor Linn and has two children. Retired in Pueblo, CO, as CW2 and presently resides in Pueblo. Retired in July 1997 as a real estate appraiser and is enjoying retirement.

JOSEPH D. SCHOLAR JR., S1/c, born May 28, 1926, in Rome, NY. Inducted into the service Sept. 1, 1944, at Albany, NY. Military locations and stations included "boots" at Sampson, NY; Seabees, Camp Parks, CA; Treasure Island, CA; Lido Beach, NY; Eniwetok and Parry Islands, Marshall Islands; Saipan and Tinian Islands, Marianas Islands; Okinawa Japan, Ryukyu Islands (saw action at Okinawa); and Tsingtao, China.

Awarded the Purple Heart, Combat Action, Meritorious Unit Commendation, China Service Medal, American Campaign Medal, Asiatic-Pacific Campaign Medal, WWII Victory Medal, WWII Occupation Medal, USN Sea Service, USN Overseas Medal, USN Expert Rifle, New York State Conspicuous Service Cross and Navy Unit Commendation. Discharged July 3, 1946, at Lido Beach, NY.

Memorable experiences: Founded Island X-9, Kingston, NY; New York State Navy Seabee Veterans of America commander, elected for two years in 1998.

He has two daughters, two sons, four grandsons, one granddaughter and three great-granddaughters. Current activities: Service officer, Island X-9, Kingston and New York State Navy Seabee Veterans of America; commander, New York State Navy Seabee Veterans of America; service officer, DAV, Ulster County, NY, Post 156; service officer, American Legion Post 950, Ahoenkia, NY; member, Sampson Veterans, CBI and VFW, Kingston, NY.

HENRY F. "BUD" SCHWARZSCHILD, born May 4, 1924, in Havana, Cuba of American parents, and came to the U.S. in 1936 graduating from Baltimore City College in June 1942. He joined the Seabees in October 1943 and took basic at Camp Peary, VA, and advanced training at Port Hueneme, CA.

As a member of the 23rd USNCB Special he participated in the amphibious assaults on

Kwajalein, Eniwetok, Tinian, Saipan, Guam, Iwo Jima and was on Okinawa when the war ended. He was stationed in Pearl Harbor at Iroquois Point, Ewa from December 1943 stevedoring at Ford Island until shipping out near the end of 1944.

He was discharged from Lido Beach Separation Center, Long Island, NY, in February 1946 as yeoman first class. The next two and one-half years were spent at Perry Point Veterans Hospital classified as combat fatigue and receives 10% compensation to date from VA. He has the Asiatic-Pacific Campaign Ribbon w/stars.

After 11 years with Amoco Corp. he founded the Schwarzschild Oil Co. in Baltimore, a successful gasoline and oil jobbership from 1962-89. He married in 1954 and after 37 years, his wife died. They had three children and four grandchildren. He married Wini in 1995. She has two children and three grandchildren. He lives in Baltimore in retirement, traveling, golfing and enjoying life.

ALBERT V. SELLS, CM2/c, born March 16, 1926, in Kent, WA. Enlisted March 8, 1944. Entered Farragut NTC for training. Transferred to the Constr. Bn. Det. 1067 at Camp Parks, CA, in October 1944. He was sent to Port Hueneme, CA, to prepare for embarkation. The detachment was based on Calicoan Island just south of Guiuan, Samar in the Philippines.

After the war was over, he was transferred to the 83rd Bn. at Guiuan and sent to Tanggu, China (near Tientsin and Peking). Completing the work for the Navy GroPac 13, he was transferred to the 32nd Spec. Bn. at Tsingtao, China for repair work on the airfield.

Returned to the States for discharge June 6, 1946. Married "Audrey" and the two have six children and nine grandchildren. A member of the American Legion, Navy Seabee Veterans of America and has held offices in the Junior Chamber of Commerce and the Greater Kent Historical Society. Retired as a battalion chief from the city of Kent Fire Dept. in 1978.

BELA O. SHORT, UTCS, USN (Ret), born Jan. 23, 1925, in Oneida, NY. Inducted into the service Aug. 5, 1943, at Albany, NY. Discharged Dec. 30, 1945, at Lido Beach, Long Island, NY. He later enlisted on Oct. 5, 1950, at Denver, CO.

Military locations and stations were boot camp at Camp Peary, VA, Aug. 5, 1943; advanced training, Camp Parks, CA; NCB-66,

Adak, AK, 1943-44; NCB-66, Okinawa, R.I., 1945; NCB-74, Okinawa, R.I., 1945; CBMU-533, Okinawa, R.I., 1945; CBD-1506 NAS Agana, Guam, M.I., 1950-52; MCB-5, Subic Bay, R.P., 1953-54; USN Station, Subic Bay, R.P., 1955-56; USN Station, Midway Island, T.H., 1956-58; USN Air Station, Alameda, CA, 1958-60; MCB-3 Camp Kubisaki, Okinawa, R.I., 1961-62; USMC Air Facility, Futema, Okinawa, R.I., 1963; MCB-5, Camp Kinser, Okinawa, R.I., 1964; MCB-5, Guam, Chichi Jima, Vietnam (Da Nang), 1964-65; MCB-40, Vietnam Chu Lai, RVN, 1966-67 (second tour); MCB-40 Vietnam Chu Lai, RVN, 1967-68 (third tour), USNAS South Weymouth, MA, 1969; U.S. Naval Facilities Engineering Command, Washington, D.C., 1970-72; USN Nuclear Power School, Ft. Belvoir, VA, 1972; USN Station, Diego Garcia, BIOT, 1973-74; and USN CBC Davisville, RI.

Awarded the Good Conduct Medal (6th award), American Campaign Medal, Asiatic-Pacific Campaign Medal w/2 Bronze Stars, WWII Victory Medal, Navy Occupation Service Medal w/Asia Clasp, National Defense Service Medal, Combat Action Ribbon, Navy Achievement Medal w/Combat "V," Vietnam Armed Forces Meritorious Unit Commendation w/Gallantry Cross, Vietnam Service Medal w/2 Bronze Stars, National Defense Service Medal (2nd award), Armed Forces Expeditionary Medal (Vietnam), Navy Unit Commendation Ribbon (Vietnam) and Expert Pistol Medal. Retired from the service June 15, 1974, at USN CBC Davisville, RI.

Worked overseas for civilian contractors as bulk petroleum superintendent. Totally retired in December 1983. Member U.S. Navy Seabee Veterans of America, MAL.

WILLIAM C. SNEFKEY, born Aug. 19, 1925, in Toledo, OH. BM2/c, Co. D, 32nd Spec. Entered Seabees in November 1943 at Camp Peary, VA. Took stevedore training at Davisville, RI, as a winch driver. Loaded ships at NSD Oakland, CA. Unloaded ships in the Philippines. Then on to Tsingtao, China. Discharged in February 1946.

As fate would have it the six months he spent in Oakland kept him just behind the action. He could hear it in the distance but he did not have to fire a gun. Thus his 25 months in the Seabees was one of the most rewarding times of his life, next to his wife and family. Has been a self-employed public accountant for 52 years. Ready to retire.

Past district commander, VFW. He and his wife, Dorothy, love to travel and enjoy their two daughters, one son and their spouses. Has found one of his buddies since leaving the service. Where are the rest?

GEORGE H. SPAFFORD, S1/c, born Oct. 22, 1926, joined the USN in New York City in September 1944. Was shipped out to Camp Parks, CA, to join the 20th NCB. Then they were shipped out to Saipan with the 20th NCB. Landed on Okinawa in April 1945. When the war was over they were transferred to the 79th NCB.

Awarded the WWII Victory Medal, Asiatic-Pacific Medal and Occupation Medal. Sent home to be discharged June 18, 1946, from Lido Beach, NY.

Worked for the city of New York and is now retired and living in Brewster, NY. Married to Mary M. Spafford and they had seven children: Mary, George, Anne, Margaret, Susan, John and Claire, all are married. They also have 14 grandchildren. Spafford enjoys traveling.

FRED SPEERS, BM2/c, inducted into the service Aug. 14, 1943, at Springfield, IL. Military locations and stations were Camp Peary, VA; Gulfport, MS; Banika Island; and Peleliu Island.

Speers was awarded the Asiatic-Pacific Campaign Medal. Discharged March 7, 1946, at St. Louis, MO.

Memorable experiences: Transformation of Peleliu Island from a backward island to a modern base for the war. Seabees were mostly responsible for this.

Now retired, he owned and operated outdoor advertising (billboard) company for 30 years, Speers Signs. Married to Patricia (47 years) and has two children, Sue and Stuart.

GEORGE W. SPICER, MM2/c, born Feb. 23, 1921, in Norwalk, CT. Enlisted in the Seabees Sept. 21, 1942, in New Haven, CT, at a rating of seaman second class and was placed on inactive duty until Nov. 19, 1942, at which time he reported for active duty to Camp Allen, Norfolk, VA, for boot training.

The 49th Bn. was transferred to Williamsburg, VA, Dec. 18, 1942. On Jan. 6, 1943, the battalion moved to Davisville, RI. On Feb. 25, 1943, the battalion was shipped to Staten Island, NY, for embarkation and arrived in Bermuda Feb. 27, 1943, then on Jan. 18, 1944, the battalion returned to Davisville, RI.

The battalion left Davisville and arrived in Camp Parks, Shoemaker, CA, Sept. 5, 1944. They left Camp Parks for Port Hueneme arriving the next day. On Sept. 12, 1944, the battalion embarked and arrived at Guam Oct. 24, 1944.

The 49th was decommissioned in July 1945 and he was transferred to the 53rd Bn. It was rotated and he was again transferred to the 23rd Bn.

He left Guam Dec. 14, 1945, and arrived at the Separation Center, Lido Beach, Long Island, NY, on Dec. 26, 1945. Reported back and was discharged at a rating of MM2/c.

Awarded the American Theater Medal, Asiatic-Pacific Campaign Medal, Victory Ribbon, Expert Rifleman and Good Conduct Medal.

He now lives in Deltona, FL, with his wife, Mary, and is an active member of the Navy Seabee Veterans of America, X-4, Orlando, FL, and a past commander of the Island. Spicer is now retired and his hobby is radio control model airplanes.

DOUGLAS A. SPLADY, SK3/c, inducted into the service in October 1942 at Minneapolis, MN. Military locations and stations were Camp Allen and Camp Bradford, Norfolk, VA; Camp Peary, Williamsburg, VA; and Port Hueneme, CA. The 2nd Spec. left for Noumea, New Caledonia Feb. 25, 1943, then to Guadalcanal. Next to Guam for D-Day (Co. B) with the 3rd Marines.

Awarded two Unit Commendations and Asiatic-Pacific Medal w/star. Discharged in January 1945 at Great Lakes, IL.

Memorable experiences: Munitions dump explosion at Noumea Nov. 1, 1943, many of the 2nd Spec. were killed. D-Day landing on beach Red One from the USS *Warren* (APA-53).

Civilian activities included sales and marketing with Chrysler Corp. for many years in Minneapolis, Kansas City, Tulsa, Milwaukee and Chicago. Moved back to Minnesota where he had four marinas until retirement. Married to Yvonne and has three children: Charles, Mary and Teri; and seven grandchildren: Jed, Joe, Anna, Jamie, Jacob, Brad and Aaron.

WALTER JAMES STANG, CM3/c, Seabee, born June 25, 1925, in Libertyville, IL. Inducted into the service Aug. 16, 1943, at Chicago, IL. Military locations and stations were Camp Peary, VA, August 1943; Camp Endicott, RI, September 1943; Camp Holliday, MS, October 1943; transferred from 133rd to 135th Bn., Camp Rousseau, CA, April 1944; Moanaloa Ridge, Oahu, HI, May 1944; Tinian, 1944; Okinawa, 1945; shipped home in November 1945; naval armory February 1946 until discharged.

Awarded the Asiatic-Pacific Campaign Medal, American Campaign Medal and Victory Medal. Discharged March 22, 1946, at Great Lakes NTS, Great Lakes, IL.

Stang is a widower with three children, seven grandchildren and two great-grandchildren. Civilian employment as carpenter and in general contracting business from 1946-70; building commissioner, Grays Lake, IL, 1970-91; retired in 1991. Member of Island X-2, Chicago, IL.

GEORGE ARTHUR STAPLES JR., born in Factoryville, PA, July 13, 1942. Entered the service May 26, 1966. Boot camp with Co. 350, Great Lakes. Military locations and stations were PWT NAS Memphis; NSA Da Nang, Republic of Vietnam; ACB-2, Norfolk; CBMU-302 Bien Hoa, Republic of Vietnam; PWT NTC San Diego; MCB-3 Port Hueneme; NCTC Port Hueneme; CBU-417 Whidbey Island; PWT NSA Diego Garcia; PWT NS Adak; ACB-2 Norfolk; NMCB-62 Gulfport; NMCB-1 Gulfport; and CBU-401 Great Lakes.

Awarded Navy Commendation Medal (2) w/"V" Device (1), Navy Achievement Medal (4) w/"V" Device (1), Combat Action Ribbon, Presidential Unit Citation, Joint Meritorious Unit Award, Navy Unit Commendation, Meritorious Unit Commendation (4), Navy "E" Ribbon (2), Good Conduct Award (6), Navy Expeditionary Medal, National Defense Service Medal (2), Vietnam Service Medal w/ Bronze Star, Sea Service Deployment Ribbon (5), RVN Presidential Unit Citation, RVN Gallantry Cross Unit Citation, RVN Civil Actions Unit Citation (First Class), RVN Campaign Medal, Expert Rifleman Medal, Expert Pistol Shot Medal and Enlisted Combat Warfare Insignia. Retired June 30, 1994.

Life member of Seabee Veterans of America, Island X-18, Citrus County, FL, and VFW; and member, American Legion and Fleet Reserve Assoc.

Currently construction manager for Brown and Root Services Corp. Resides in Homosassa, FL, with his wife, the former Nancy Thompson. They have two daughters, Eileen and Valarie, and one son, George III (Buck).

VERNON STAR, CE2/c, born April 9, 1929, in Corsica, SD. Inducted into the service Jan. 16, 1952, at Omaha, NE. Military locations and stations were boot camp, Great Lakes, MI; Electrician's School (three months), Port Hueneme, CA; homeport, MCBI Davisville, RI; electrical work, Guantanamo Bay, Cuba; Argentina, Newfoundland; electrical maintenance.

Awarded the National Defense Service Medal. Star was discharged Jan. 5, 1956, at Brooklyn, NY.

Married to LuVerne and has one son, Jerry, born in Argentina, Newfoundland. Star is now semi-retired and active in the American Legion and other organizations.

LEROY VERNON ST. AUBIN, Coxswain, born Dec. 16, 1918, in Kankakee, IL. Inducted into the service Aug. 14, 1944, at Great Lakes, IL. Served with 37th and 35th NCB. Military locations and stations were Great Lakes, IL; Davisville, RI; and Pearl Harbor, HI.

Memorable experiences: Stevedore and gang leader, Pearl Harbor. He loved serving in the Seabees and says he should have made a career of the Navy.

Awarded the Asiatic-Pacific Campaign Medal and Victory Medal. Discharged Feb. 9, 1946, at Great Lakes, IL.

St. Aubin is married to Violet and has two sons, Darrel Lee (b. 1944) and Rodney (b. 1946). Employed in the trucking business until 1991. He became ill in March 1996 and is now in the VA home in Manteno, IL.

LESTER A. STAY, MoMM3/c, born and educated in Schenectady, NY. Enlisted in October 1944 and sent to Sampson NTS in January 1945, completing basic in April 1945. Took advanced Marine training at Davisville, RI, Seabee Base. Then was sent to Camp Parks, CA. Departed there in July 1945 for Okinawa but was diverted to CBMU-573 in Espiritu Santo, New Hebrides after the surrender of Japan. Then was transferred to CBD-1056 in Noumea, New Caledonia. Then flown to Pago Pago, Samoa. Was then assigned to a ship, the USAT *Howe*-7 as engineman and sailed for Pearl Harbor, HI. Was put aboard a troop ship and sailed for the USA, discharging in August 1946 at Lido Beach, Long Island, NY.

Married to Anna, has one daughter and three grandchildren. Retired from the USPS in October 1987. Hobbies: Amateur radio and life member of ARRL with the call W2LES, scuba, flying and cycling. Past president of Albany Ostomy Assoc.; charter member and past vice commander/treasurer, Island X-10, New York; past knight in Elks; life member of Sampson WWII Vets #758; and life member, Navy Seabee Veterans of America #3050. Presently resides in Clifton Park, NY.

RALPH J. STORTI, CM3/c, born Nov. 30, 1948, in Philadelphia, PA. Enlisted in the USN July 17, 1968, and took basic training in Gulfport, MS.

Assigned to Mobile Constr. Bn. 53 in Davisville, RI. Took advanced training at Camp Lejeune, NC. Shipped out in March 1969 for a tour of duty in South Vietnam.

After being discharged in 1970 Storti went

to work for, and is still employed by, PECO Energy Co. Married to the former Linda Hummel, the couple has two children and now reside in Willow Grove, PA.

Active in veterans organizations, Storti is a past commander and life member of VFW Post 3612, a member of American Legion Post 308, founder and past president of the Mobile Constr. Bn. 53 Alumni Assoc. and the secretary and life member of Navy Seabee Veterans of America Island X-76, Pennsylvania.

ROLAND A. SWANSON, born April 26, 1925, in Jamestown, NY. Entered Navy Seabee service in August 1943 at Buffalo, NY. Following "boot" he received advanced training at Davisville, RI. Shipped out from Gulfport, MS. Member of first replacements for 78th NCB during Admiralty Islands battle. Served on Los Negros, Panama and Manus Islands. Following New Caledonia 78th served on Okinawa constructing Bolo Point airstrip.

Served on USS *Minos*, amphibious repair landing ship, Little Creek, VA, during Korean Conflict.

Employed 22 years with Sears, Roebuck and Co., Sunset Hill Cemetery, also in Jamestown, NY, in sales prior to retiring.

He and wife, Doris, have three children and three grandchildren. Doris is a retired registered nurse.

Active memberships include town of Poland, NY, Seniors; First Lutheran Church, Jamestown; life member, Navy Seabee Veterans of America; former charter member and chaplain, Island X-5, Buffalo, NY; charter member and commander, Island X-11, Chautauqua Region, Jamestown, NY; serving as Dept. New York chaplain since 1993. Named Navy Seabee Veterans of America National Chaplain along with wife as Navy Seabee Veterans of America Auxiliary National Chaplain in 1998.

NORMAN L. SZEWCZYK, S1/c, inducted into the service Oct. 2, 1943, at Detroit, MI. Boot camp at Camp Peary, VA; advance training, Camp Parks, CA (132nd NCB); shipped out of San Francisco to Noumea, New Caledonia. Then to Guadalcanal to join the 4th Spec. NCB. Later transferred to join the 9th Spec. NCB at Munda and Sasavele Islands in New Georgia, Solomons in October 1945. Joined CBD-1056 (Spec.) at Noumea, New Caledonia.

Awarded the American Theater Medal, Asiatic-Pacific Campaign Medal w/star, Victory Medal, two Letters of Commendation (involved in collision of two LCVPs at midnite in channel off Sasavele Island, New Guinea. All hands were rescued).

Self-employed and retired as operator of cab business in Hamtramck, MI. Life member of VFW Post 4404; past commander and past district commander, Dept. of Michigan; member, Island X-4, Navy Seabee Veterans of America, Toledo, OH. Also member of Polish Legion American Veterans Post No. 6, Hamtramck, MI. Szewczyk is single.

JOHN H. TAGGART, raised in Phoenixville, PA. Enlisted in USNCB Nov. 6, 1942, inducted Dec. 28, 1942, Philadelphia, PA. Trained in Camp Bradford, VA; Gulfport, MS; Port Hueneme, CA; then to Aleutians from May 1943-November 1944. Left California in January 1945 to Saipan then to Okinawa in April 1945. Discharged from Bainbridge, MD, as a Y3/c, all the time with the 79th USNCB.

Attended University of Pennsylvania, worked as union plumber/pipefitter until going into business as mechanical contractor from 1962-89. Still active in consulting business but retired at age 75.

Married to Cecilia, has six children, nine grandchildren and two great-grandchildren. Life member, Island X-16, South Hillsborough County, FL, but resides in Collegeville, PA.

Accomplishments in his career he owes to the men of the 79th. He will not forget them and he's grateful for what they taught him both in construction and about life. He was proud to be a Seabee and he salutes you one and all.

FRED TANNER, born Sept. 11, 1923, in Elfrida, AZ. Enlisted in the Navy Seabees, SF3/c, at Bisbee, AZ, in September 1943. Basic training and advanced training at Camp Peary, VA. Their company was sent to Camp Pendleton, CA, now attached to the Marines. Then shipped to Camp Parks in Oakland, assigned to the 13th NCB as a welder. Shipped to Hawaii via Port Hueneme in June 1944. Took part in the construction of John Rogers Airfield before shipping to Tinian arriving in October 1944. The 13th participated in building the world's largest operational air base accommodating B-29 bombers.

Ten months later left for Okinawa leaving their camp to the 509th Composite Group who later dropped the Atomic Bombs. On October

9 a typhoon they named "World War II" hit Okinawa destroying many buildings and all of their tents.

Arrived stateside Christmas Eve 1945. Erma was waiting for him; they married in March 1946. Discharged in April 1946 at San Pedro, CA, MM1/c. They have five wonderful children, seven grandchildren and two great-grandchildren. He owned and operated a heating and cooling business until retirement. Presently serving as vice-commander Southwest Dist. Seabee Veterans of America, member of Island X-3, Tucson, AZ.

JACK C. TANNER, enlisted in the USNCB July 28, 1943, at the age of 17. He was sent to Camp Peary, Williamsburg, VA, for basic training. He was assigned to the 126th USNCB Bn. and sent to Camp Endicott, RI, for advanced construction training and then to Camp Parks, CA, for combat training.

They embarked from Port Hueneme, CA, in February 1944 for the invasion of the Marshall Islands. After completing an air base and other Navy assignments he was transferred to the 110th USNCB Bn. for the invasions of Saipan and Tinian in the Marianas Islands for the construction of B-29 airfields and related construction. He served on a 40mm gun crew through over 100 air raids.

He received the following citations: Asiatic-Pacific Area w/2 stars, American Area, Philippine Liberation Medal, Philippine Independence Medal and American Medal.

FRANK THOMAS, BTCM, enlisted at Newark, NJ, Aug. 24, 1944. Trained at Sampson, NY. Sent to Davisville, RI, for Pontoon-Barge Operation and Truck Driving Schools. Shipped out to Port Hueneme, CA. Their train took 14 days, through 14 states and Canada to reach California. Transferred to 4th NBC (Spec.).

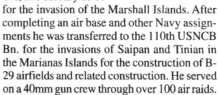

Shipped out on board SS *Wentley*, stopped at Pearl Harbor. Slow ride to Ulithi. Beach party got two cans of coke. Landed Awase, Okinawa, trucked across island to Mochinato. Unloaded ships between air raids. USS *Control* (AM-164) minesweeper entered Buckner Bay with his brother, Lloyd Thomas MoMM1/c aboard. Got a two day pass to see him. Thomas left camp in full battle gear and carbine. Crossed the island to Buckner Bay a ride out on a "M" boat. His brother and other "SNIPS" sitting on the fantail. They saw the boat with a fully armed man coming to his ship. He told

Thomas later they thought that he carried secret orders from Gen. MacArthur. He had to leave after three hours. Storm warning; they went to sea. It was the worst typhoon in 20 years. Wind instruments stopped working after 120 mph. He lost all his gear. The war was over and he was transferred to USS *Alcor* (AD-34). Three months at Sasebo and Yokosuka, Japan. Homeward bound stops at Pearl Harbor, Treasure Island, Panama, Norfolk, VA, Lido Beach, NY. Discharged in June 1946. Enlisted in the Naval Reserves at Port Newark, NJ.

Awarded the American Theater Medal, Asiatic Theater Medal w/star, Victory Medal, Occupation Medal, National Defense Service Medal, Naval Reserve Meritorious Service Medal, Armed Forces Reserve Medal (four awards). Retired Aug. 24, 1987, Naval Reserve Center, Fort Wadsworth, Staten Island, NY, as the command master chief boilerman technician. Was in the naval service for 43 years.

He is retired from the city of Newark Fire Dept. Married to Carole Ann Thomas and has five children: Karen, Kathie, Vikie, Gerrie and Micheal; six grandchildren; and 11 great-grandchildren.

JOHN F. THOMPSON, MM3/c, born Jan. 28, 1918, in Juniata, PA. Inducted into the service in September 1943 at Altoona, PA. Military locations and stations were Camp Peary, Hawaii, Marshall Islands and Tinian (Marianas Islands). Discharged in November 1945 at Bainbridge, MD.

Memorable experiences: Construction work on Pacific Islands.

Married to Eleanor and has one son and two grandchildren. Currently enjoys woodworking. He is a retired trans. supervisor.

CLAY TOUPS, CD3/c, born Feb. 19, 1930, in Thibodaux, LA. Inducted into the service Aug. 5, 1947, at New Orleans, LA. Military locations and stations were USS *Columbus* (CA-74), 1947-50; staff, USN Fleet Sonar School, Key West, FL, 1950-53; and Seabees HD equipment operator, 1953-54.

Awarded the Occupational Service Medal, China Service Medal, National Defense Service Medal, Good Conduct Medal and United Nations Service Medal.

Married to Merle and has four children and seven grandchildren. Toups is a retired automobile salesman. At present he is operating a commercial bingo hall.

GEORGE A. TREANTAFEL, SWC, inducted into the service Nov. 23, 1953, MAARNG; Jan. 15, 1955, Regular Army. Discharged Aug. 3, 1966. Served in the USNR

RNMCB-27 from May 10, 1974-Dec. 31, 1989.

Military locations and stations were Army, Ft. Bliss, TX; Ft. Leonard Wood, MO; Ft. Polk, LA; Ft. Benning, GA; Ft. Riley, KS; Camp McCoy, WI; Hawaii; and Germany. Navy, Cuba; Spain; Panama; and Ft. Drum, NY.

Awarded the U.S. Army Good Conduct Medal w/2 clasps, National Defense Service Medal, Navy Expert Rifle and Pistol, excellence in competition (Leg Medal) and Flt. Adm. Nimitz Award (1984).

Memorable experiences: Seabee Jam, Seacoast party, retiring at "Bee" in Rhode Island.

Civilian activities include sled hockey, shooting, woodworking, crafts, metal sucplurs and ornamental iron. Treantafel is single.

JOHN DONALD TURNER, BUCN, born Nov. 22, 1947, in Macon, GA. Inducted into the service Oct. 10, 1967, at Atlanta, GA. Military locations and stations were Mayport, FL; Davisville, RI; Gulfport, MS; and Great Lakes, IL (boot camp).

Memorable experiences: Clean-up after Hurricane Camille and crossing Equator.

Awarded the National Service Medal. Discharged March 17, 1971, at Orlando, FL.

Married to Mary L. Turner and has two daughters, Jill Darden and Janice Turner. He is a locomotive engineer for Norfolk Southern and a member of Navy Seabee Veterans, Island X-2.

JOHN S. VERFURTH, BU3/c, inducted into the service Aug. 22, 1952, at Milwaukee, WI. Military locations and stations included boot camp, Great Lakes Training Center, August-November 1952; USN Ceremonial Guard in Washington, D.C., November 1952-June 1954; Builders School, Port Hueneme, CA, June-September 1954; and MCB-10, Guam, Marianas Island in National Defense, September 1954-July 1956. Discharged July 7, 1956, at Treasure Island, CA.

Memorable experiences: 1955, when the French left Vietnam, they were going to be the first Seabee unit sent there.

He was just introduced to the Navy Seabee Veterans of American about four years ago and since then has renewed some old friendships and looks forward to the *Can Do* newsletter.

After discharge he took an apprenticeship in brick laying and worked at the trade for 30 years and then was a construction inspector for the city of Milwaukee for 13 years. He retired in August 1996. Married to Patricia and has three children: Michael, Karen and Kathleen; and two grandchildren, Nicole and Bradley.

RENALDO A. "VIC" VICTORIO, born April 27, 1921, in Staten Island, NY, and worked as a welder at Bethlehem Steel until enlisting in November 1942.

He enlisted in the Seabees as seaman second class. Taking basic training at Camp Peary, VA, and then becoming 6th NCB Spec. He left for Port Hueneme, CA, in June 1943, continuing to New Caledonia and Guadalcanal. There he became attached to the 1st Marine Amphibious Corps continuing on to the Solomon Islands. Afterwards he took part in invasions in Vella LaVella and Bougainville. Next, there was a short stop at Treasury Island and Bougainville. A seven month invasion of the Philippines at Leyte Gulf and Samar Island followed in May 1945. He returned to Hawaii and then to California for discharge in January 1946.

Some of his awards include a Good Conduct Medal, Philippine Liberation Ribbon w/ star, Asiatic-Pacific Theater Ribbon w/3 stars, Victory Medal and Letter of Commendation.

Since his discharge as a coxswain he has been in construction. In 1955 he moved from New York to St. Petersburg, FL, where he became a general contractor, retiring in 1992. He is married to Carolyn, has four children and seven grandchildren.

WILLIAM T. WALLS, SK1/c, enlisted at Tampa, FL, Nov. 8, 1942. Service began at Jacksonville NRS. Then to boot indoctrination at Camp Peary, VA (his first winter snow). Then to be charter member of 96th NCB at Camp Endicott, Davisville, NC, Training Center.

The 96th was sent to Terciera in the Azores where they built an air base for the British air force. While there he was promoted to SK1/c. On completion they were returned to Davisville to await reassignment. He secured a job in Endicott's Ship's Co., in the supply office where he remained several months building points for discharge which occurred at NRS Jacksonville, FL, Nov. 10, 1945. He returned to Tampa and to his interrupted Federal civil service career at MacDill AFB. There he was deputy base procurement officer and unlimited Air Force contracting officer for Tactical Air Command.

On June 30, 1972, he retired after 30 years of service. Based on a hobby since childhood he became a full time violin maker/restorer and violinist/violist in the symphony orchestra. He also taught violin making and violin playing. In October 1935 he married his high school sweetheart and in 1998 they celebrated their 63rd anniversary. They have a daughter who is a personnel manager and talent agent.

ROBERT F. WEBB, CMC, USNR (Ret), born Feb. 25, 1922, in Oregon City, OR. In 1940 he enlisted in the U.S. Army for six years with duty in South Pacific. Discharged Dec. 23, 1945, then to construction.

In 1953 he enlisted in the Seabee Reserve as CD2/c, requested active duty in Korea. Received orders to public works, Guam. Discharged in 1955, returned to construction. Also graduated from Oregon Tech. in diesel technology.

In 1960 he re-enlisted in the Seabee Reserve as CMD-2 with CB Unit 11-16 and MCB-17 Port Hueneme, CA.

In 1965 again requested active duty to Vietnam as CM1/c. Received orders to NAVSTA Adak, AK.

Returned to Port Hueneme in 1967 and MCB-11 later released to 31st RNCR. Also employment as heavy duty mechanic at CBC-CED Port Hueneme.

Retired in 1982 from 31st RNCR as CMC with 10 years active duty and 30 years total military service.

Retired in 1983 from USN-CBC.

Webb is a life member of Navy Seabee Veterans of America, Island X-2, Tacoma, WA; NERA; VFW; and American Legion. He is also a member of the Fleet Reserve Assoc.

KENNETH L. WENDT, CD3/c, inducted into the service April 12, 1956, at Buffalo, NY. Basic training at Bainbridge, MD. Assigned to MCB-7, while en route to Antisua and waiting for a flight out of NAS Jacksonville, FL, his orders were changed by Adm. Cornwall. Was his driver for nine months. "What great duty!" After being rated to CD3/c was transferred to the Navy Early Warning Station, Cape May, NJ, second in charge of motor pool. Finished his tour there. Discharged April 5, 1958.

Memorable experiences: Monument chairman of U.S. Navy Seabee Memorial, built by Island X-8, New York in North Tonawanday, NY, near the mighty Niagara River on Rte. #265. Chairman, Board of Director, membership secretary, Island X-8, New York. Also Navy Seabee Veterans of America life membership chairman.

Owned and operated Ken Wendt's Propane Gas Service since 1968 with wife, Dianne and sons, Paul and Todd. Todd left the business in May 1998 to be a helicopter pilot, he is doing very well. He has four children: Mark, Paul, Todd and Dana; and 10 grandchildren: Kyle, Josh, Kari, Jake, Kati, Janice, Diana, Trevor, Kimberly and Erick.

JOHN B. WEST, CM2/c, 41st Bn., born in Plattsburgh, NY, June 5, 1921. Enlisted Sept. 16, 1942, married Peg Slack Oct. 11, 1942, reported for duty Oct. 31, 1942. Trained at Camp Allen and Camp Peary, VA. After a tour of duty in Kodiak, AK, transferred to Ship's Co. at Port Hueneme, CA.

Discharged from Camp Peary Nov. 7, 1945. On Dec. 21, 1945, first of seven children was born at Plattsburgh, NY, where he lived for 10 years before moving back to his hometown of Chazy, NY. Worked as a brick mason until 1972; served on Town Board and as one of the original trustees of Clinton County Community College.

Moved to Hyde Park, NY, in 1972 and taught masonry at a vocational school until retirement in 1983. Moved to Plattsburgh, NY, in 1997.

Life member and past commander of American Legion Post #769 and VFW Post #125; life member of Seabee Island X-6, New York. Member of Knights of Columbus and charter member of BPOE Lodge 2778 in Hyde Park, NY.

JOHN E. WHARE JR., YN3/c, born Sept. 18, 1928, in York, PA. Inducted into the service Aug. 28, 1946. Military locations and stations were NTC Bainbridge, MD; CBNTC, Port Hueneme, CA; refrigeration training, 103rd NCB, Guam, Marianas Islands. Discharged July 15, 1949, at Rec. Station, San Francisco, CA.

Memorable experiences: He was a member of the first football team of Seabees in 1948. Charter member, Island X-1, Pennsylvania (recruited over 200 members). Editor *Keystone Islander* (1991-96) and advocate for Navy Seabee Veterans of America (life member).

Civilian activities in educational administration (local, state and national level). Whare has four children, six grandchildren and two great-grandchildren. He is now retired and is an advocate for honest government.

DARRELL T. WIDDOWS, member of Island X-7, Seabee Veterans of America, Effingham, IL. Was disbanded June 30, 1998.

GARY E. WILLIAMS, SMC(SW), USN (Ret), inducted into the service Jan. 31, 1962, at Syracuse, NY. Military locations and stations were Phib. CB-2, various fleet units, and instructor SM "A" School, Orlando, FL.

Awarded the Good Conduct Medal (four awards), National Defense Service Medal, Meritorious Unit Commendation, Naval Meri-

torious Service (two awards), Sea Service Medal, Vietnam Service Medal, various Letters of Commendation, Master Training Specialist. Discharged Sept. 31, 1987, in Orlando, FL.

Memorable experiences: Tutelage under EOC Peter Wohl. Having a bulldozer battery blow up in his face. Making SM3/c due to overmanning in Group 8 ratings.

Civilian activities include student at Onondoga Community College, Syracuse, NY; poultry farmer; golf; bowling; hunting; fishing; and reading. His first wife, Zandra A., is deceased. He is now married to Priscilla Ann. Williams has four children: David, Richard, Debra and Gary Jr.; seven grandchildren; and one great-grandchild.

HAROLD ELDRIDGE WILLIAMS, Coxswain, enlisted in the USN at Detroit, MI, Nov. 24, 1941. This was 13 days before Pearl Harbor. Sent to Newport, RI, for boot camp training. After only 14 days of training he went to the Longwharf Section Base for a short time, and then on to Quonset Point for combat training by the Marines. After that he was transferred to the

Sixth Naval Dist. Three days later his group was commissioned the First Naval Constr. Det. They were the first Seabees to be commissioned and the first to go overseas, which was in January 1942.

They arrived at Bora Bora, Society Islands Feb. 17, 1942. They were to build a refueling base for ships and planes. He was a coxswain and operated a tank lighter and barges. They left Bora Bora around Sept. 11, 1943, and traveled to quite a few other islands. Then they were attached to the 22nd Marines Reinforced and engaged the Japanese in the Marshall Islands. After 27 months they finally headed back to the States. They got a 30 day leave, then back to California and then back overseas.

They had just entered Mindoro Bay in the Philippines when they were attacked by enemy aircraft, two suicide planes (Betty Bombers) crashed into them. They also were strafed and on top of this, 90 drums of high octane gas went off in the hole of the ship, plus ammunition in the hole caught fire and started exploding. They dumped as much as they could while waiting for a rescue ship to take them off the ship. This was an LST they were being transferred to the Philippines in.

Military locations and stations were Bora Bora; American Samoa; Maui, HI; Honolulu,

HI; Pearl Harbor, HI; Kwajalein, Marshall Islands; Eniwetok, Marshall Islands; Engibe, Marshall Islands; Parry, Marshall Islands; Namgie Roy, Marshall Islands; Guadalcanal, Solomon Islands; Espiritu Santo, New Hebrides; Capinitu Santo, New Hebrides, Noumea, New Caledonia; Mindoro, Philippines; and New Guinea.

Awarded the WWII Victory Medal, Good Conduct Medal, American Defense Service Medal, American Campaign Medal, Asiatic-Pacific Campaign Medal, Philippine Liberation Medal and five Battle Stars. He was discharged Nov. 20, 1945, on the point system.

Williams is a retired mechanic. Married to Wanda F. and has two children, Harold D. and Gale Vozar, and one grandchild, Shane Vozar.

STEVEN B. WILLIAMS, born June 25, 1949, in Princeton, IN. Inducted into the service Oct. 24, 1967, at Great Lakes NTC. Military locations and stations were Davisville, RI; Da Nang, Phu Bai, Camp Deshirley, Phu Hoc, Hatien, Hue, Republic of Vietnam; and Keflavik, Iceland.

Awarded the Vietnam Service Medal, Vietnam Campaign Medal and National Defense Service Medal. Discharged March 18, 1971, in Philadelphia, PA.

Williams is single. His current activities include knife collecting and church.

WALTER A. WILSON, member of the 7th/36th Special Island at Large. He reported for service in Portland, OR, Dec. 9, 1942. Transferred to Williamsburg, VA, for basic training and then to Port Hueneme, CA. He arrived at Dutch Harbor in the Aleutians in July 1943 and was transferred to Adak in November 1943. In both locations he operated clothing warehouses.

Most memorable were the selfless visits by movie stars such as Errol Flynn and Olivia DeHaviland who braved 90 mile an hour williwaws and sub zero temperatures to visit the men.

He returned to Camp Shoemaker, CA, where he was discharged with the chief storekeeper rating Oct. 17, 1945. He returned to Portland, OR, where he pursued his career representing Simonds Saw & Steel Co. He joined the Naval Reserve and served for five years. His interests were travel, fishing, reading and gardening.

He married Dorothy in 1966 and has one son, Gary J. and two grandchildren, Christopher and Corrie. Mr. Wilson passed away Sept. 15, 1998. *Submitted by Dorothy K. Wilson, wife.*

ROBERT R. WINDER, enlisted in the U.S. Naval Constr. Bn. in 1942 and reported for active duty Jan. 25, 1943. He trained at Camp Peary, VA. He was part of a replacement group that joined the 24th Bn. in New Caledonia. He stayed with the 24th through training, Rendova, Munda and Okinawa, from where he shipped home for discharge Jan. 31, 1946.

After discharge as CM2/c he married Lee and had two children. Spent eight years in night school graduating Fairleigh Dickinson University where he earned a BS degree. He spent 31 years in the cosmetic field. He left the firm of Yardley of London as director of production to join the USPS as a principal program manager in the engineering group at USPS HQ in Washington, D.C. He retired in 1988 and now enjoys meeting old friends at Navy Seabee Veterans of America reunions.

JAKE WOLFFE, SK2/c, V-6, USNR, inducted into the service April 13, 1943, at Macon, GA. Military locations and stations were NRS, Macon, GA; Camp Peary, Williamsburg, VA; 15th Spec. NCB (41st NCB Spec.) Milne Bay, Dutch New Guinea; and Hollandia, New Guinea. Discharged Oct. 23, 1945, at Jacksonville, FL.

Memorable experiences: The battalion left him at Milne Bay and Base Hospital 13 after the burns he received at Milne Bay. He spent 66 days at Base Hospital, where his burns were treated and was told that he could rejoin the outfit. This was an awful ordeal because he had to get back on his own. He did hitch a ride on an LST and got to Hollandia. There his problems started again. The commander of the LST would not let him go ashore until days later. And then with a lot of problems. He did get ashore. And lucky for him he was only about 10 miles from dockside where his outfit was housed on the hillside. It was a glorious day when he first saw his many many buddies. Cmdr. McMullen did work to get him back into the battalion. So Wolffe was ever grateful when he checked into McMullen's office to report back for duty after almost 90 days away. He too remembers he was among the first nine men to be sent home on leave and he left Hollandia on July 4th and it was while he was on his 30 day leave that the Japanese surrendered. After his leave he reported back to Davisville and marked his time until his discharge in October 1945.

Moved to Bainbridge, GA, in 1948 and

opened Jake's Pawn Shop. Very active in Lions Club (president, district governor, recipient of Melvin Jones Award), Decatur County Man of the Year, VFW, American Legion, Chamber of Commerce and Temple Beth El.

Married to Bella Turetzky Wolffe and has two children, Edward H. (Atlanta) and Roslyn W. Palmer (Bainbridge), and three grandchildren: Ryan and Julie Wolffe and Mycla Ann Palmer.

WILLIAM J. WOLTER, born March 12, 1948, in Suffern, NY. Inducted into the service March 26, 1968, at Gulfport, MS, Naval Station. Military locations and stations were basic training at Gulfport, MS; Port Hueneme, CA; and Naval Support Facility, Cam Ranh Bay, Vietnam, CBMU-302.

Awarded the National Defense Service Medal, Vietnam Service Medal and Republic of Vietnam Campaign Medal.

Memorable experiences: Treasurer of Island X-9, Kingston, NY.

Married to Cheryl and has one daughter and one grandson. Current activities include Navy Seabee Veterans of America Island X-9, Kingston, NY; VFW; commissioner at fire department; and captain of fire police.

CRAIG T. WOOD, EO2/c, inducted into the service Oct. 26, 1965, at Chicago, IL. Military locations and stations were Davisville, RI; Chu Lai, South Vietnam; and Phu Loc, South Vietnam.

Awarded the Purple Heart and regular Vietnam ribbons. Discharged Dec. 20, 1968, at Davisville, RI.

Memorable experiences: Recommission of MCB-71 and crushing rock in South Vietnam.

Civilian employment as air traffic controller at O'Hare Airport for 12 years and nuclear plant operator for 12 years. Married to Holly and has three children: Stephanie, Tracy and Elizabeth; and three grandchildren: Cassie, Anthony and Michael.

C. BRUCE "CB" WRIGHT, served in the military from Jan. 23, 1943-Feb. 26, 1946. Trained at Camps Allen and Peary, VA; left Camp Endicott, Davisville, RI, in March 1943 with 64th Bn. for Newfoundland. Wright became a mail censor in August 1943.

Returning to the U.S. in January 1944 he transferred to the V-12 Officers' Training Program, Williams College. In July 1945 he was reassigned to Camp Endicott, then to Camp Parks, Oakland, CA, soon back to the regular Navy, Separation Center, Camp Shoemaker, until discharged at Boston's Fargo Building.

His awards include North Atlantic, Good

Conduct and WWII Victory Medal. Wright belongs to New Hampshire Seabee Island X-1 and Navy Seabee Veterans of America.

His career included vice presidential level positions in public relations at hospitals and colleges, speech writing and public relations for Air Force generals and high school teaching. Wright has been a member of the National Defense Executive Reserve since 1972.

JOSEPH R. YANARELLA, GM2/c, born June 10, 1925, in Peekskill, NY. Attended school in Yonkers and graduated in 1941 from Saunders Technical High School. Went to work at Eastern Aircraft and just after 17th birthday, enlisted in the Seabees as seaman second class.

Took basic and advanced training at Camp Peary, VA, then Gulfport and Camp Magu, CA. He left for Hawaii and took part in the invasion of the Marshall Islands in 1944. Returned to Hawaii and then left for the Philippines. Discharged in 1946. Married Rena and they have two children and two grandchildren. Initially worked for the U.S. Maritime Commission, but later became a journeyman electrician and taught high voltage cable splicing. Retired in 1987 after 41 years of service.

Active in veterans organizations, he is past commander of American Legion, past state commander and past national commander, LaSociete 40/8, past Grand Knight in Knights of Columbus and department treasurer, Navy Seabee Veterans of America Island X-17, Florida.

GEORGE J. YOCUM JR., MM1/c, inducted into the service at Williamsport, PA, in March 1943. Military locations and stations were Camp Peary, VA; Pearl Harbor; Okinawa; and Philadelphia Navy Yards.

Awarded the Pacific Theater Ribbon, American Theater Ribbon and Victory Medal. Discharged in February 1946 at Bainbridge, MD.

Memorable experiences: While at Pearl Harbor he helped build the "Magic City of the Pacific," which was the advance reshipment depot at Iraque Point. While on Okinawa he was a heavy equipment operator doing maintenance work and maintaining roads. While there he experienced two typhoons. It destroyed seaplanes and freighter which they had to dredge the beach to refloat it.

Has been an operating engineer for 45 years. Is now retired but still operates equipment. Has horses and enjoys riding. Married

Shirley Yocum 52 years ago and has one daughter, Dixie A. VanDyke and two grandchildren, Matthew and Jason VanDyke.

ANTHONY THOMAS ZAMBITO, born Dec. 10, 1924, in Brooklyn, NY. Enlisted in the service in New York in 1942. Took basic training at Camp Peary, VA. Then to Port Hueneme, CA. Left there to Bremerton Navy Yard, Washington, then on to join the 12th NCB in the Aleutians, Dutch Harbor, Adak and outer islands. Returned to  Camp Parks and was transferred to the 14th NCB. His second tour overseas was to Hawaii, Saipan and invasion of Okinawa. Back to the U.S. to Pier 92 in New York and on to Lido Beach, Long Island.

Memorable experiences: How they lived through the hurricane on Okinawa in September 1945 tied under a bulldozer.

Awarded the American Theater Medal, Asiatic-Pacific Medal w/star, Good Conduct Medal and Victory Medal. Discharged in February 1946.

He is married to Flory and has two sons, one daughter and six grandchildren. Civilian employment as a real estate broker. Retired after 35 years in business.

RICHARD ZANDER, MM3/c, drafted into the Seabees Nov. 12, 1943, in Chicago, IL. Had boot training at Peary and advanced training at Endicott as a crane, dragline and shovel operator. From there to Parks and then to Hueneme. On Oct. 11, 1944, left Hueneme with the 41st NCB for Guam. This was the 41st's second tour of duty and the unit had all older experienced enlisted men. He was 18 but was trained well by a very experienced coal strip mine dragline operator from Texas. He'll never forget this very patient, older instructor. One day Pitman gave him a lot of confidence. He said, "Dick, I'm getting off the machine and don't tip it over." Zander performed to his satisfaction and graduated from the school.

On Guam he worked on road building and also delivered supplies by truck from the ships to units on the island.

Currently he is married to Pat, has eight children and 14 grandchildren. He is a retired self-employed carpenter.

ALAN D. ZANGER, MCB-9, CE2/c, born Oct. 22, 1944. Enlisted in the USNR Seabees after watching John Wayne in *The Fighting Seabees*, 1963. After graduating from Samuel Gompers High School, went to Construction Electrician School at Port Hueneme, CA, and was assigned to MCB-9. Discharged in 1966 after two tours in Vietnam.

Worked for Con Edison, New York for two years, went on to advanced Construction Electrician School at Port Hueneme as part of the Naval Reserve program, then got a job offer at Southern California Edison.

After two years as Southern California Edison went on to use the G.I. Bill and obtained an AA degree from Pasadena City College and a BA degree from the School of Journalism at the University of Southern California.

Served with the Army Reserve and CANG and retired in 1992. Worked for United Press International as a staff photographer for 10 years. Presently a freelance photographer, covering assignments for magazines all over the world.

LEE CHARLES ZIMMER, Boatswains Mate First Class (CB), inducted into the service March 29, 1942, at Spokane, WA. Military locations and stations were boot camp at Camp Peary, VA; port of debarkation, Port Hueneme, CA; South Pacific Islands; and Okinawa. Discharged Nov. 27, 1945, at Puget Sound Navy Yard, Bremerton, WA.

Memorable experiences: They were 27 days aboard a liberty ship before they reached their destination in the Solomon Islands in the South Pacific. After 18 months as a stevedore unit in the Solomon Islands their battalion, the 12th Spec., was then assigned to take part in the invasion of Okinawa. They were on Okinawa when the war ended.

Started out as a machinist for Kaiser Aluminum and Chemical Corp. Advanced to supervisor in the maintenance department. Retired after 35 years with Kaiser.

John Turner, Sr., Oct. 1944

Seabees would cheer upon seeing this sight-the Golden Gate Bridge in San Francisco, CA. Home was not far away. Dec. 1945. Courtesy of Alan Burns.

Billy Meredith, Lt. J.E. Holt and Leo L. Stubler with what we called big sticks.

Two Veterans in San Francisco, back from the war. Courtesy of Gino Sacchetti.

THE
THICK & THIN LBR. CO. LTD.
"We Rip and Tear!"
TWO SIZES ONLY
TOO THICK and TOO THIN

The 59th Navy Construction Battalion lumber detail. August/September 1943. Courtesy of Clifford W. Miner.

More big boards, 59th Seabees in Hilo, Hawaii, August, 1943.

Chauncey Nutter on the 59th NCB lumber carrier.

Lumber detail building, B.O.Q.S. at Naval Air Station in Hilo, Hawaii August 1943.

Ed McDermott on the left, John Taggart on the right. Okinawa circa June 1945. McDermott was photographer for 79th USNCB-from Providence RI, during Aleution and Okinawa campaign. Courtesy of John H. Taggart.

Okinawa 1945. Fleet Post Office after Typhoon. Courtesy of M.J. Etters, Jr.

John H. (Jack) Taggart at fuel storage area, Okinawa, April 1945. Courtesy of John H. Taggart.

CBMU-541, 1945. Courtesy of M.J. Etters, Jr.

First Echelon arrived on Okinawa on LST's 899, 850 and 763, April 20, 1945. Courtesy of William Andressi.

December 1944, 59th Seabees finishing an underground fuel storage tank on Guam, Marianas Islands.

Putting up a pre-fab on Guam.

Guam M.I. MCB 10 1955, buildings in background are the concrete block housing being built by MCB 10 for Navy dependants. Courtesy of John Verfurth.

Guam M.I. MCB 10 1955, Offices and supply huts. Courtesy of John Verfurth.

Chapel built by Seabees on Iwo Jima, before and after, 1945. Courtesy of Phillip J. Newman.

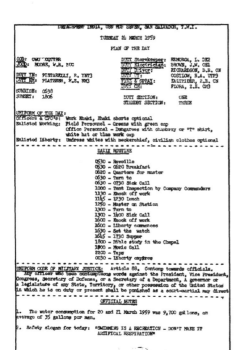

Officers Building, Coast Guard, San Salvador 1959; Atlantic Ocean in rear. Courtesy of Ernest B. Hauer.

This was taken on top of the 40' x 100'. The fellow on the right side half way down looking up is Charlie Payment. Courtesy of Ernest B. Hauer.

Bob Hope visits troops at Chulia during the war in SE Asia, 28 Dec. 1965. Courtesy of W.J. Ferland, III.

New enlisted mens barracks going up with our tent-camp on left side, Atlantic Ocean in rear. 1959. Courtesy of Ernest B. Hauer.

Celebrities have always helped U.S. Veterans in time of war. Errol Flynn visits with Seabees during WWII. Courtesy of Ernest Hauer.

U.S.O. troop in San Salvador, 1959. Courtesy of Ernest B. Hauer.

Building two breakwaters, Tilbury docks, Buzz Bomb Alley, cement mixing area. Aug-Sept 1944. Courtesy of Raymond B. Dierkes.

CBMU 505, British Samoa, 1944. Courtesy of Ernest E. Brown.

Courtesy of Ernest B. Hauer.

Page Kelly, Oahu 1944. Courtesy of Carl E. Bergstrom.

1971 Seabee team 7107, Mytho S. Vietnam. Courtesy of C.C. Cochran.

Barracks Building, San Salvador Island. Courtesy of Ernest B. Hauer.

Christmas Day 1966, Monsoon season. Courtesy of George Baldwin.

Well drilling, Danang 1967. Courtesy of George Baldwin.

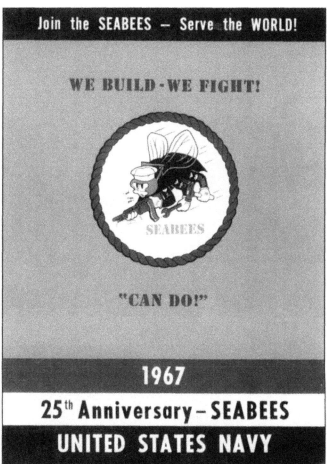

Join the SEABEES — Serve the WORLD!

WE BUILD - WE FIGHT!

"CAN DO!"

1967
25th Anniversary – SEABEES
UNITED STATES NAVY

Iwo Jima. Courtesy of Carl E. Bergstrom.

Iwo Jima. Courtesy of Carl E. Bergstrom.

Commander Naval Construction Troops at muster on Okinawa, WWII. Courtesy of Mel Koch.

Ralph Liden on mobil crane, Barbados, B.W.I.,1958.

Chu Lia, 1966, Warren J. Ferlandy,III.

Our chow line and gally, Camp Shields, Feb. 1966.

Unloading Barbados, L.S.U. B.W.I., while natives watch.

P. Finazzo and F.M. Erickson. Courtesy of Carl E. Bergstrom.

L.A. Wents, C.F. Caldwell, Ralph Laird, F.W. Willaby, Walter Roberts, Joel Feldstein, J.B. Miller, J.P. Contor. Courtesy of G. Windham.

Iwo Jima. Courtesy of Carl E. Bergstrom

LST 282 hit by bomb during landing. Seabees were aboard with pontoons.

Ernest B. Hauer on a "UKE", San Salvador, BWI, R.I.

Courtesy of Bill Patrick.

B-29 bearing 110 USNCB insignia, dropped leaflets and bombs over Japan.

Left (standing) Cliff Mirier, left (seated) Westley Huston.

Front view of Post Office.

40th NCB presented with the Army Presidential Unit Citation.' - "as public evidence of deserved honor and distinction for having operated effectively as combat troops on Los Nergros, in the Admiralty Islands."

Regimental dress review for President Roosevelt, Dec 22, 1944.

Hoyt Bryson stacking pontoons. New Guinea 1944-45.

Courtesy of Bill Patrick.

14th U.S. Naval Const. Battalion, Company "C", August 1945, Okinawa. The 14th Battalion was commissioned at Camp Allen in July 1942, and transferred to Camp Bradford on July 14. In August the outfit was moved to Hueneme via Davisville, and Oakland, Calif., arriving at Hueneme on Sept. 8, 1942. The following day the unit embarked for overseas duty and arrived at Noumea, New Caledonia on Sept. 29. At Noumea, the Battalion was split into two sections with the first section departing for Guadalcanal on Oct. 19, and arriving on Nov. 4. The second section left Noumea Nov. 5, 1942. The second section joined the first section at Guadalcanal in two detachments arriving on Guadalcanal Nov. 29 and Dec. 23, 1942. On Nov. 9, 1943 the entire outfit left Guadalcanal and reported at Pearl Harbor Nov. 27. Three days later the Battalion sailed for the States, arriving at Camp Parks Dec. 11. Beginning its second tour, the outfit moved out of Camp Parks Oct. 21, 1944, arriving at Pearl Harbor Oct. 29. War's end found them on duty at Okinawa.

Members of the 27th N.C.B.

Courtesy of Bill Patrick.

INDEX

Printed in the USA
CPSIA information can be obtained
at www.ICGtesting.com
JSHW060056150824
68134JS00032B/2745

9 781681 621364